IF THERE IS ONE PLACE that can bring friends and family together, it's a Target store. You already know it's one-stop-shopping for all things Whole30, but it's also a treasure trove of inspiration for entertaining and gatherings.

First, let's talk about the food. Target carries dozens of Whole30 Approved and compliant brands like Applegate, Primal Kitchen, Organicville, LaCroix, bubly, hint, Rethink Water, Lucini, Tribali, Vital Proteins, Veggie Noodle Co., Epic, Wild Planet, Coconut Secret, and more—not to mention tons of fresh produce, meat, seafood, and eggs. Stocking up on Whole30 staples, emergency food, and ingredients for your *Friends & Family* menu all in one place saves you time and money . . . but we all know nobody runs into Target *just* for groceries.

Whether you're buying reusable melamine dishes for your next beach picnic, picking up trinkets from the dollar bin for your kid's birthday party, or searching for the perfect "chip"-and-dip holder for your Game Day feast, Target's got you covered. (Ooh—grab a few portable camp chairs for tailgating while you're at it.)

Then, take a spin through the kitchen and home goods sections and look for creative ways to make meal prep easier, serve food fancier, and generally level up your host or hostess game. (Even if you don't buy anything, the displays and offerings will inspire you to create your own game night or book club setting using things you already own.)

Finally, make prepping for your Whole30 into a social gathering itself by browsing or shopping with friends or family. Picking up Whole30 ingredients at Target is a great way to introduce people to the accessibility, variety, and deliciousness of Whole30 cooking and eating, and shopping is always more fun with a friend. (Unless that "friend" is under four feet tall and insists on being "helpful" by dropping RXBARs into other people's carts. But my Target stories are for another day.)

Just don't forget to "casually" stop by the book section, where you'll find the other Whole30 books, often available at a discount. Hey, all's fair in love and Whole30—and if you want your loved ones to get excited about the program too, all it's gonna take is for them to flip through our delicious recipes. Winning!

Now, go put that basket back and grab a cart, because you're gonna need it. It's time to stock up for your next Whole30 gathering—see you at Target!

Best in health,
Melissa

THE WHOLE30

FRIENDS & FAMILY

150 RECIPES FOR EVERY SOCIAL OCCASION

TARGET EDITION

MELISSA HARTWIG URBAN

Photography by Ghazalle Badiozamani

HOUGHTON MIFFLIN HARCOURT
Boston • New York • 2019

Whole30® is a registered trademark of Thirty & Co., LLC.
The Whole30® logo is a trademark of Thirty & Co., LLC

Photography © 2019 by Ghazalle Badiozamani
Food styling by Monica Pierini
Prop styling by Paola Andrea
Hair and makeup styling by Toby Klinger
Wardrobe styling by Andrew Gelwicks

For information about permission to reproduce selections from this book, write to
trade.permissions@hmhco.com or to Permissions, Houghton Mifflin Harcourt
Publishing Company, 3 Park Avenue, 19th Floor, New York, New York 10016.

hmhbooks.com

Library of Congress Cataloging-in-Publication Data is available.
ISBN 978-0-358-11579-3 (hbk); 978-0-358-20219-6 (hbk Target edition)
ISBN 978-0-358-11213-6 (ebk)

Book design by Vertigo Design NYC

Printed in China

C&C 10 9 8 7 6 5 4 3 2 1

To my Whole30 team,
who inspires me daily

CONTENTS

acknowledgments x

introduction xii

what is the whole30? xiv

the whole30 rules xvi

getting started with
the whole30 xix

family
game night
1

parent and
tot group
11

beach picnic
19

date night
29

baby shower
39

road trip
57

adults-only dinner party
65

kid-friendly family dinner
77

game day
87

book club
97

camping
105

office potluck
119

family movie night
129

kids' birthday party
137

adult party time
151

study group
165

weekend houseguests
173

backyard bbq
181

friendsgiving
195

church picnic 209

tailgating 219

sunday brunch 229

basics 240

◎ **ew year's eve** 267

◎ **valentine's day date night** 279

◎ **independence day** 289

whole30 resources 244
whole30 inspiration 248
whole30 approved 251
whole30 support 256
cooking conversions 257
index 258

acknowledgments

To Justin Schwartz, my editor at Houghton Mifflin Harcourt, thank you for believing in me and this project, which is so dear to my heart. We make the best team.

To Bruce Nichols, Ellen Archer, Marina Padakis, Lori Glazer, Brianna Yamashita, Breanne Sommer, Allison Chi, Rebecca Springer, and the entire Houghton Mifflin Harcourt team, I love working with you more with each project we bring to life. Thank you for making me part of the HMH family.

To Andrea Magyar and Tonia Addison at Penguin Canada, my Canadian Whole30'ers are forever grateful for your continued encouragement and support, as am I.

To Christy Fletcher, you are so much more than an agent, and I don't know how I ever managed without you, especially this year. You are my greatest advocate and a true friend.

To Melissa Chinchillo, Liz Resnick, Sarah Fuentes, Alyssa Taylor, and the Fletcher & Company team, thank you for all of your guidance and support, and for always being in my corner.

To Ghazalle Badiozamani, I'm so glad we're now friends in real life, as you're even cooler than I imagined. Your creative talents, like your dad jokes, are unlimited. To Paola Andrea and Monica Pierini, your skills and creativity continue to astonish me. This is the most beautiful book I have ever done, thanks to you. To Andrew Gelwicks and Toby Klinger, you came in clutch for this cover shoot, and I'm so grateful to have you both on my team.

To my Whole30 team—Kristen Crandall, Shanna Keller, Jen Kendall, Karyn Scott, Stephanie Greunke, Bill Ferrante, Maggie Lopez, Alyssa Anthony, Stephanie Kelley, Erica Rozetti, Chelsea Long, and Autumn Michaelis—as with everything I do, this is 100 percent a team effort. You are Whole30, and I am forever grateful for your contributions and friendship.

To my team of Whole30 Certified Coaches sharing the message and connecting in your local communities: you are the future of this program, and we are just getting started.

To Sarah Steffens, our in-house recipe creative, thank you for sharing your talents, your careful review skills, and your impeccable feedback for this project.

To Brandon, forty years at least. Team Us, forever, babe (although you still have to be in a tie with Kelly for "biggest fan").

To my sister, my most vocal cheerleader, honest-est feedback giver, and unconditional love shower-er . . . there is no one on this earth who could take your place, and I'm so lucky to have you.

To my family and friends, your love, support, pride, and encouragement fill me up. Thank you, thank you, thank you.

To my son, you are my whole world.

Finally, to YOU, my Whole30'ers. Everything I do is for you. It's always for you. My loyalty to you is fierce and undying, and I love you all.

introduction

"Dear Melissa, how can I maintain a social life on the Whole30?" Love, Everyone.

Dear Everyone, there is often a misconception (sometimes from the media, sometimes in your social circles, or maybe just inside your head) that in order to complete the Whole30, you essentially have to become a hermit. How can you possibly survive happy hours without beer, birthday parties without cake, and game days without pizza?

Spoiler: If you've ever had a pleasant conversation *without* a piece of bread in your hand, you're already well on your way!

Okay, it's not exactly that simple, but it doesn't have to be that complicated either. First, here's why I definitely want you to be social on your Whole30.

The biggest lesson to be learned is that socializing isn't about what's on your plate or in your glass. The gathering is about the people, connections, and good feelings. You can toast the boss with sparkling water, celebrate the birthday with a bowl of fruit, or shout-out the touchdown holding a ranch-dipped chicken wing. (Yeah, that can be compliant. I told you it's not that hard.) With some practice, you'll gain confidence in holding your self-care boundaries and still have just as good a time (if not better). Bonus: You'll also wake up with boundless energy, a happy belly, and a clear head.

Second, after the Whole30, you're going to want to take what you've learned and create your own "food freedom" lifestyle—and you can't avoid social situations forever. Use your Whole30 as practice ground for saying no to what doesn't serve you and yes to real, whole foods that you know make you look and feel your best. Frankly, it's even *easier* to say no when you're on the program, because you can just blame me. ("The Whole30 Lady says no alcohol. I'm not sure I even like her, but I made a promise to myself, and I'm going to keep it.")

Third, I want you to be social because if there is anyone in your life who you think would benefit from the Whole30, you have to lead by example. If they see you turning down invitations, leaving parties early, or standing around uncomfortably, you have zero chance of getting them on board. So get out there and socialize! Show them (and yourself) that you don't need sugar, booze, or carbs to enjoy the company or the surroundings.

Finally, you do have a secret weapon here . . . *this book.*

I created *The Whole30 Friends and Family* to help you be social while upholding your Whole30 commitment, whether you're hosting, contributing to, or attending the gathering. I've given you 22 colorful, creative, drool-worthy menus for everyday social occasions like backyard BBQs, baby showers, and birthday parties, and every. single. thing. is Whole30-compliant. No asking about ingredients, picking off the cheese, or gnawing on a dry broccoli floret because the ranch has sugar. NEVER AGAIN.

This cookbook is unlike anything I've ever done, so it probably should come with some specific instructions. Here's how I want you to use *Friends and Family*: *any gosh-darn way you please*. Create the entire Book Club menu and serve it to your actual book club. Give the book to your mom and tell her you want the Birthday menu for your birthday. Make half of the Office Potluck dishes and bring them to your church picnic. Grab one dish from Road Trip, one from Dinner Party, and the drink from Friendsgiving and make 'em for dinner on Wednesday.

This book has menu ideas for every kind of gathering you might encounter, but you don't have to serve the menus exactly as written. Yes, our expert assembly of main dishes, sides, shareable bites, and mocktails makes planning any event effortless . . . but I want you to *use* this book, so please don't wait for the big game to whip up those Pulled Pork Potato Skins with Chipotle Slaw (page 223).

A Word on Desserts

This book features a few fruity creations intended as dessert, which is unusual for a Whole30 cookbook, but hear me out: special occasion desserts (especially these fruit-based dishes) *are not the problem*. Feeling like you *need* something sweet at the end of every meal is a problem. Prowling through the pantry like a starving raccoon every night is a problem. Telling yourself you'll only have one handful/square/spoonful, then eating the whole thing is a problem. These are the habits the Whole30 is helping you break. But enjoying Cardamom-Ginger Poached Pears (page 207) with friends after a relaxing, laughter-filled gathering is the not that scenario. Use these dishes the way they were intended, and you'll also discover a changed relationship with "dessert."

One last thing—I've had thousands of conversations, written dozens of articles, and penned three whole chapters in *Food Freedom Forever* about how to talk to people about the Whole30 . . . so I know a few things about the social challenges you might face. I've sprinkled my best tips and talking points throughout this book, to help you gracefully navigate questions about your "new diet" and introduce the program to family and friends. And trust: zero persons are going to look at any of these dishes at their party and say, "This looks like weird diet food." In fact, if I were you, I'd not even tell them until the end. "Oh, you loved those BLT Potato Skins? Yeah, those are totally Whole30. Yes, I *do* eat like that every day. Oh sure, I'd be happy to tell you more . . ."

I think you can take it from here. So get on out there and eat, drink, and be merry . . . all while changing your life with the Whole30. Save me a seat at Friendsgiving, okay?

Best in health,
Melissa

what is the whole30?

Think of the Whole30 like pushing the reset button with your health, habits, and relationship with food.

The premise is simple: Certain foods could be having a negative impact on how you look, how you feel, and your quality of life without you even realizing it. Are your energy levels inconsistent or nonexistent? Do you have aches and pains that can't be explained by overuse or injury? Are you having a difficult time losing weight no matter how hard you try? Do you have a condition (like skin issues, digestive ailments, seasonal allergies, or chronic fatigue) that medication hasn't helped? Your symptoms may be directly related to the foods you eat—even the "healthy" stuff.

So how do you know if (and how) these foods are affecting you? Eliminate them from your diet completely. Cut out all the psychologically unhealthy, hormone-unbalancing, gut-disrupting, inflammatory foods for a full 30 days. Give your body a break from these foods and see what changes. Push the reset button on your metabolism, systemic inflammation, and the downstream effects of the food choices you've been making. Learn once and for all how the foods you've been eating are actually affecting your day-to-day life and your long-term health.

HOW IT WORKS

For a full 30 days, you'll completely eliminate the foods that the scientific literature and my clinical experience have deemed the most commonly problematic in one of four areas: cravings, metabolism, digestion, and immune system. During the elimination period, you'll experience what life is like without these commonly problematic triggers while paying careful attention to improvements in energy, sleep, digestion, mood, cravings, focus, anxiety, self-confidence, chronic pain or fatigue, athletic performance and recovery, and any number of other symptoms or medical conditions. This elimination period will leave you with a new "normal"—a healthy baseline where, in all likelihood, you will look, feel, and live better than you ever imagined you could.

> It's important to note that we're not eliminating these foods because they're "bad"; they're just *unknown*. Sure, they can be problematic, but I don't know if they're problematic for *you* . . . and neither will you, until you eliminate and reintroduce. Think of the Whole30 as a scientific experiment or a learning tool, not a prescriptive "you have eat like this forever" diet.

At the end of the 30 days, you will carefully and systematically reintroduce the foods you've been missing, again paying attention to any changes in your health, habits, or mindset. Do your 2 p.m. energy slumps return? Does your stomach bloat? Does your face break out, your joints swell, your pain return? Does your Sugar Dragon rear his ugly head? The reintroduction period teaches you how specific foods are having a negative impact on *you*, and which foods are making you look and feel less than your best.

Put it all together, and for the first time in your life, you'll be able to make educated decisions and create the perfect diet for *you*. You'll be able to eliminate the specific foods that just aren't serving you and level up your quality of life forever. More important, you'll know when, how often, and in what amount you can include the problematic-but-still-worth-it foods in your diet in a way that feels balanced and sustainable, but still keeps you looking and feeling as awesome as you now *know* you can look and feel.

THE RESULTS

I'll make a bold statement here—the next 30 days will change your life.* They will change the way you think about food; they will change your tastes; they will change your habits and your cravings.

They could, quite possibly, change the emotional relationship you have with food, and with your body. They have the potential to change the way you eat for the rest of your life. I know this because I did it, and millions of people have done it in the last ten years, and it changed my life (and their lives) in a permanent fashion.

The physical benefits of the Whole30 are profound. A full 96 percent of participants lose weight and improve their body composition without counting or restricting calories. Also commonly reported? Consistently high energy levels, better sleep, improved focus and mental clarity, a return to healthy digestive function, improved athletic performance, and a sunnier disposition. (Yes, many Whole30 graduates say they felt "strangely happy" during and after their program.)

The psychological benefits of the Whole30 may be even more dramatic. Through the program, participants report effectively changing long-standing, unhealthy habits related to food, developing a healthier body image, and dramatically reducing or eliminating cravings, particularly for sugar and carbohydrates. The words so many Whole30 participants use to describe this place?

"Food freedom."

Finally, testimonials from thousands of Whole30 participants document the improvement or resolution of symptoms associated with a number of lifestyle-related diseases and conditions.[†]

• high blood pressure • high cholesterol • type 1 diabetes • type 2 diabetes • asthma • allergies • sinus infections • hives • acne • eczema • psoriasis • endometriosis • PCOS • infertility • migraines • depression • anxiety • heartburn • GERD •arthritis • joint pain • ADHD • spectrum disorders • thyroid dysfunction • Lyme disease • fibromyalgia • multiple sclerosis • chronic fatigue • lupus • leaky gut syndrome • Crohn's disease • IBS • celiac disease • diverticulitis • ulcerative colitis

---

*In a 2016 survey of nearly 8,000 Whole30 alumni, 88 percent said the Whole30 really did change their life.

[†]These testimonials are not a guarantee, promise, or indicator of results and/or experiences while participating in and after completing the Whole30 program.

the whole30 rules

For the next 30 days, you'll be eating meat, seafood, and eggs; lots of vegetables and fruit; natural, healthy fats; and fresh herbs and spices. Oh yeah, and on this program, there are no slips, cheats, or special occasions. Below are the program rules. (Please refer to *The Whole30: The 30-Day Guide to Total Health and Food Freedom* for a complete list of rules, and use that book to prepare for and succeed with your program.)

> The "no cheat" thing isn't me playing the tough guy or turning the Whole30 into a hazing. It's grounded in the science of an elimination diet, during which you have to *completely* eliminate suspected triggers to accurately evaluate them. (Otherwise, how will you know if life could be better without them?) Plus, the Whole30 is about keeping your promise to yourself. You committed to 30 days of evaluating your health, habits, and relationship with food, and I want you to honor that commitment. Want the program to *actually* change your life? Follow the rules 100 percent for 30 straight days.

DO NOT CONSUME ADDED SUGAR OF ANY KIND, REAL OR ARTIFICIAL. No maple syrup, honey, agave nectar, coconut sugar, Splenda, Equal, Nutrasweet, xylitol, stevia, etc. Read your labels, because companies sneak sugar into products more often than you realize.

DO NOT CONSUME ALCOHOL IN ANY FORM. No wine, beer, champagne, vodka, rum, whiskey, tequila, etc., whether consumed on its own or used as an ingredient—not even for cooking.

DO NOT EAT GRAINS. This includes wheat, rye, barley, oats, corn, rice, millet, bulgur, sorghum, sprouted grains, and pseudo-cereals like amaranth, buckwheat, or quinoa. This also includes all the ways we add wheat, corn, and rice into our foods in the form of bran, germ, starch, and so on. Again, read your labels.

DO NOT EAT LEGUMES. This includes beans of all kinds (black, red, pinto, navy, white, kidney, lima, fava, etc.), peas, chickpeas, lentils, and peanuts. This also includes all forms of soy— soy sauce, miso, tofu, tempeh, edamame, and all the ways we sneak soy into foods (like soybean oil or soy lecithin). No peanut butter, either. The only exceptions are green beans and snow/snap peas.

DO NOT EAT DAIRY. This includes cow's-, goat's-, and sheep's-milk products such as cream, cheese, kefir, yogurt, and sour cream. The only exceptions are clarified butter and ghee.

DO NOT CONSUME CARRAGEENAN, MSG, OR ADDED SULFITES. If these appear in any form in the ingredient list of your processed food or beverage, it's out for the Whole30.

DO NOT RE-CREATE BAKED GOODS, "TREATS," OR JUNK FOODS WITH APPROVED INGREDIENTS. No banana-egg pancakes, Paleo tortillas, avocado oil potato chips, or coconut-milk ice cream. (See Let's Get Specific below for more details.) Your cravings and habits won't change if you keep eating these foods, even if they are made with Whole30 ingredients.

DO NOT STEP ON THE SCALE OR TAKE MEASURE-MENTS. Your reset is about so much more than just weight loss; focusing on your body composition means you'll miss out on the most dramatic and lifelong benefits this plan has to offer. So no weighing yourself, analyzing body fat, or breaking out the tape measure during the 30-day elimination.

LET'S GET SPECIFIC

A few off-limits foods that fall under the "No baked goods, treats, or junk foods" rule include pancakes, bread, tortillas, biscuits, crepes, waffles, cereal or granola, muffins, cupcakes, cookies, pizza crust, store-bought chips of any kind (even plantain), and restaurant French fries. While this list of off-limits foods applies to everyone (even those who "don't have a problem" with pancakes), you may decide your personal Off-Limits List includes additional foods that you already know make you feel out of control, like RXBARs or almond butter. (See page 95 in *The Whole30* for guidance.)

THE FINE PRINT

These foods are exceptions to the rules and are allowed during your Whole30.

CLARIFIED BUTTER OR GHEE. Clarified butter (page 241) and ghee are the only sources of dairy allowed during your Whole30, as they've had their milk solids rendered out. Plain old butter is *not* allowed, as its milk proteins could impact the results of your program.

FRUIT JUICE AS A SWEETENER. Products or recipes that include orange, apple, or other fruit juices are permitted on the program, although we encourage you not to go overboard here.

GREEN BEANS AND SNOW/SNAP PEAS. While these are technically legumes, they are far more "pod" than "bean," and green plant matter is generally good for you.

VINEGAR AND BOTANICAL EXTRACTS. Most vinegar (including white, red wine, balsamic, apple cider, and rice) and alcohol-based botanical extracts (like vanilla, lemon, or lavender) are allowed during your Whole30 program. (Just not *malt-based* vinegar or extracts, which will be clearly labeled as such, as they contain gluten.)

COCONUT AMINOS. All brands of coconut aminos (a brewed and naturally fermented soy sauce substitute) are acceptable, even if you see the word "coconut nectar" in the ingredient list.

IODIZED SALT. All iodized salt contains a tiny amount of dextrose (sugar) as a stabilizer, but ruling out table salt would be unreasonable. This exception will not impact your Whole30 results in any way.

IT'S FOR YOUR OWN GOOD

Here comes the tough love, heavy on the love—perhaps the most famous part of the Whole30. This is for those of you who are considering taking on this life-changing month, but aren't sure you can actually pull it off, cheat-free, for a full 30 days. This is for people who have tried comitting to health initiatives before, but "slipped" or "fell off the wagon" or "just *had* to eat [fill in food here] because of this [fill in event here]." This is for you, said with love.

THIS IS NOT HARD. Fighting cancer is hard. Birthing a baby is hard. Losing a parent is hard. Drinking your coffee black is. not. hard. You've done harder things than this, and you have no excuse not to complete the program as written. It's only 30 days, and it's for the most important cause: the only physical body you will ever have in this lifetime.

DON'T EVEN CONSIDER THE POSSIBILITY OF CHEATING. Unless you physically trip and your face lands in a box of doughnuts, there is no "slip." It is always a choice to eat something unhealthy, and if you open the door now to "Whole30 but . . ." you will bail on the program, and I cannot allow you to bail on yourself again. Commit to the program 100 percent for the full 30 days. Don't give yourself an excuse to fail before you've even started.

YOU NEVER, EVER, EVER HAVE TO EAT ANYTHING YOU DON'T WANT TO EAT. You're all adults. Stand up for yourself. Learn to say, "no, thank you" and hold the line without defending, explaining, or excusing your decision. Just

because it's your sister's birthday, best friend's wedding, or office party does not mean you *have* to eat or drink anything. It is always a choice, and I hope we all stopped succumbing to peer pressure in seventh grade.

THIS DOES REQUIRE EFFORT. Meal planning, grocery shopping, cooking, dining out, explaining the program to friends and family, and dealing with stress will all prove challenging at some point during your program. I've given you all the tools, guidelines, and resources you'll need in the eight Whole30 books and on our website, and our community is here 24/7 with accountability, resources, advice, and support . . . but you also have to take responsibility for your own program. Improved health, habits, and relationship with food don't happen automatically just because you're now taking a pass on bread. This will be work, but it will be worth it.

YOU CAN DO THIS. You've come this far—don't back out now. You want to do this. You *need* to do this. And I believe in you, even if you're not quite ready to believe in yourself. So stop thinking about it, and start doing it. Right now, this very minute, commit to the Whole30—and tell someone you're doing it.

I want you to have this experience. I want you to join our community, complete the program, and see amazing results in every area of your life. Even if you aren't convinced this will *actually* change your life, just give me 30 short days. You are that important, and I believe in our efficacy that much. It changed my life, and I want it to change yours, too.

Welcome to the Whole30.

getting started with the whole30

Planning and preparation are THE key to Whole30 success. Here are some basic steps for getting your home and your head Whole30-ready. For a more detailed step-by-step plan for getting started with the program, see pages 17 to 31 in *The Whole30*.

STEP 1: CHOOSE YOUR START DATE

Start *as soon as possible*, but plan carefully. If you've got a once-in-a-lifetime vacation, a planned trip to an unfamiliar location, or a wedding (especially your own) in your immediate future, consider starting the Whole30 after those events. It's also important not to have your Whole30 end the day before a vacation, holiday, or special event where you'll want to eat All the Things. The systematic reintroduction process is just as critical as the 30-day elimination. Ideally, you'll allow at least 10 days after your Whole30 is done to go through the reintroduction schedule as outlined—so for planning purposes, block out 40 full days for the program.

Finally, take a look at your calendar during the proposed 30-day period and see what business or personal commitments you have in place. If you've got a family dinner, a backyard BBQ, or a bridal shower in your imminent future, excellent! You've got a variety of menus right here in this book, so whether you're hosting or a guest, you'll know exactly what to make or bring to wow the crowd and stick to the program. It's still a good idea to create a plan for how to navigate social occasions (see Step 4), but don't let these common social gatherings push your Whole30 off.

Finally, write your start date on a calendar in permanent marker (or add a bunch of emojis to your electronic calendar). Really—write it down. Habit research shows that putting your commitment on paper makes you more likely to succeed.

STEP 2: BUILD YOUR SUPPORT TEAM

Finding the right support network will be critical to keeping you motivated, inspired, and accountable during your program. The first step is sharing a bit about the program and your motivation about why it's important to you. A few tips on the first part:

DON'T HAVE THIS CONVERSATION OVER DINNER!
Try introducing it during a walk or car ride, a relaxed moment before bed, or after a fitness class.

DEVELOP A WHOLE30 "ELEVATOR PITCH"— a way to explain the program quickly on the off chance someone hasn't heard of it. Don't use the word "diet" or they'll get the wrong idea. Try, "The Whole30 is a 30-day self-experiment designed to teach me which foods work for my body."

LEAD WITH THE THINGS YOU *WILL* BE EATING, NOT THE "NO" LIST. Give examples! "A typical Whole30 breakfast is a vegetable frittata with hot sauce and bacon crumbles, and a side of avocado with fresh berries."

You should also share *why* you are choosing to embark upon this journey. Make it as personal as is appropriate. Share your current struggles, your goals, and all the ways you believe the program will make you healthier and happier. Be specific, and choose talking points that will resonate with your conversation partner. Maybe, "Every day after lunch, I feel like I need a nap—so instead, I have some sugar, which leaves me fuzzy and hungry again. I'm hoping the Whole30 will give me an energy and focus boost without needing a soda and granola bar."

Finally, don't forget to let them know how they can help you, and *ask* for their support. Be clear about whether you want them to be a cheerleader, accountability partner, resource, or butt-kicker, and say, "I'm really committed to this. Will you help me?" Their buy-in will feel good and let them know how important this is to you and how much you value their support.

Unfortunately, despite all your best efforts, family and friends may be less than supportive of your Whole30 efforts. If you're having a hard time talking to friends and family about the Whole30 or are dealing with pushback during your conversations, read the Friends, Family, and Food section in *The Whole30's Food Freedom Forever* for guidance.

STEP 3: GET YOUR HOUSE READY

First, get all the stuff you won't be eating out of the fridge and pantry. Be thorough; throw out the foods you won't be eating, give that favorite bottle of wine to a neighbor for safekeeping, or donate your pantry goods to a local food bank. (Warning: Do NOT throw yourself a Carb-a-pa-looza and eat it all up the night before your program starts. I promise, that will not go well.)

If you're the only one at home doing the Whole30, dedicate one drawer in your fridge, one out-of-the-way cabinet, and one covered bin in the pantry for your family's off-plan items. You don't want to have to reach around the Oreos every time you need a can of coconut milk.

Make a plan for what you'll eat for breakfast, lunch, dinner, and emergency food (grab-and-go foods you can keep at work, in your bag, and at home) for at least the first few days of your Whole30. (Trust me—this is not the time to "wing it," as the Whole30 is different from anything you've ever done, and a sugar-hungry brain without a plan is *highly* likely to just hit the vending machine.) Then, go grocery shopping and buy what you need for your first set of meals, emergency food, and pantry staples. (See whole30.com/pdf-downloads for a detailed shopping list.)

STEP 4:
PLAN FOR SUCCESS

Think about the next 30 days, and write down every potentially stressful, difficult, or complicated situation you may encounter during your Whole30. These may include business lunches, family dinners, travel plans, a long day at work, birthday parties, office gatherings, family stress, job stress, financial stress . . . anything you think could derail your Whole30 train. Then, make a plan for how you'll handle it, using if/then statements. Some examples might include:

BUSINESS LUNCH: If my coworkers pressure me to have a drink, then I'll say, "No, thanks, not today" and will keep repeating it with a smile until they stop.

FAMILY DINNER: If Mom invites me out for dinner, then I'll ask if I can cook for her instead.

TRAVEL DAY: If I get to the airport and my flight is delayed, then I'll snack on the DNX Bar, carrot sticks, and single-serve almond butter I brought in my carry-on.

Finally, plan three quick and easy "go-to" simple Whole30 meals. (I call them "ingredient meals" because they're less recipe and more meat + veggies + fat + sauce/dressing.)

Write your list down and post it on your fridge so you'll always have a plan for nights when things get busy.

STEP 5:
TOSS THAT SCALE

Your last step, but a hard one for many—for the next 30 days, get rid of your scale. Put it in the garage, give it to a friend to "hold," or better yet, take it out back and introduce it to your sledgehammer because aren't you tired of letting that thing dictate your self-confidence?

We don't want you to ignore your body for the next 30 days—it'll be obvious if your clothes are fitting differently, your stomach is flatter, your rings are looser, or your skin is clearer. But remember the Whole30 isn't about weight loss, and to hyper-focus on your body composition means you'll be missing so many other incredible benefits. (If you really want to, you can weigh yourself or take measurements and/or photos on Days 0 and 31 . . . but many Whole30'ers don't, and they report feeling *so free* because of it.)

READY, SET, WHOLE30!

Now it's time to re-read the program details, FAQs, and Whole30 Timeline in *The Whole30;* write your goals in *Whole30 Day by Day;* and choose some recipes from this book for your first week's meal plan. Yes, these dishes were designed for special occasions . . . but I think the first day of your Whole30 is a very special occasion indeed.

family game night

Turn off the TV! It's time for a little friendly face-to-face competition among your nearest and dearest. Game night is a tradition for many families; there's usually a fair amount of good-natured ribbing and belly-laughter too! If your family has a regular game night, you probably have some favorite games *and* some favorite foods, but if you're doing a Whole30, pizza, popcorn, and nachos are not part of the game plan. This menu of family-friendly finger foods, featuring potato skins, "tacos," creamy dip, and a bacon-y nut snack mix, frees hands up for throwing dice, moving game pieces, shuffling cards, and high-fives! (Just have lots of napkins on hand.)

• •

blt potato skins

**charred pepper steak tacos
with citrus chimichurri**

layered mexican dip

**smashed potatoes with everything
seasoning and garlic mayo**

**peppery pecan chicken drumsticks
with cider barbecue sauce**

**double peppered bacon-
nut snack mix**

everyone wins!

SERVING A SPREAD OF HEALTHY WHOLE30 FOODS TO YOUR KIDS, whether they're at the age for Candyland or Monopoly, offers up an opportunity to talk about the benefits of eating whole, real food as a family. It's a chance to model good behavior and reinforce the idea that food that's healthy for our bodies can be even more fun and delicious than food that isn't. ("It's nice that no one fights during game night anymore. I think all that sugar was making us cranky.")

KEEP THINGS LIGHT. Emphasize that the real fun isn't in winning, but enjoying one another's company and sharing the yummy food you prepared together.

LET THE KIDS HELP PLAN AND PREPARE YOUR GAME NIGHT MENU. Families on the Whole30 report spending more quality time with their kids in the kitchen, and getting the kids involved will make a transition away from pizza and soda easier.

INSTITUTE A SCREEN-FREE RULE; no TV in the background and no phones at the table. Family game night (emphasis on "family") is all about interacting with real live humans you love. Parents, this is your chance to model, too. Airplane mode, engage!

blt potato skins

This recipe takes the elements of a favorite summer sandwich and turns them into a yummy something to munch on when you're engaged in a little friendly competition with those you love best.

· ·

PREP: 10 MINUTES **COOK:** 5 MINUTES
ROAST: 30 MINUTES **TOTAL:** 45 MINUTES

· ·

1 pint grape tomatoes

2 sprigs fresh thyme

2 tablespoons extra-virgin olive oil

½ teaspoon coarse salt

¼ teaspoon black pepper

4 slices Whole30-compliant bacon

4 medium red and/or Yukon gold potatoes, sliced ¼ inch thick

¼ cup Basic Mayonnaise (page 240) or Whole30-compliant mayonnaise

1 cup shredded romaine lettuce

PREHEAT the oven to 425°F. Line a large rimmed baking pan with parchment paper.

ARRANGE the tomatoes and thyme sprigs on the baking pan, drizzle with 1 tablespoon of the olive oil, and sprinkle with ¼ teaspoon of the salt and the pepper. Roast for 20 to 25 minutes, until lightly browned and tender. Let cool; discard the thyme sprigs.

MEANWHILE, in a large skillet, cook the bacon over medium heat until crisp, about 5 minutes. Transfer to paper towels to drain. When cool, crumble and set aside.

ARRANGE the potatoes on another large rimmed baking pan. Brush both sides of the potatoes with the remaining 1 tablespoon olive oil and sprinkle with the remaining ¼ teaspoon salt. Roast for 10 to 12 minutes, turning once, until lightly browned and tender.

IN a medium bowl, gently stir together the roasted tomatoes and mayonnaise. To serve, spoon the tomato mixture on the potatoes. Top with the crumbled bacon and shredded lettuce.

charred pepper steak tacos with citrus chimichurri

SERVES 4

The chimichurri sauce—spiked with orange and lime juice—is a refreshing addition to the rich flavor of the ancho-and-cumin-rubbed steak. These tacos are a little messy to eat, but they sure are tasty! Serve with lots of napkins and a sense of humor.

....

PREP: 20 MINUTES   **COOK:** 15 MINUTES
STAND: 15 MINUTES   **TOTAL:** 50 MINUTES

....

FOR THE CITRUS CHIMICHURRI

1 orange

1 lime

1 cup lightly packed, roughly chopped fresh parsley

1 cup lightly packed, roughly chopped fresh cilantro

⅓ cup extra-virgin olive oil

2 tablespoons red wine vinegar

¼ cup chopped shallot

2 cloves garlic, coarsely chopped

FOR THE STEAK AND PEPPERS

2 red, yellow, and/or orange bell peppers, halved lengthwise and seeded

2 tablespoons extra-virgin olive oil

½ teaspoon ancho chile powder

½ teaspoon cumin seeds

¼ teaspoon garlic powder

⅛ teaspoon salt

⅛ teaspoon black pepper

1 flank steak or skirt steak (8 to 10 ounces)

TO SERVE

Shredded cabbage

Diced avocado

Roasted and salted pepitas

MAKE THE CITRUS CHIMICHURRI: Remove 1 teaspoon zest and 1 tablespoon juice from the orange. Remove ½ teaspoon zest and 1 teaspoon juice from the lime. In a blender or food processor, combine the orange juice and zest, lime juice and zest, parsley, cilantro, olive oil, vinegar, shallot, and garlic. Pulse several times, then puree until almost smooth. Transfer to a bowl and cover until ready to serve.

MAKE THE STEAK AND PEPPERS: Adjust the oven racks so one is about 6 inches from the broiler heat. Preheat the broiler. Line a large rimmed baking pan with foil. Place the peppers on the foil, cut sides down, and drizzle with 1 tablespoon of the olive oil. Broil the peppers for about 8 minutes, until charred and just tender. Carefully enclose the peppers with the foil; let stand for 10 to 15 minutes. Peel and discard some of the charred skin.

MEANWHILE, preheat a grill or grill pan over medium-high heat. In a small bowl, combine the ancho chile powder, cumin seeds, garlic powder, salt, and pepper. Rub the steak with the remaining 1 tablespoon olive oil; sprinkle both sides with the seasoning.

GRILL the steak, turning once halfway through, for 7 to 8 minutes, or to desired doneness (145°F for medium). Transfer the steak to a cutting board; tent with foil and let rest for 5 minutes.

THINLY slice the steak.

FOR each taco, place four or five slices of steak inside a pepper half. Drizzle with the chimichurri. Top with cabbage, avocado, and pepitas.

layered mexican dip

SERVES 4

The only thing you have to plan a little bit ahead for in this recipe is the creamy base of the dip, made with soaked pureed macadamia nuts. The rest of it goes together in less than 30 minutes.

....

PREP: 20 MINUTES **STAND:** 8 HOURS
COOK: 10 MINUTES **TOTAL:** 8 HOURS 30 MINUTES

....

1½ cups macadamia nuts

¼ cup extra-virgin olive oil

1 (4-ounce) can diced mild green chiles, drained slightly

1½ teaspoons ground cumin

½ teaspoon salt

½ pound lean ground beef

1½ teaspoons Whole30-compliant chili powder

1 teaspoon dried oregano, crushed

⅛ teaspoon black pepper

1 avocado, halved, pitted, peeled, and roughly chopped

1 teaspoon fresh lime juice

1 cup Whole30-compliant pico de gallo

2 cups shredded iceberg lettuce

Sliced carrots, cucumbers, and/or jicama

PLACE the macadamia nuts in a small bowl and add enough water to cover by 1 inch. Cover the bowl and let stand for 8 to 12 hours. Drain the nuts and rinse under cold water.

COMBINE the macadamia nuts, olive oil, green chiles, cumin, and ¼ teaspoon of the salt in a blender or food processor. Cover and pulse until finely chopped, then blend or process until smooth, 4 to 5 minutes. Spread the mixture in the bottom of a 9-inch pie plate. (This can be made up to 2 days ahead.)

HEAT a large skillet over medium-high heat. Add the ground beef, chili powder, oregano, remaining ¼ teaspoon salt, and pepper. Cook, stirring with a wooden spoon to break up the meat, until browned, about 10 minutes. Remove from the heat. Let cool slightly, then spread over the nut mixture.

IN a small bowl, use a fork to mash the avocado with the lime juice. Spoon the avocado in small mounds over the beef. Top with the pico de gallo and iceberg lettuce.

SERVE the dip with sliced carrots, cucumbers, and/or jicama.

smashed potatoes with everything seasoning and garlic mayo

SERVES 4

No bagel is needed when you serve these crispy oven-roasted potatoes seasoned with an "everything" blend of dried onion flakes, sesame seeds, poppy seeds, garlic powder, and salt.

PREP: 15 MINUTES   **COOK:** 20 MINUTES
ROAST/BROIL: 20 MINUTES   **TOTAL:** 60 MINUTES

1 teaspoon dried onion flakes

1 teaspoon sesame seeds

½ teaspoon poppy seeds

½ teaspoon garlic powder

½ teaspoon salt

¼ cup Basic Mayonnaise (page 240) or Whole30-compliant mayonnaise

1 small clove garlic, minced

¾ to 1 pound baby Yukon Gold or red potatoes

2 tablespoons Clarified Butter (page 241) or ghee

2 tablespoons chopped fresh parsley

ADJUST the oven racks so one is 4 to 6 inches from the broiler heat. Preheat the oven to 400°F. Line a large rimmed baking pan with parchment paper.

IN a small bowl, combine the onion flakes, sesame seeds, poppy seeds, garlic powder, and salt. Set aside.

IN another small bowl, stir together the mayonnaise and minced garlic. Set aside.

PLACE the potatoes in a medium saucepan. Add enough water to cover by 1 inch. Bring to a boil. Reduce the heat and simmer, stirring occasionally, until just tender, 20 to 25 minutes. Drain; return the potatoes to the saucepan. Add the butter and 2 teaspoons of the seasoning; gently stir to combine. Arrange the potatoes on the baking pan.

USE the bottom of a glass to smash each potato until about ½ inch thick. Roast on the upper rack for 17 to 20 minutes, until the potatoes are golden brown. Turn the oven to broil. Broil for about 3 minutes, until the potatoes are crisp on top.

ARRANGE the potatoes on a platter. To serve, spoon about 1 teaspoon of the garlic mayonnaise on each potato. Sprinkle with the remaining seasoning and the parsley.

peppery pecan chicken drumsticks with cider barbecue sauce

SERVES 4

A light brushing of mayonnaise helps the savory pecan coating stick to the chicken, resulting in maximum crunch after it's baked. The smoky barbecue sauce is the perfect foil for the richness of the chicken.

· ·

PREP: 15 MINUTES   **BAKE:** 30 MINUTES
COOK: 5 MINUTES   **TOTAL:** 50 MINUTES

· ·

FOR THE CHICKEN

1 cup pecan pieces

1½ teaspoons ground Aleppo pepper, ancho chile powder, or paprika

¾ teaspoon salt

¾ teaspoon black pepper

¾ teaspoon garlic powder

¾ teaspoon onion powder

8 chicken drumsticks

⅓ cup Basic Mayonnaise (page 240) or Whole30-compliant mayonnaise

2 tablespoons Clarified Butter (page 241) or ghee, melted

FOR THE BARBECUE DIPPING SAUCE

1 (8-ounce) can Whole30-compliant tomato sauce

½ cup apple cider

2 tablespoons balsamic vinegar

1 teaspoon smoked paprika

½ teaspoon celery seeds

¼ teaspoon salt

PREHEAT the oven to 425°F. Line a large rimmed baking pan with parchment paper.

MAKE THE CHICKEN: Place the pecans in a food processor. Pulse until finely ground, about 45 seconds. In a medium bowl or shallow dish, combine the ground pecans, Aleppo pepper, salt, black pepper, garlic powder, and onion powder. Brush the chicken drumsticks with mayonnaise. Dip each drumstick into the pecan coating. Arrange the chicken on the baking pan. Drizzle with the butter.

ROAST the chicken for about 20 minutes. Turn and roast about 10 minutes more, until the chicken is lightly browned and the internal temperature is 170°F.

MAKE THE BARBECUE DIPPING SAUCE: Meanwhile, in a medium saucepan, combine the tomato sauce, cider, balsamic vinegar, smoked paprika, celery seeds, and salt. Bring to a boil. Reduce the heat and simmer, until slightly thickened, 5 to 10 minutes. Transfer the sauce to a serving bowl.

ARRANGE the chicken on a platter and serve with the sauce for dipping.

double peppered bacon-nut snack mix

SERVES 4

You will want to savor every crunchy bite of this delicious nut-based nosh. Aleppo pepper and cracked black pepper give it just the mildest bit of heat, while freeze-dried apples add pops of airy sweetness.

....

PREP: 12 MINUTES   BAKE: 28 MINUTES   TOTAL: 40 MINUTES

....

4 slices Whole30-compliant bacon

1 teaspoon freshly cracked black pepper

1 teaspoon ground Aleppo pepper
or ancho chile powder

1 cup walnut halves

1 cup raw almonds

1 tablespoon extra-virgin olive oil

½ teaspoon dried thyme

½ teaspoon dried oregano

½ teaspoon salt

¾ cup freeze-dried apples, broken
into bite-size pieces

PREHEAT the oven to 375°F. Line a large rimmed baking pan with foil.

PLACE a cooling rack on the baking pan. Arrange the bacon on the cooling rack. Sprinkle both sides of the bacon with the black pepper and Aleppo pepper.

BAKE about 20 minutes, until the bacon is crisp. Transfer to a paper towel-lined plate. Crumble when cool.

ON another large rimmed baking pan, combine the walnuts, almonds, olive oil, thyme, oregano, and salt; toss to combine. Spread into a single layer. Bake for 8 to 10 minutes, stirring once halfway through, until lightly toasted. Cool completely.

IN a large bowl, combine the bacon, nuts, and apple pieces.

parent and tot group

If you are an at-home parent of a small child (or children), getting together with other parents provides much-needed interaction and support. Doing puzzles, coloring, and singing along with the Wiggles is certainly rewarding, but everyone in your house will be happier if Mom or Dad can engage in conversation that doesn't involve a rhyming couplet. For your next playdate, try this menu. Perfect for parent-tot gatherings, it gives both the kids and adults something to nibble on: grown-ups will enjoy the sophisticated Basil-Balsamic Cucumber Bites and beverages, while the Prosciutto-Wrapped Apple Slices and Cinnamon-Toasted Oranges will appeal to tiny teeth and inquisitive taste buds. And it's light enough that it can be served between meals without ruining lunch or dinner.

....

basil-balsamic cucumber bites
prosciutto-wrapped apple slices
cinnamon-toasted oranges
with pistachios
cranberry-pear rooibos iced tea
choco-vanilla rooibos tea

let's play!

ONE OF THE TOPICS that comes up most often among parents of toddlers is how to get them to eat their veggies. Invite all your guests to bring a dish or snack their child enjoys, and share their best tricks for successfully serving new foods.

PLAN A FUN FOOD-RELATED ACTIVITY (that isn't too messy!) for the kids to get them interested in noodling around in the kitchen. Cutting bananas with a dull knife, putting the "ants" on your almond butter-covered "log," or washing vegetables and fruit are all tasks that are appropriate for toddlers.

KEEP THE KIDS BUSY and physically active with a treasure hunt, either indoors or outside. Search online for printable scavenger hunts for toddlers and preschoolers.

REMEMBER, this time is as much for you as it is for your kids. Allow yourself to share openly, ask for help if you need it, and lean on others for support. We've all had "parenting fails," and it's nice to remember that you're not alone.

basil-balsamic cucumber bites

SERVES 8

Be sure to get English cucumbers—also called hothouse cucumbers—to make these refreshing nibbles. English cucumbers are seedless, more slender than regular cucumbers, and not waxed. Look for them wrapped in plastic in the produce section.

······································

PREP: 10 MINUTES   COOK: 5 MINUTES
COOL: 20 MINUTES   TOTAL: 35 MINUTES

······································

½ cup balsamic vinegar

2 English cucumbers, sliced 1 inch thick
(you need 24 slices)

⅔ cup drained roasted red peppers

24 fresh basil leaves

24 Whole30-compliant Kalamata olives,
pitted

IN a small saucepan, bring the vinegar to a boil over medium heat. Reduce the heat to a gentle simmer. Cook, uncovered, until the vinegar is reduced to 3 tablespoons, 5 to 6 minutes. Transfer to a small bowl and cool completely, about 20 minutes.

MEANWHILE, arrange the cucumber slices on a serving platter. Dry the peppers with a paper towel. Cut the peppers into 24 pieces; place on the cucumber slices. Top each with a basil leaf, folded in half if necessary. Top with an olive. Insert a cocktail pick to hold all the pieces in place. Drizzle with the reduced vinegar.

prosciutto-wrapped apple slices

SERVES 8

Fresh basil and lemon zest are wrapped up in these fruit-and-prosciutto bundles for a pop of flavor. Make these right before you serve them to keep the apples from turning brown, or you can brush the cut sides of the apples with a little lemon juice.

PREP: 10 MINUTES **TOTAL:** 10 MINUTES

¼ cup chopped fresh basil

3 tablespoons grated lemon zest

12 very thin slices Whole30-compliant prosciutto, halved lengthwise

4 medium apples, cored and cut into 6 wedges each

IN a small bowl, combine the basil and lemon zest. Lay the prosciutto slices on a large cutting board. Spoon 1 teaspoon basil mixture among the prosciutto slices.

WRAP each apple wedge with a prosciutto slice to almost fully cover it.

REPEAT with the remaining prosciutto slices, basil mixture, and apple wedges.

cinnamon-toasted oranges with pistachios

SERVES 8

Even the pickiest tots at the gathering will gobble up these yummy cinnamon-spiced roasted orange slices. Because both the peel and flesh are eaten, it's best if you can find cara cara oranges—they have a thinner peel than navel oranges.

PREP: 10 MINUTES **BAKE:** 5 MINUTES
TOTAL: 15 MINUTES

½ teaspoon ground cinnamon

¼ teaspoon ground nutmeg

4 medium cara cara oranges or navel oranges, cut into ¼-inch slices (you need 24 slices)

3 tablespoons Clarified Butter (page 241) or ghee, melted

½ cup roasted pistachios, chopped

ADJUST an oven rack to the upper third of the oven. Preheat the oven to 475°F. Line a large rimmed baking pan with parchment paper.

IN a small bowl, combine the cinnamon and nutmeg. Set aside. Brush the tops of the orange slices with butter and sprinkle with the cinnamon and nutmeg. Bake until the tops of the orange slices are lightly browned, 5 to 7 minutes.

TO serve, transfer the orange slices to a serving platter. Sprinkle with the pistachios and serve warm.

cranberry-pear rooibos iced tea

SERVES 8

Rooibos (*ROY-bos*) tea—also called redbush tea—is an herbal infusion made from the leaves of a shrub that's native to South Africa. Beyond its beautiful color and interesting flavor—described in turns as smoky, spicy, honey, and caramel—it is packed with health-promoting antioxidants.

·····························

PREP: 10 MINUTES   **STAND:** 15 MINUTES   **CHILL:** 4 HOURS
TOTAL: 4 HOURS 25 MINUTES

·····························

1½ cups frozen cranberries

1 large ripe pear, peeled, cored, and thinly sliced

¼ cup loose rooibos tea leaves
or 10 rooibos tea bags

Ice

IN a large saucepan, bring 2 quarts of water to a boil. Add 1 cup of the cranberries and the pear slices. Boil for 1 minute. Remove the pan from the heat; cover and steep for 10 minutes.

BRING the water to a boil again; remove from the heat. Add the tea; cover and steep for 5 minutes. Strain to remove the tea leaves and fruit. Transfer the tea to a large heatproof pitcher. Cover and chill until cold, at least 4 hours.

TO serve, pour the tea into ice-filled glasses. Garnish each with 1 tablespoon frozen cranberries.

choco-vanilla rooibos tea

SERVES 8

Guests will settle in for some much-needed grown-up conversation with mugs of this sweetly spiced, ruby-hued hot tea.

·····························

PREP: 10 MINUTES   **STAND:** 15 MINUTES
TOTAL: 25 MINUTES

·····························

2 (3-inch) cinnamon sticks, plus more for garnish (optional)

½ vanilla bean, split lengthwise

1 tablespoon cacao nibs

¼ cup loose rooibos tea leaves
or 10 rooibos tea bags

IN a large saucepan, bring 2 quarts of water to a boil. Add the 2 cinnamon sticks, vanilla bean halves, and cacao nibs. Remove from the heat; cover and steep for 10 minutes.

BRING the water to a boil again; remove from the heat. Add the tea; cover and steep for 5 minutes. Strain the tea through a fine-mesh sieve into a large heatproof glass pitcher or teapot.

SERVE hot. Garnish each serving with a cinnamon stick, if desired.

beach picnic

Kelsey Preciado

LITTLE BITS OF REAL FOOD
LITTLEBITSOF.COM

Kelsey Preciado loves to share real-food recipes perfect for everyone from babies to grown-ups. She wants everyone to find joy in their kitchen and their life, and she finds hers somewhere between baked sweet potato fries and a dance party.

It's a sunny summer weekend, and nothing sounds better than some fresh air, warm sand, and splashing around in the water. If you're going to spend all day lake- or oceanside, you need good food to fuel all of that fun. Given all of the other stuff you'll have to pack up, you'll want to keep your meals as simple as possible. This menu featuring a selection of salads (including one that's served on skewers!) is perfect for toting to the beach in a big ice-packed cooler. When it's time to eat, drizzle the Cobb spears with ranch and scoop the curried chicken salad and potato salad onto plates, then finish the meal off with a lemony poppy seed–speckled fruit salad.

. . . .

pesto-bacon potato salad
almond butter–curry chicken salad
cobb spears
**fruit salad with lemon–
poppy seed vinaigrette**
sparkling lemon iced tea

fun in the sun

IF YOU WANT TO GET AN EARLY START TO YOUR DAY, you can make everything the night before. Store the chicken and potato salads in tightly sealed containers in the refrigerator. Toss the cut-up apples with a tiny bit of lemon juice to keep them from turning brown, and dress the Cobb spears and the fruit salad right before serving.

PACK IT IN, PACK IT OUT. If you're going somewhere remote, it might be up to you to keep your park or beach clean. Be sure to bring along a trash bag, zip-top plastic bags, and plastic storage containers so you can easily pack up leftover food and disposables and get rid of them at home.

THE SAFEST SERVEWARE FOR A BEACH PICNIC IS UNBREAKABLE. Look for disposable plates, glasses, forks and spoons that are compostable or bio-degradable. You can find eco-friendly plates made from wheat straw, palm leaves, sugar cane fiber, or bamboo—or pick up some inexpensive melamine dishes and reuse them. Natural baby wipes are also a great idea for cleaning up basically everything.

ENGAGING IN PHYSICALLY ACTIVE FUN with family and friends is a great way to socialize in an environment that isn't food-focused. Beach days create an opportunity to model healthy behaviors for your kids, soak up some nourishing Vitamin D, and have a good excuse for a mid-day nap in the shade.

pesto-bacon potato salad

SERVES 6

Be careful not to overcook the potatoes so that they will hold their shape after being cut and tossed with the pesto. If they get too soft, they won't stay in distinct shapes and your nice potato salad will look mushy.

....

PREP: 20 MINUTES   **COOK:** 10 MINUTES   **TOTAL:** 30 MINUTES

....

2 pounds baby potatoes

1¼ teaspoons coarse salt

2 cups lightly packed fresh basil leaves

½ cup extra-virgin olive oil

½ cup pine nuts or walnuts

4 teaspoons fresh lemon juice

1 tablespoon nutritional yeast

1 large clove garlic, chopped

¼ teaspoon black pepper

6 slices Whole30-compliant bacon

PLACE the potatoes and ½ teaspoon salt in a large pot of water to cover by 1 inch. Bring to a boil, reduce heat to a simmer. Cook until just fork-tender, about 10 to 15 minutes. Drain and set aside.

MEANWHILE, in a food processor or blender, combine the basil, olive oil, pine nuts, lemon juice, nutritional yeast, garlic, pepper, and the remaining ¾ teaspoon salt. Cover and blend or process until almost smooth.

WHEN the potatoes are cool enough to handle, cut in half or quarters. In a large bowl, combine the potatoes and ½ cup of the pesto; stir gently to coat. If desired, add more pesto.

IN a large skillet, cook the bacon over medium heat until crisp, about 10 minutes. Drain on a paper towel–lined plate. Chop the bacon and add to the potatoes. While the bacon grease is still hot, add 1 tablespoon to the potatoes. Stir gently to coat.

STORE the salad in an airtight container in a cooler or refrigerator until ready to serve.

tip: STORE LEFTOVER PESTO in an airtight container in the refrigerator for up to 1 week.

almond butter–curry chicken salad

SERVES 6

This chunky salad is a jumble of chicken, sweet potato, crunchy celery, and raisins— all swathed in an almond butter–curry dressing. Scooping it up with mini bell pepper halves eliminates the need for toting flatware to the beach.

....

PREP: 20 MINUTES **BAKE:** 25 MINUTES
COOL: 30 MINUTES **TOTAL:** 1 HOUR 15 MINUTES

....

3 large boneless, skinless chicken breasts (about 8 ounces each)

¾ teaspoon salt

½ teaspoon black pepper

1 large sweet potato, peeled and diced

1 tablespoon extra-virgin olive oil

¼ cup coconut oil, melted

¼ cup Whole30-compliant almond butter

1 tablespoon cider vinegar

1 teaspoon Whole30-compliant curry powder

1 teaspoon garlic powder

2 stalks celery, finely chopped

¼ cup raisins or currants

9 mini bell peppers, halved

PREHEAT the oven to 375°F. Line two large rimmed baking pans with foil.

ARRANGE the chicken breasts on one pan and season with ½ teaspoon salt and ¼ teaspoon pepper. Spread the sweet potato on the other baking pan; drizzle with the olive oil and toss to coat.

BAKE the chicken for 10 minutes. Add the sweet potato pan to the oven. Bake about 15 minutes more, until the chicken is cooked through (165°F) and sweet potatoes are tender. Transfer to a wire rack to cool. When the chicken has cooled, chop it into bite-size pieces.

IN a large bowl, whisk together the coconut oil, almond butter, vinegar, curry powder, garlic powder, and the remaining ¼ teaspoon each salt and pepper. Add the chicken, sweet potato, celery, and raisins; gently stir until well combined.

STORE the chicken salad and pepper halves separately in airtight containers in a cooler or refrigerator until ready to serve.

TO serve, scoop the chicken salad into bowls or cups; add 3 pepper halves for diners to scoop up the salad.

cobb spears

SERVES 6

Folding the lettuce and bacon into tidy packages before threading them onto the skewers helps give the skewers a nice shape—and also makes for easier eating.

....

PREP: 1 HOUR   TOTAL: 1 HOUR

....

FOR THE RANCH VINAIGRETTE

1 cup extra-virgin olive oil

¼ cup white wine vinegar

1 teaspoon dried dill

1 teaspoon dried parsley

1 teaspoon garlic powder

½ teaspoon onion powder

¾ teaspoon coarse salt

¼ teaspoon black pepper

FOR THE SPEARS

18 (8- or 10-inch) wooden skewers

3 hearts of romaine, ends trimmed and separated into 12 leaves

12 slices Whole30-compliant bacon, cooked (not crisp), cut into 3 pieces

5 large hard-cooked eggs, peeled and quartered (see Tip)

2 cooked chicken breasts, each cut into 9 cubes (see Tip)

18 cherry tomatoes

MAKE THE RANCH VINAIGRETTE: In a blender, combine the olive oil, vinegar, dill, parsley, garlic powder, onion powder, salt, and pepper. Cover and blend the vinaigrette until well combined. Transfer to an airtight container; place in a cooler or refrigerator until ready to serve.

MAKE THE SPEARS: On each skewer, thread a folded piece of lettuce, folded piece of bacon, an egg quarter, a cube of chicken, another folded piece of bacon, a cherry tomato, and another folded piece of lettuce. Store the spears in airtight plastic containers with lids or large resealable plastic bags in a cooler or refrigerator until ready to serve.

TO serve, drizzle spears with the dressing.

tips: PLACE THE EGGS IN A LARGE SAUCEPAN; add cold water to cover by 1 inch. Bring the water to a rolling boil. Remove from the heat. Let stand, covered, for 15 minutes. Drain the eggs. Add cold water to the pan to cover the eggs. Add a few handfuls of ice cubes. Let stand until the eggs are cool enough to handle, about 15 minutes. Drain the eggs and peel.

PREHEAT THE OVEN TO 350°F. Place 2 chicken breasts (about 7 ounces each) on a medium rimmed baking pan lined with parchment paper or foil. Drizzle with olive oil and season with salt and pepper. Bake at 350°F for about 25 minutes, until cooked through (165°F).

fruit salad with lemon–poppy seed vinaigrette

SERVES 6

Even the simplest vinaigrette—just lemon juice, olive oil, poppy seeds, and a little salt—enhances the flavors of the fruits in this colorful salad.

••••••••••••••••••••••••••••••

PREP: 20 MINUTES **TOTAL:** 20 MINUTES

••••••••••••••••••••••••••••••

2 small apples (such as Honeycrisp), cored and chopped

1 cup chopped pineapple

1 cup chopped cantaloupe

1 cup grapes, halved

1 cup quartered strawberries

3 clementines, peeled and sectioned

¼ cup fresh lemon juice

¼ cup extra-virgin olive oil

1 teaspoon poppy seeds

Pinch salt

IN a large bowl, combine the apples, pineapple, cantaloupe, grapes, strawberries, and clementines.

IN a blender, combine the lemon juice, olive oil, poppy seeds, and salt. Cover and blend on high, just until the lemon juice and oil have emulsified, 10 to 20 seconds. Pour the dressing over the fruit; stir gently to combine.

STORE the salad in an airtight container in a cooler or refrigerator until ready to serve.

sparkling lemon iced tea

SERVES 6

For many people, a tall glass of cold, freshly brewed iced tea is the ultimate summer refreshment. Adding sparkling lemon-flavored water makes it even better. Be sure to pack plenty of ice in your cooler for refills.

••••••••••••••••••••••••••••••

PREP: 15 MINUTES **STAND:** 30 MINUTES **TOTAL:** 45 MINUTES

••••••••••••••••••••••••••••••

6 black tea bags

24 ounces Whole30-compliant lemon-flavored sparkling water, chilled

Ice

BRING 3 cups water to a boil. Add the tea bags and steep for 10 minutes. Remove the bags. Allow the tea to cool to room temperature, about 30 minutes. Transfer to an airtight pitcher.

TO serve, pour ½ cup of the tea concentrate into an ice-filled glass. Add ½ cup sparkling water. Stir gently.

date night

The classic date activity is dinner out, but when you're doing a Whole30, eating at a restaurant can be tricky. (Plus, you don't want to be "that person" on a first date.) How about our date night dinner *in*? This menu offers up restaurant-quality food so elegant and delicious, it's sure to impress. Plus, it's romantic to cook together! If you're ambitious, you can make every dish, or pick and choose to build your own menu. Start with one of the seafood first courses, and select a vegetable side to serve with the Mustard and Coriander-Crusted Pork Tenderloin. End the night cozied up on the couch with warm coconut milk infused with turmeric, cinnamon, and ginger.

•••••••••••••••••••••••

**sautéed snap peas with
lemon and tarragon**

**coriander-crusted pork tenderloin
with tangy apple-mustard compote**

**angels on horseback with
grapefruit-fennel-radish relish**

**roasted root vegetables
with horseradish cream**

fish in crazy water

spicy golden milk

love is in the air

IF THIS IS A FIRST DATE, set the expectation for an alcohol-free night. "I'm not drinking right now" is my favorite way of offering explanation, but you can also say "I'm doing the Whole30" and see how they respond.

YOU DON'T HAVE TO SAY A WORD ABOUT THE WHOLE30, but if your date asks questions about the program, have a short "elevator pitch" ready, explaining what the program is and why you're committed to it.

IF COOKING AND EATING IS THE PRIMARY ENTERTAINMENT FOR THE EVENING, do it in stages. Have the first course(s) ready to serve, and enjoy them while you prepare the pork tenderloin and vegetable side(s). Turn up a fun kitchen playlist and use dinner to see how well you work together!

TURN OFF YOUR PHONE—and ask your date to do the same. Date night is about focusing on each other, whether you've known each other for just a few days or have been married for years. (And not picking up your phone during dinner scores *big* points these days.)

sautéed snap peas with lemon and tarragon

SERVES 2

Snap peas are at their best when they are still crunchy and bright green, so be careful not to overcook—3 minutes max is perfect.

······································

PREP: 10 MINUTES **COOK:** 4 MINUTES **TOTAL:** 15 MINUTES

······································

8 ounces sugar snap peas, trimmed (about 2½ cups)

1 tablespoon extra-virgin olive oil

2 tablespoons fresh lemon juice

¼ teaspoon coarse salt

⅛ teaspoon black pepper

1 tablespoon minced fresh tarragon

1 teaspoon grated lemon zest

PLACE the peas and ¼ cup water in a large skillet. Cover and bring to a boil over high heat. Cook for 2 minutes. Reduce to medium-high. Cook, uncovered, shaking the pan occasionally, until the water evaporates, about 1 minute.

REMOVE from the heat. Add the olive oil, lemon juice, salt, and pepper; stir to combine.

TO serve, sprinkle with the tarragon and lemon zest.

coriander-crusted pork tenderloin with tangy apple-mustard compote

SERVES 2

This entrée has serious restaurant-quality flair. The highly flavorful and aromatic crust brings some black-pepper heat that complements the sweetness of the apple compote.

....

PREP: 15 MINUTES   **COOK:** 15 MINUTES   **ROAST:** 10 MINUTES
STAND: 5 MINUTES   **TOTAL:** 45 MINUTES

....

3 tablespoons plus 1 teaspoon Whole30-compliant Dijon mustard

1 Whole30-compliant pork tenderloin (1 to 1½ pounds), trimmed

3 tablespoons coriander seeds, lightly crushed (see Tip)

1 tablespoon black peppercorns, lightly crushed (see Tip)

¾ teaspoon coarse salt

2 tablespoons extra-virgin olive oil

1 large shallot, thinly sliced

1 tart-sweet apple (such as Pink Lady), cored and thinly sliced

½ teaspoon dried thyme leaves, crushed

½ cup unfiltered apple cider

1 tablespoon cider vinegar

⅛ teaspoon black pepper

PREHEAT the oven to 400°F.

SPREAD 3 tablespoons of the mustard over the tenderloin. Evenly press the coriander seeds and peppercorns onto the tenderloin. Season with ½ teaspoon salt.

IN an extra-large ovenproof skillet, heat 1 tablespoon olive oil over medium-high heat. Add the tenderloin, top side down, and brown on all sides, 8 to 10 minutes. (If the mustard-and-seed crust falls off in places, use a spoon to press it onto the top of the tenderloin after you turn it.)

TRANSFER the skillet to the oven. Roast for 10 to 15 minutes, until the tenderloin is 145°F. Carefully remove the skillet from the oven; transfer the tenderloin to a cutting board. Tent with foil and let rest for 5 minutes.

MEANWHILE, in a medium skillet, heat the remaining 1 tablespoon olive oil over medium heat. Add the shallot, apple, and thyme. Cook, stirring frequently, until the shallot and apple are crisp-tender, 4 to 5 minutes. Add the cider and simmer until reduced by half, about 3 minutes. Whisk in the vinegar and remaining 1 teaspoon mustard. Season with the remaining ¼ teaspoon salt and the pepper.

TO serve, slice the tenderloin into medallions. Arrange 3 medallions on each of two plates. Top with a generous ⅓ cup of the apple compote. (You will probably have some leftover pork and compote.)

tip: YOU CAN CRUSH THE CORIANDER SEEDS and black peppercorns with a mortar and pestle. If you don't have one, place them in a small plastic bag. Seal the bag and roll over it with a rolling pin a few times.

angels on horseback with grapefruit-fennel-radish relish

SERVES 2

No one really knows how this classic hors d'oeuvre got its name, but it always refers to some version of scallops wrapped in bacon. The first mention of it in a cookbook goes back to the late nineteenth century, and it experienced popularity among foodies in the 1960s. This contemporary take features a refreshing and super-flavorful relish.

....

PREP: 30 MINUTES **COOK:** 10 MINUTES **TOTAL:** 40 MINUTES

....

½ red grapefruit, peeled and cut into segments (see Tip)

½ cup shaved fennel (see Tip)

¼ cup julienned red radishes

3 tablespoons fresh grapefruit juice

2 tablespoons minced shallot

2 tablespoons chopped fresh parsley

2 tablespoons extra-virgin olive oil

½ teaspoon smoked paprika

½ teaspoon anise seeds, lightly crushed (see Tip)

¼ teaspoon coarse salt

¼ teaspoon black pepper

6 sea scallops (about 8 ounces total)

3 slices Whole30-compliant bacon, halved crosswise

PREHEAT the broiler to high. Line a large rimmed baking pan with foil.

IN a small bowl, combine the grapefruit, fennel, radishes, grapefruit juice, shallot, parsley, olive oil, paprika, and anise. Season with ⅛ teaspoon each of the salt and pepper. Stir to combine.

RINSE the scallops and pat dry with a paper towel. Season with the remaining ⅛ teaspoon each salt and pepper. Wrap a half slice of bacon around each scallop, secure with a toothpick, and arrange on the baking pan.

BROIL for 8 to 10 minutes, turning once halfway, until the scallops are translucent and the bacon is cooked. To serve, divide the relish between two appetizer plates and top each with three scallops.

tips: IF YOU HAVE A FEW EXTRA MINUTES, you can supreme the grapefruit segments (remove the membrane from the fruit so it can easily be served in slices). With a sharp knife, trim the fruit's ends. Set one end on a cutting board and slice off the peel and pith in sections. Set the fruit on its side. Cut toward the center, along a membrane. Then slice along the adjacent membrane until the cuts meet, releasing the segment. Repeat with the remaining segments.

TO TRIM A FENNEL BULB, cut off the stalk about 1 inch from the bulb. Cut a thin slice from the root end and discard. Remove any wilted outer layers. Stand the bulb upright and cut in half. Cut away and discard the tough core from each half. Use a mandoline set at ⅛ inch or sharp knife to thinly slice.

YOU CAN CRUSH THE ANISE SEEDS in a mortar and pestle. If you don't have one, place them in a small plastic bag. Seal the bag and roll over it with a rolling pin a few times.

roasted root vegetables with horseradish cream

SERVES 2

A drizzle of zesty horseradish cream is the finishing touch on these simple but delicious herb-and-lemon roasted roots. Get them prepped and put them in the oven when you start to brown the tenderloin for the Coriander-Crusted Pork Tenderloin with Tangy Apple-Mustard Compote (page 33).

PREP: 20 MINUTES **ROAST:** 25 MINUTES **TOTAL:** 45 MINUTES

2 small carrots, peeled and cut into ½-inch pieces

2 small parsnips, peeled and cut into ½-inch pieces

1 medium turnip (about 8 ounces), peeled and cut into ½-inch pieces

3 red potatoes, cut into ½-inch pieces

1 tablespoon extra-virgin olive oil

½ teaspoon coarse salt

¼ teaspoon black pepper

1 (14-ounce) can Whole30-compliant coconut milk, refrigerated overnight

1 tablespoon Whole30-compliant horseradish

1 teaspoon grated lemon zest

1 teaspoon fresh lemon juice

2 tablespoons chopped fresh parsley

PREHEAT the oven to 400°F. Line a large rimmed baking pan with parchment paper.

IN a medium bowl, combine the carrots, parsnips, turnip, and potatoes. Drizzle with the olive oil and sprinkle with ¼ teaspoon salt and ⅛ teaspoon pepper. Toss to combine. Arrange in a single layer on the pan. Roast, stirring once halfway through, until tender, about 25 minutes.

MEANWHILE, open the refrigerated can of coconut milk; drain off the liquid and reserve for smoothies. Spoon the coconut cream into a medium bowl. Beat with an electric mixer on medium-high until fluffy, about 5 minutes. Stir in the horseradish, lemon zest and juice, and the remaining ¼ teaspoon salt and ⅛ teaspoon pepper.

SPRINKLE the vegetables with parsley and serve with the horseradish cream.

fish in crazy water

SERVES 2

Gently poaching in "crazy water," or *acqua pazza*, as the Italians call it, is a beautiful way to cook meaty white fish such as mahi-mahi or halibut. As it simmers, it absorbs the flavor of water infused with lemon, capers, garlic, red pepper flakes, citrus juice, and fresh herbs. The texture of the finished fish is always perfect—moist, tender, and buttery.

PREP: 15 MINUTES **COOK:** 10 MINUTES **TOTAL:** 25 MINUTES

1 tablespoon extra-virgin olive oil, plus more for serving (optional)

1 small lemon, thinly sliced and seeded

1 tablespoon Whole30-compliant drained capers

2 cloves garlic, thinly sliced

Pinch red pepper flakes

½ cup grape tomatoes, halved

2 tablespoons fresh lemon juice

2 tablespoons fresh orange juice

2 sprigs fresh thyme, plus more leaves for garnish

2 fillets (3 to 4 ounces each) fresh mahi-mahi or halibut

¼ teaspoon coarse salt

Pinch black pepper

Finishing salt, such as Maldon (optional)

IN a small skillet or saucepan, heat 1 tablespoon olive oil over medium-high heat. Add the lemon and capers. Cook, turning once halfway, until the lemons begin to brown around the edges and the capers shrivel slightly, 3 to 4 minutes. Remove the lemons and capers from the pan. Set aside.

ADD the garlic and red pepper flakes to the pan, and cook just until fragrant, about 30 seconds. Add 1 cup water and the tomatoes, lemon juice, orange juice, and thyme sprigs; bring to a simmer. Carefully add the fillets; cover and reduce heat to medium-low. Cook until the fish flakes when tested with a fork, 6 to 8 minutes. (Adjust the heat if necessary to ensure the liquid doesn't hard boil.) Transfer the fillets to shallow serving bowls. Top with the lemon and capers. Tent loosely with foil to keep warm.

COOK the poaching liquid over high heat to reduce and intensify the flavor, 1 to 2 minutes. Season with the coarse salt and black pepper.

SPOON the poaching liquid into the bowls. Drizzle with the olive oil. Sprinkle with the finishing salt and thyme leaves.

spicy golden milk

SERVES 2

Warming and slightly spicy, this beautifully colored beverage is the perfect thing to sip at the end of the evening while you're all snuggled up on the sofa.

···································

PREP: 5 MINUTES **COOK:** 10 MINUTES
STAND: 5 MINUTES **TOTAL:** 20 MINUTES

···································

1 cup Whole30-compliant almond milk
1 cup Whole30-compliant coconut milk (see Tip)
½ teaspoon ground turmeric
¼ teaspoon Whole30-compliant
vanilla bean powder
⅛ teaspoon black pepper
1 cinnamon stick
2 whole star anise
1 piece (1 inch) fresh ginger, peeled and sliced
Ground cinnamon, for serving

IN a small saucepan, combine the almond milk, coconut milk, turmeric, vanilla bean powder, and black pepper. Whisk to combine. Stir in the cinnamon stick, star anise, and ginger. Gently heat over medium heat until steaming, 10 to 12 minutes. Remove from the heat. Cover and let steep for 5 minutes. Strain out the solids.

TO serve, divide the milk between two mugs and sprinkle with the cinnamon.

tip: CANNED COCONUT MILK separates in the can, with the cream rising to the top. Make sure to whisk the coconut milk well before measuring.

baby shower

There's a baby on the way, and everyone's gathered to shower mama, but this table is so gorgeous, it could almost be the star of the show. Our Whole30 baby shower menu is both sophisticated and highly Instagrammable. There's also a fruity mocktail—a pretty pink punch garnished with edible rose petals or pomegranate seeds—to help you toast to the new arrival. Cheers to the future Whole30'er!

· ·

beet-parsnip fritters with
arugula pesto

cucumber cups with red
curry shrimp salad

hot artichoke-parsley dip with
roasted fingerling dippers

plantain crostini with
avocado-jicama topping

masala-mango chicken
salad lettuce cups

spicy collard roll-ups with
macadamia hummus

smoky salmon rillettes with
caramelized shallots

teriyaki beef–cauliflower
rice cabbage cups

roasted berries and grapes with
sesame-pistachio crumble

flower power punch

healthy mama, happy baby

PEOPLE ARE ALWAYS OFFERING UNSOLICITED ADVICE during pregnancy, so if this baby shower is for you, be prepared for questions about your diet. Remind yourself they have good intentions, but also remember that *your* pregnancy is not *their* business.

IF YOU DON'T WANT TO TALK ABOUT YOUR DIET, keep it short and sweet. "Thanks for asking. I talk about my diet with my doctor often, and the baby and I are both healthy." Then change the subject: "Doesn't this artichoke dip look incredible?"

IF YOU CHOOSE TO EXPLAIN your Whole30 to close friends or family, keep it personal and focus on the benefits. "Whole30 meals keep my energy up and stomach happy. I'm not waking up with heartburn anymore!"

FINALLY, ask friends or family to prepare this menu, and tell them not to say a word to your guests! No one will miss the added sugar, and no one will go home disappointed. The event isn't about the food anyway—it's about showering you and your baby with love. (And you don't need gluten for that.)

beet-parsnip fritters with arugula pesto

SERVES 15

The flavor of these crispy herb-and-shallot-infused fritters is wonderful on its own, but the fresh and peppery pesto takes it over the top. Made with red beets, they're a pretty shade of pink—with yellow beets, a beautiful pale yellow.

PREP: 20 MINUTES   **COOK:** 20 MINUTES   **TOTAL:** 40 MINUTES

FOR THE PESTO
2 cups lightly packed baby arugula

1 cup lightly packed basil leaves

¾ cup chopped walnuts

2 cloves garlic, chopped

2 tablespoons fresh lemon juice

½ teaspoon salt

⅔ cup extra-virgin olive oil

FOR THE FRITTERS
¾ cup almond flour or meal

3 large eggs

¼ cup chopped fresh parsley

1 medium shallot, finely chopped

½ teaspoon salt

½ teaspoon black pepper

1 teaspoon grated lemon zest

3 medium parsnips, peeled and shredded (about 12 ounces total)

1 pound red or yellow beets, peeled and shredded

7 to 8 tablespoons Clarified Butter (page 241) or ghee

MAKE THE PESTO: Combine the arugula, basil, walnuts, garlic, lemon juice, and salt in a food processor. Cover and pulse until finely chopped. With the food processor running, add the olive oil and process until well combined and nearly smooth. Cover and chill until ready to serve.

MAKE THE FRITTERS: Preheat the oven to 200°F. In a large bowl, stir together the almond flour, eggs, parsley, shallot, salt, pepper, and lemon zest. Fold in the parsnips and beets.

IN two large skillets over medium heat, melt 1 tablespoon Clarified Butter. Working in batches, use a ¼ cup measuring cup to add fritter batter to the skillet. (You will be able to cook 4 fritters at a time.) Cook, until browned on the bottom, about 3 minutes. Turn, add 1 tablespoon butter, and cook until browned on the bottom, about 3 minutes more. Transfer the fritters to a large rimmed baking pan or serving platter. Place in the oven to keep warm, or cover.

TOP each fritter with about 2 teaspoons pesto.

cucumber cups with red curry shrimp salad

SERVES 15

Red curry paste is an awesome (and compliant!) ingredient—it provides so much complex flavor in just a few spoonfuls. Here, it gives the shrimp salad a touch of heat that contrasts perfectly with the crisp, cool cucumber.

··

PREP: 30 MINUTES TOTAL: 30 MINUTES

··

1 teaspoon grated lime zest

3 tablespoons fresh lime juice (about 1 lime)

¼ cup Whole30-compliant coconut milk (see Tip)

3 tablespoons Whole30-compliant red curry paste

1 pound peeled and deveined cooked shrimp, chopped

1 small red bell pepper, finely chopped

4 green onions, finely chopped

¼ cup chopped fresh cilantro

¼ cup chopped fresh basil

2 tablespoons chopped fresh mint

5 English cucumbers, about 2 inches in diameter

IN a medium bowl, whisk together the lime zest and juice, coconut milk, and curry paste. Add the shrimp, bell pepper, green onions, cilantro, basil, and mint. Toss gently to combine.

TRIM the ends from the cucumbers. Cut each cucumber into 1½-inch pieces (you need 30 pieces). Using a melon baller or small measuring spoon, scoop out about 1 tablespoon from the center of one side of each cucumber piece, creating small cups.

TO serve, arrange the cucumber cups on a platter. Spoon a generous tablespoon of the shrimp salad into each cup.

tip: CANNED COCONUT MILK separates in the can, with the cream rising to the top. Make sure to whisk the coconut milk thoroughly before measuring.

hot artichoke-parsley dip with roasted fingerling dippers

SERVES 15

Crisp-baked fingerling potatoes are the perfect vehicle for this creamy warm dip. Nutritional yeast gives it an awesome cheesy flavor.

....

PREP: 25 MINUTES **STAND:** 4 HOURS OR OVERNIGHT
BAKE: 50 MINUTES **TOTAL:** 5 HOURS 15 MINUTES

....

1 cup raw cashews

1½ pounds fingerling potatoes, halved lengthwise

2 tablespoons extra-virgin olive oil

1 tablespoon chopped fresh rosemary

2 teaspoons chopped fresh thyme

1 teaspoon salt

1 teaspoon black pepper

1 cup Basic Mayonnaise (page 240) or Whole30-compliant mayonnaise

Grated zest and juice of 1 lemon

2 tablespoons nutritional yeast

2 cloves garlic, chopped

1 (9- to 12-ounce) package frozen artichoke hearts, thawed and drained, or 2 (14-ounce) cans Whole30-compliant quartered artichoke hearts, drained

1 cup lightly packed fresh parsley leaves

RINSE the cashews and drain. Place the cashews in a bowl and add enough water to cover by 1 inch. Cover the bowl and let stand for 4 hours or up to overnight. Drain the cashews and rinse under cold water. Set aside.

PREHEAT the oven to 400°F. Line a large rimmed baking pan with parchment paper.

PLACE the potatoes in a large bowl. Drizzle with olive oil and sprinkle with the rosemary, thyme, ½ teaspoon salt, and ½ teaspoon pepper; toss to coat. Arrange in a single layer on the baking pan, cut sides down. Roast for about 25 minutes, until the potatoes are tender and bottoms are lightly browned.

MEANWHILE, combine the soaked cashews, mayonnaise, ½ cup of water, lemon zest and juice, nutritional yeast, garlic, and the remaining ½ teaspoon salt and ½ teaspoon pepper in a blender or food processor. Cover and pulse until finely chopped and then puree until smooth, about 2 minutes. Roughly chop the artichoke hearts. Add the artichokes and parsley to the blender or food processor. Cover and pulse until the artichokes and parsley are finely chopped. Transfer the mixture to a 9-inch glass pie plate.

BAKE for 25 to 30 minutes at 160°F, until the top is lightly browned and heated through. Serve hot with the potatoes for dipping.

plantain crostini with avocado-jicama topping

SERVES 15

Plantains—sometimes called cooking bananas—are a popular Mexican ingredient. Lightly toasted slices pair perfectly with a fresh salsa-like topping of avocado, jicama, and tomato flavored with cilantro and garlic.

PREP: 25 MINUTES   **ROAST:** 15 MINUTES   **TOTAL:** 40 MINUTES

FOR THE PLANTAIN CROSTINI

4 ripe plantains (see Tip)

3 tablespoons extra-virgin olive oil

¾ teaspoon coarse salt

¼ teaspoon black pepper

FOR THE TOPPING

3 tomatoes, cored, seeded, and finely chopped

2 avocados, halved, pitted, peeled, and finely chopped

1 medium (about 14 ounces) jicama, peeled and finely chopped

4 green onions, thinly sliced

¼ cup chopped fresh cilantro

3 cloves garlic, minced

2 tablespoons extra-virgin olive oil

2 tablespoons red wine vinegar

PREHEAT the oven to 450°F. Line a large rimmed baking pan with parchment paper.

MAKE THE PLANTAIN CROSTINI: Peel and bias-cut the plantains into ¼- to ½-inch slices (you should have 45 slices). Arrange the slices in a single layer on the baking pan. Brush both sides with 3 tablespoons olive oil; sprinkle with the salt and the black pepper. Roast for about 15 minutes, turning once, until lightly browned on both sides. Transfer to a wire rack to cool.

MAKE THE TOPPING: Meanwhile, in a medium bowl, combine the tomatoes, avocados, jicama, green onions, cilantro, and garlic. Drizzle with the remaining 2 tablespoons of olive oil and the red wine vinegar; gently stir to combine.

TO serve, arrange the plantain slices on a platter. Top each slice with a scant tablespoon of the topping.

tip: THE PLANTAINS should be yellow with some black spots.

masala-mango chicken salad lettuce cups

SERVES 15

Diced mango provides freshness and a bit of sweetness to this Indian-spiced chicken salad with a twist that's flavored with garam masala in place of the usual curry powder.

....

PREP: 30 MINUTES **TOTAL:** 30 MINUTES

....

¾ cup Basic Mayonnaise (page 240) or Whole30-compliant mayonnaise

1 tablespoon Whole30-compliant coarse-grain brown mustard

1 jalapeño, seeded and minced

1 piece (½ inch) fresh ginger, peeled and grated

1 teaspoon Whole30-compliant garam masala

1 teaspoon cumin seeds, toasted (see Tip)

½ teaspoon ground turmeric

½ teaspoon black pepper

3 cups diced cooked chicken

1 mango, pitted, peeled, and diced (see Tip)

½ small red onion, finely chopped

½ teaspoon salt

1 head Bibb lettuce, leaves separated (15 leaves)

Chopped fresh cilantro or parsley

IN a large bowl, whisk together the mayonnaise, mustard, jalapeño, ginger, garam masala, cumin seeds, turmeric, and black pepper. Add the chicken, mango, and red onion. Toss gently to combine. Season to taste with salt.

TO serve, arrange the lettuce leaves on one or two large platters or trays. Spoon about ½ cup chicken salad into each leaf. Sprinkle with the cilantro or parsley.

tips: To TOAST CUMIN SEEDS, heat in a skillet over medium heat, stirring, until fragrant and lightly browned, about 2 minutes.

To CUT A MANGO, use a "Y" peeler to peel it, then use a sharp knife to trim the stem. Set the mango on one of its narrow sides and, holding it in one hand and a sharp knife in the other, slice through the flesh slightly off center to avoid the pit. Repeat with the other side. Dice or cut as desired.

spicy collard roll-ups with macadamia hummus

SERVES 15

Parboiling the collard leaves for just 1 minute (and plunging them into ice water to stop the cooking process) leaves them just tender enough to be pleasant to eat but sturdy enough to hold a bundle of fresh veggies, nut hummus, and a drizzle of hot sauce.

·····················

PREP: 25 MINUTES   **STAND:** 15 MINUTES
CHILL: 1 HOUR   **TOTAL:** 1 HOUR 40 MINUTES

·····················

1½ cups macadamia nuts

2 tablespoons fresh lemon juice,
plus 1 teaspoon grated zest

¼ cup Whole30-compliant tahini

¼ cup extra-virgin olive oil

2 cloves garlic, minced

1 teaspoon ground cumin

½ teaspoon ground coriander

½ teaspoon salt

8 collard green leaves, stems removed
and inner rib of leaves trimmed

2 small red and/or yellow bell
peppers, cut into matchsticks

2 large carrots, peeled and cut into matchsticks

1 English cucumber, sliced and cut into matchsticks

4 radishes, trimmed and cut into matchsticks

Whole30 Sriracha (page 242) or
Whole30-compliant hot sauce

PLACE the macadamia nuts in a small bowl; add enough boiling water to cover. Let stand 15 minutes. Drain and rinse well.

IN a food processor, combine the nuts, lemon juice and zest, tahini, olive oil, garlic, cumin, coriander, and salt. Pulse until the nuts are finely chopped. Add ¼ cup of water. Puree until smooth, about 2 minutes (adding more water as necessary to reach desired consistency). Cover and chill until needed or for up 24 hours.

BRING a large pot of water to a boil. Prepare a large bowl of ice water. Add the collard greens to the boiling water to cook for 1 minute; transfer to the ice water. Let stand 2 minutes. Drain well and pat leaves dry with paper towels.

PLACE one leaf on a clean work surface with the top of the leaf facing down and the stem end toward you. Spread with 3 to 4 tablespoons of the hummus. Arrange some of the peppers, carrots, cucumber, and radish matchsticks on the hummus in a row about 2 inches from the wide stem end of the leaf (crosswise along the length of the leaf). Drizzle with Sriracha. Starting from the stem end, roll the leaf up into a log, working toward the tip. Repeat with remaining leaves to make 8 rolls. Cover and chill for 1 hour.

TO serve, trim the ends of the rolls; cut in 1½- or 2-inch slices. Arrange the slices, cut sides up, on a platter.

smoky salmon rillettes with caramelized shallots

SERVES 15

Rillettes (*ree-YEHTS*) is a French invention of meat, poultry, or fish that's slowly cooked in seasoned fat and then pounded into a paste, chilled, and served spread on toast or bread as an appetizer—a bit like pâté. This version features a blend of poached fresh salmon and hot-smoked salmon with mayo, caramelized shallots, parsley, and lemon. It's then served on endive or radicchio leaves, of course!

....

PREP: 15 MINUTES   **COOK:** 3 MINUTES   **STAND:** 5 MINUTES
CHILL: 2 HOURS   **TOTAL:** 2 HOURS 25 MINUTES

....

1 pound skinless salmon fillet, cut into 4 or 5 pieces

2 tablespoons white wine vinegar

1 teaspoon black peppercorns

1½ teaspoons coarse salt

2 sprigs fresh parsley

2 tablespoons Clarified Butter (page 241) or ghee

2 large shallots, finely chopped

4 ounces hot-smoked salmon, finely flaked

½ cup Basic Mayonnaise (page 240) or Whole30-compliant mayonnaise

2 tablespoons chopped fresh parsley

1 teaspoon grated lemon zest

4 heads Belgian endive or radicchio

PLACE the salmon in a large saucepan. Add enough water to just cover. Add the vinegar, peppercorns, 1 teaspoon of the salt, and parsley sprigs. Bring to a simmer over medium heat; reduce heat to low. Cover and simmer for 3 minutes. Remove from the heat. Let stand until the fish just begins to flake, about 5 minutes. Transfer the salmon to a plate; cover and refrigerate until chilled, about 1 hour. Discard poaching liquid.

IN a small skillet, melt the butter over medium heat. Add the shallots. Cook until golden brown and tender, stirring occasionally, about 5 minutes. Remove from the heat and cool.

FINELY flake the poached salmon with a fork. In a medium bowl, combine the poached salmon, smoked salmon, mayonnaise, caramelized shallots, chopped parsley, remaining ½ teaspoon salt, and lemon zest. Transfer to a serving dish. Cover and chill for at least 1 hour or up to 24 hours.

TO serve, separate leaves from the Belgian endive. Serve the rillettes with the endive leaves, or spoon the rillettes onto endive leaves and serve on a platter.

teriyaki beef–cauliflower rice cabbage cups

SERVES 15

The beef-and-cauliflower filling for these crunchy cups has great Asian flavor without the use of any soy or sugar—just fresh ginger, garlic, a hint of sweetness from pineapple juice, coconut aminos, and sesame.

PREP: 20 MINUTES **COOK:** 15 MINUTES **TOTAL:** 35 MINUTES

5 tablespoons coconut oil

1 (16-ounce) package cauliflower crumbles or cauliflower rice

2 tablespoons Whole30-compliant coconut milk (see Tip)

3 green onions, finely chopped, plus more for garnish

¾ teaspoon coarse salt

1¼ to 1½ pounds boneless sirloin, thinly sliced then cut into bite-size pieces

¼ teaspoon black pepper

4 cloves garlic, minced

1 piece (2 inches) fresh ginger, peeled and grated

¼ cup 100% pineapple juice

2 tablespoons coconut aminos

2 teaspoons toasted sesame oil

1 tablespoon sesame seeds, toasted (see Tip)

30 small napa cabbage leaves

OVER medium-high heat in a large skillet, heat 1 tablespoon of the coconut oil. Add the cauliflower. Cook, stirring occasionally, until lightly browned and tender, about 5 minutes. Remove from the heat. Stir in the coconut milk, green onions, and ¼ teaspoon salt.

IN a large skillet over medium-high heat, heat 2 tablespoons of the coconut oil. Sprinkle the steak with the remaining ½ teaspoon salt and the pepper. Add half of the steak to the skillet. Cook, stirring occasionally, until browned and slightly pink in the center, 4 to 5 minutes. Transfer the steak to a shallow dish. Repeat with the remaining 2 tablespoons coconut oil and steak; transfer to the shallow dish.

ADD the garlic and ginger to the skillet. Cook over medium heat, stirring, for 1 minute. Add the pineapple juice, coconut aminos, and sesame oil. Simmer until slightly thickened, about 2 minutes. Return the steak to the skillet. Stir in the sesame seeds.

FOR each cabbage cup, place a heaping tablespoon of the cauliflower and tablespoon of the steak onto the center of a cabbage leaf. Sprinkle with additional green onions for garnish.

tips: CANNED COCONUT MILK separates in the can, with the cream rising to the top. Make sure to whisk the coconut milk well before measuring.

TO TOAST THE SESAME SEEDS, heat in a dry skillet over medium heat, stirring, until fragrant and lightly browned, about 2 minutes.

roasted berries and grapes with sesame-pistachio crumble

SERVES 15

This simple dessert is a study in contrasts. Each spoonful is a beautifully balanced bite of sweet, juicy roasted fruit and crunchy, nutty-flavored almond–sesame seed–pistachio topping.

....

PREP: 12 MINUTES   ROAST: 15 MINUTES
COOK: 8 MINUTES   TOTAL: 35 MINUTES

....

1 pound red or green seedless grapes, halved

1 (6- to 8-ounce) container blueberries

1 (6-ounce) container raspberries

1 vanilla bean, split lengthwise and cut into 6 pieces

¼ cup extra-virgin olive oil

¼ cup almond flour or meal

4 teaspoons sesame seeds

1 cup roasted salted pistachios, chopped

2 teaspoons coconut oil

Chopped fresh mint for garnish

PREHEAT the oven to 425°F.

COMBINE the grapes, blueberries, raspberries, and vanilla bean pieces on a large rimmed baking pan. Drizzle with the olive oil; gently stir to coat. Spread into an even layer. Roast for 15 to 20 minutes, stirring once, until the fruit is tender and caramelizes in some places. Remove the vanilla bean pieces. Spoon the fruit into a shallow serving dish or 15 small ramekins.

IN a small skillet, combine the almond flour and sesame seeds. Cook over medium heat, stirring frequently, until lightly toasted, about 5 minutes. Stir in the pistachios and coconut oil. Cook, stirring, until fragrant, about 3 minutes.

TO serve, spoon the crumble over the fruit and garnish with mint.

flower power punch

SERVES 15

A splash of rose water gives this pink and sparkly punch just a hint of floral flavor. A blend of chamomile and rose hip tea creates the base (and adds a big dose of vitamin C!), while a garnish of edible rose petals or pomegranate arils provides a pretty finishing touch.

·····························

PREP: 10 MINUTES   **STAND:** 15 MINUTES
CHILL: 2 HOURS   **TOTAL:** 2 HOURS 25 MINUTES

·····························

1 (0.99-ounce) box Whole30-compliant hibiscus tea (16 bags)

4 chamomile tea bags

4 rose hip tea bags

3 cups white grape juice

2 tablespoons rose water

Ice

1 (1-liter) bottle Whole30-compliant sparkling water

Fresh edible rose petals and/or pomegranate arils

IN a medium saucepan, bring 8 cups of water to a boil. Remove from the heat; add the tea bags. Cover and let steep for 15 to 20 minutes. Remove and discard the tea bags. Cover and cool completely, about 1 hour. Transfer to a 3- or 4-quart pitcher. Stir in the grape juice and rose water. Cover and refrigerate for at least 1 hour, or until thoroughly chilled.

TO serve, fill fifteen 10- to 12-ounce glasses about half full with ice. Add ½ to ⅔ cup punch to each glass. Top with ¼ cup sparkling water. Garnish with the rose petals and/or pomegranate arils.

tips: READ THE TEA LABELS CAREFULLY, as many have added sweeteners.

POMEGRANATE ARILS are the beautiful red seeds of the pomegranate and are available in the produce section of your grocery store.

road trip

Road trip food usually consists of salty snacks and sodas from convenience stores or fast food burgers and fries, guaranteed to give you an energy crash and rumbly stomach. Finding convenient food that fits the Whole30 template is hard—so take your Whole30 on the road! This menu includes snacky foods even the driver can (carefully) eat in the car—including salty roasted Brussels sprouts and spiced pumpkin energy balls—as well as picnicky foods you can enjoy stopped at a pretty park or rest area. Pack it all into a cooler (don't forget the napkins) and hit the road!

....

**snackable spicy garlic
brussels sprouts**

chicken-asparagus roll-ups

lemon-garlic shrimp kabobs

**roasted pepper–garlic
cashew hummus**

spicy pumpkin power bites

on the road again

SOMETHING OTHER THAN PLAIN OLD WATER is a nice addition to this menu. Mix your favorite "spa water" in a reusable water bottle flavored with just a splash of juice or fruit, pack a Sound unsweetened tea, and don't forget a case of Waterloo!

THIS MENU FEATURES 100 percent no-utensils-needed foods—which is great for traveling but not so good for keeping your hands clean. Be sure to pack some hand wipes, a soft cloth for soaking up any accidental spills, and a small bag for garbage.

IF YOU'RE SHORT ON TIME (or it's a short trip), make just a few of these recipes, then supplement with dry-roasted nuts, hard-boiled eggs, Applegate deli meat, fresh fruit, homemade kale chips, compliant meat sticks, and RXBARs.

IF YOUR TRIP IS AS MUCH ABOUT THE JOURNEY as the destination, check out myscenicdrives.com, an online road trip planner that allows you to pick a pre-planned trip, plan sightseeing stops on your route, and share your trip with family and friends.

snackable spicy garlic brussels sprouts

SERVES 4

These are a perfect snack for a road trip, even for the person who's doing the driving. You can just pick them up and pop them in your mouth—easy-peasy.

••••••••••••••••••••••••••••••

PREP: 15 MINUTES   **COOK:** 30 MINUTES   **CHILL:** 2 HOURS
TOTAL: 2 HOURS 45 MINUTES

••••••••••••••••••••••••••••••

2 tablespoons extra-virgin olive oil

1 clove garlic, thinly sliced

4 cups Brussels sprouts, trimmed and halved

½ teaspoon coarse salt

¼ teaspoon black pepper

⅛ teaspoon chipotle powder or cayenne pepper

PREHEAT the oven to 425°F. Line a large baking pan with parchment paper.

IN a saucepan, heat the olive oil and garlic over medium heat, until the garlic is fragrant and starts to brown, 3 to 4 minutes. Remove from the heat; cool for 5 minutes. Remove the garlic from the oil; discard the garlic.

PLACE the Brussels sprouts in a large bowl. Drizzle with the garlic oil and sprinkle with the salt, pepper, and chipotle powder; toss to coat. Arrange the sprouts in a single layer on the pan. Roast for about 25 minutes, stirring once halfway through, until lightly browned and just tender. Transfer the pan to a wire rack to cool. Place the Brussels sprouts in an airtight container. Chill for at least 2 hours before traveling.

to travel

PLACE the container of Brussels sprouts in a cooler with ice packs or ice. Consume within 8 hours unless you replenish the cooler with fresh ice packs or ice, or are able to transfer the container to a refrigerator.

chicken-asparagus roll-ups

SERVES 4

These easy-to-eat bundles—crisp-tender stalks of asparagus wrapped up in thin slices of smoked chicken with olive tapenade, spinach, and roasted red peppers—provide hungry travelers with a veggie-and-protein boost.

·····································

PREP: 20 MINUTES **COOK:** 2 MINUTES **CHILL:** 2 HOURS
TOTAL: 2 HOURS 20 MINUTES

·····································

24 thin asparagus spears, trimmed and cut into 7-inch pieces

16 slices Whole30-compliant deli smoked chicken or turkey breast

½ cup olive tapenade

1 cup lightly packed baby spinach, stems removed

½ cup drained roasted red peppers, cut into ¼-inch slices

PLACE a steamer basket in a large, deep skillet; expand to almost flat. Add water to just below the bottom of the basket and bring to a boil. Add the asparagus. Cover and steam until crisp-tender, about 3 minutes. Place in ice water to cool. Drain.

LAYER two slices of chicken to make eight stacks. Pat dry with paper towels. Spread about 1 tablespoon of the tapenade over each chicken stack. Top it with 3 to 4 spinach leaves. Pat the pepper slices dry with paper towels and place on the spinach. Lay 3 asparagus spears in the middle of each stack. Roll the chicken around the asparagus. Secure the rolls with toothpicks. Place the roll-ups in an airtight container. Chill for at least 2 hours before traveling.

to travel

PLACE the container of roll-ups in a cooler with ice packs or ice. Consume within 8 hours unless you replenish the cooler with fresh ice packs or ice, or are able to transfer the container to a refrigerator.

lemon-garlic shrimp kabobs

SERVES 4

No need to pack utensils when you've got these shrimp-and-veggie kabobs in the cooler—just enjoy and throw the wooden skewers away!

....

PREP: 35 MINUTES **COOK:** 18 MINUTES **CHILL:** 2 HOURS
TOTAL: 2 HOURS 55 MINUTES

....

16 large peeled, deveined shrimp, thawed if frozen

¼ cup extra-virgin olive oil

¼ cup fresh lemon juice

¼ teaspoon black pepper

¼ teaspoon salt

⅛ teaspoon cayenne pepper (optional)

1 clove garlic, minced

8 ounces Yukon Gold potatoes, cut into 1-inch pieces

1 medium zucchini, trimmed and cut into 8 1-inch pieces

16 cherry tomatoes or grape tomatoes

8 10- to 12-inch wooden skewers

PLACE the shrimp in a medium bowl; set aside. In a small bowl, whisk together the olive oil, lemon juice, and pepper. Transfer ¼ cup of the oil mixture to another small bowl; whisk in the salt and, if using, cayenne. Set aside. Stir the garlic into the remaining oil mixture; drizzle over the shrimp; toss to coat. Cover and marinate in the refrigerator for 15 to 30 minutes (see Tip).

MEANWHILE, place a large steamer basket in a deep skillet; expand to almost flat. Add the water to just below the bottom of the basket. Bring the water to a boil. Add the potatoes to the basket. Cover and steam for 12 minutes. Place the zucchini on the potatoes. Cover and steam until the zucchini is crisp-tender and the potatoes are just tender, 2 to 3 minutes more. Transfer the vegetables to a large bowl. Drizzle with the remaining oil mixture; toss gently to coat. Set aside to cool.

HEAT a large nonstick skillet over medium-high heat. Use a slotted spoon to transfer the shrimp from the marinade to the hot skillet; discard the marinade. Cook, turning once halfway through, until the shrimp are opaque, 4 to 5 minutes. Transfer to a large plate. Let cool completely.

THREAD the potatoes, zucchini, tomatoes, and shrimp onto the skewers. Place the kabobs in an airtight container. Chill for at least 2 hours before traveling.

to travel

PLACE the container of kabobs in a cooler with ice packs or ice. Consume within 8 hours unless you replenish the cooler with fresh ice packs or ice, or are able to transfer the container to a refrigerator.

tip: DO NOT MARINATE any longer than 30 minutes or the shrimp will "cook" from the lemon juice in the marinade.

roasted pepper–garlic cashew hummus

SERVES 4

When you need a little nibble to tide you over, this veggie and hummus snack is just the thing. The peppers and garlic are roasted before being pureed with soaked cashews. Roasting mellows the garlic and adds a touch of sweetness to the dip that's balanced by a splash of lemon juice.

....

PREP: 15 MINUTES   **STAND:** 1 HOUR 15 MINUTES
ROAST: 20 MINUTES   **CHILL:** 2 HOURS
TOTAL: 3 HOURS 50 MINUTES

....

⅓ cup raw cashews

1 small yellow bell pepper, quartered

1 small head garlic

2 tablespoons plus 1 teaspoon extra-virgin olive oil

2 tablespoons Whole30-compliant tahini

2 tablespoons fresh lemon juice

½ teaspoon salt

⅛ teaspoon black pepper or cayenne pepper

Assorted vegetables, such as sugar snap peas, bell pepper strips, grape tomatoes, and/or carrot sticks

PLACE the cashews in a small bowl and add boiling water to cover by 1 inch. Cover the bowl and let stand for 1 hour. Drain the cashews and rinse under cold water.

MEANWHILE, preheat the oven to 450°F. Line a large rimmed baking pan with foil.

PLACE the peppers on the pan, skin sides up. Cut about ¼ inch from the top of the garlic to expose the cloves, keeping the head intact. Place the garlic on a 4-inch piece of foil; drizzle with 1 teaspoon olive oil. Fold and seal the foil. Roast until the pepper skins are charred and tender, and the garlic is tender, 20 to 25 minutes. Remove the garlic packet. Enclose the peppers in the foil to cool, about 15 minutes.

SQUEEZE the roasted garlic cloves into a food processor or blender. Use a small sharp knife to peel the charred skin off the pepper quarters. Add the peppers and cashews to the food processor. Cover and process or blend until finely chopped. Add the 2 tablespoons olive oil, tahini, lemon juice, salt, and pepper. Cover and process or blend until smooth.

TRANSFER the hummus to an airtight container. Place the vegetables in a separate airtight container. Chill the hummus and vegetables for at least 2 hours before traveling.

to travel

PLACE the containers of hummus and vegetables in a cooler with ice packs or ice. Consume within 8 hours unless you replenish the cooler with fresh ice packs or ice, or are able to transfer the container to a refrigerator.

spicy pumpkin power bites

SERVES 4

A dash of cayenne pepper gives these energy balls a little bit of heat that balances out the sweetness of the dried fruit. If that's not your thing, just leave it out.

....

PREP: 25 MINUTES **TOTAL:** 25 MINUTES

....

½ cup Whole30-compliant sunflower seed butter

⅓ cup plain canned pumpkin

½ teaspoon ground cinnamon

¼ teaspoon ground ginger

⅛ teaspoon cayenne pepper

¼ cup coconut flour

2 tablespoons unflavored collagen powder

¼ cup finely chopped toasted almonds or walnuts

2 tablespoons finely chopped unsweetened raisins or dried figs

2 tablespoons unsweetened flaked coconut

IN a medium bowl, stir together the sunflower seed butter, pumpkin, cinnamon, ginger, and cayenne until well combined. Add the coconut flour and collagen powder. Stir until well combined. Add in the almonds and raisins. (You may need to use your hands at the end to mix everything well.)

SHAPE the mixture into 8 balls about 1½ inches in diameter. (Use 2 heaping tablespoons of the mixture per ball.) Roll in the flaked coconut. Place the balls in an airtight container.

to travel

THESE bites do not need to be chilled for traveling unless they will be sitting in a hot car. In that case, store them in an insulated cooler with several ice packs.

adults-only dinner party

Bailey Fischer
WHOLEKITCHENSINK.COM
Bailey Fischer is a Whole30
Certified Coach, writer, and
cookbook author passionate about
developing easy recipes that
create lifestyle changes through
food. Beginning from a need to
teach herself to cook real, good-
tasting food in ways that didn't
stress her limited time or budget,
she is now dedicated to helping
others find health and healing.

Everyone you know works hard on the job and at home with kids, pets, and housework. One of the best ways to unwind is to get together with a few good friends around a table full of good food . . . and hire a babysitter. If you're feeling the need for some uninterrupted adult conversation *now* but you happen to be doing a Whole30, you don't need to wait to schedule a grown-up dinner party. This totally compliant menu featuring Garlic-Roasted Lamb is elegant and sophisticated, and a bubbly Mocktail Mule made with ginger kombucha is a perfect way to get things started. You won't miss the vodka (or the kids) at all, I promise.

....

apple-bacon bites
dijon brussels and butternut squash
seared scallops with avocado whip
citrus kale salad
garlic-roasted lamb
**fingerling potatoes with
parsley pesto**
coconut ambrosia salad
mocktail mule

let's get together

WHEN YOU'RE HOSTING A DINNER PARTY, you want to have fun, not be stuck in the kitchen. Make a simple but elegant roast the centerpiece of your meal—just season it and put it in the oven. Your house will smell glorious, and your brow will be perspiration-free.

JUST BECAUSE YOU'RE DOING A WHOLE30 doesn't mean you have to forego premeal nibbles—they just have to be compliant. (Cheese and crackers are boring anyway.) If you want to simplify the starters on this menu, just put out bowls of compliant olives; roasted, salted nuts; and raw veggies with a Mesa de Vida dipping sauce.

HALF THE FUN OF A DINNER PARTY is the atmosphere you create, taking you out of your everyday world of hurried weeknight meals scheduled around homework, soccer games, and meetings. Dim the lights and put out some candles. Get some fresh flowers for the table. Put on music that sets the vibe you're looking for—try my "Whole30 Dinner Party" playlist on Spotify!

AS FOR DESSERT, it doesn't have to be a piece of molten chocolate cake or cheesecake to satisfy. The light and fresh Coconut Ambrosia Salad on this menu will impress and leave your guests sugar-coma-free.

apple-bacon bites

SERVES 4

This appetizer is short on ingredients but big on flavor! Each bite of tender, sweet apple is complemented by crispy bacon. Be sure to cut the apples in approximately the same-size pieces so that they cook evenly.

·····

PREP: 20 MINUTES **BAKE:** 24 MINUTES
TOTAL: 45 MINUTES

·····

2 Gala apples, peeled, cored, and
cut into 8 wedges

½ teaspoon ground cinnamon

8 slices Whole30-compliant bacon,
cut in half crosswise

PREHEAT the oven to 400°F. Line a large rimmed baking pan with parchment paper.

PLACE the apple wedges in a medium bowl. Sprinkle with the cinnamon; toss to coat.

WRAP each apple wedge with a half strip of bacon, pressing on the seam to seal. Arrange the bacon-wrapped apple slices, seam sides up, on the baking pan. Bake for 12 minutes. Carefully turn over, rewrapping with the bacon if necessary. Bake for about 12 minutes more, until the bacon is cooked through and crisp on the edges.

TRANSFER to a serving platter. Serve with toothpicks.

dijon brussels and butternut squash

SERVES 4

This veggie side dish is a gorgeous addition to the dinner table. An aromatic combination of ingredients—garlic, rosemary, cinnamon, cloves—enhances the sweet-salty flavor from the squash and prosciutto. To add a little extra something-something, top with compliant dried cranberries or toasted pecans!

PREP: 15 MINUTES   ROAST: 25 MINUTES
TOTAL: 40 MINUTES

FOR THE BRUSSELS SPROUTS AND SQUASH

½ pound Brussels sprouts, trimmed and halved

½ pound butternut squash, peeled, seeded, and cubed

2 tablespoons extra-virgin olive oil

2 cloves garlic, minced

1 teaspoon dried rosemary

¼ teaspoon ground cinnamon

⅛ teaspoon ground cloves

¼ teaspoon salt

¼ teaspoon black pepper

1 (2-ounce) package Whole30-compliant prosciutto, chopped

FOR THE DIJON DRESSING

4 teaspoons extra-virgin olive oil

1 tablespoon Whole30-compliant Dijon mustard

1½ teaspoons cider vinegar

⅛ teaspoon salt

⅛ teaspoon black pepper

PREHEAT the oven to 400°F. Line a large rimmed baking pan with parchment paper.

MAKE THE BRUSSELS SPROUTS AND SQUASH: Arrange the Brussels sprouts and squash on the pan. In a small bowl, combine the olive oil, garlic, rosemary, cinnamon, cloves, salt, and pepper. Drizzle the vegetables with the oil mixture; toss to combine. Arrange the vegetables in a single layer.

ROAST for 15 minutes. Turn the Brussels sprouts and squash; sprinkle with the prosciutto. Roast for 10 to 15 minutes until the vegetables are tender and lightly browned, and the prosciutto is crisp.

MAKE THE DIJON DRESSING: Meanwhile, in a small bowl, whisk together the olive oil, mustard, vinegar, salt, and pepper.

TRANSFER the roasted vegetables to a serving bowl and drizzle with the dressing; gently stir to combine.

seared scallops with avocado whip

SERVES 4

The trick to creating a garlicky, buttery crust on these scallops is to be sure they are as dry as possible before searing them—and that your pan is nice and hot. Seared scallops make one of the easiest appetizers because of their quick cook time—and they naturally have an air of sophistication. The creamy, zesty avocado whip jazzes them up and helps create a bright and colorful plate.

PREP: 25 MINUTES COOK: 5 MINUTES
TOTAL: 30 MINUTES

FOR THE AVOCADO WHIP
1 small lime

1 small ripe avocado, peeled and pitted

¼ teaspoon salt

¼ teaspoon red pepper flakes (optional)

FOR THE SCALLOPS
8 large sea scallops

¼ teaspoon salt

¼ teaspoon black pepper

1 tablespoon avocado oil

2 tablespoons Clarified Butter (page 241) or ghee

2 cloves garlic, minced

MAKE THE AVOCADO WHIP: Zest the lime; set the zest aside for garnish. Juice half of the lime (about 1 tablespoon). Place the avocado, lime juice, salt, and red pepper flakes (if using) in a blender or food processor. Cover and blend or process on high until smooth. Transfer to a bowl. Cover and refrigerate until needed.

MAKE THE SCALLOPS: Rinse the scallops and pat dry with a paper towel. Sprinkle with salt and pepper. In a large skillet, heat the oil and butter over medium-high heat. Add the garlic. Add the scallops (do not crowd the pan). Cook until the bottoms are golden brown, about 3 minutes. Turn the scallops and cook until translucent in the center, 2 to 3 minutes more.

TO serve, transfer the scallops to a serving platter. Top each scallop with a scant tablespoon of the avocado whip. Garnish with lime zest.

citrus kale salad

SERVES 4

This salad will have those who think they don't like kale going for seconds! By massaging the kale to make it silky soft, dressing it up with a lemony vinaigrette, adding sliced fennel, orange, and dried apricots—then topping it with crunchy almonds—you'll have a simple salad that will steal the show.

....

PREP: 20 MINUTES   **TOTAL:** 20 MINUTES

....

3 tablespoons extra-virgin olive oil

1 tablespoon fresh lemon juice

1 tablespoon cider vinegar

⅛ teaspoon dried dill

Pinch salt and black pepper

1 fennel bulb

4 cups chopped kale (about ½ bunch)

1 large blood orange, peeled, sectioned, and finely chopped

½ small red onion, finely chopped

½ cup chopped unsulfured dried apricots

¼ cup sliced almonds or chopped cashews

IN a small bowl, whisk together the olive oil, lemon juice, vinegar, dill, salt, and pepper. Set aside.

CUT off the fennel stalks about 1 inch from the bulb; chop two of the stalks and set aside. Cut a thin slice from the root end and discard. Remove any wilted outer layers with a vegetable peeler. Stand the bulb upright and cut in half. Cut away and discard the tough core from each half. Use a mandoline set at ⅛ inch or a sharp knife to thinly slice the fennel bulb. (You need 1 cup of fennel slices for this recipe.)

ADD the chopped kale to a large bowl. Drizzle the dressing over the kale; massage to coat. Add the sliced fennel, fennel stalks, blood orange, onion, dried apricots, and almonds. Toss to combine.

garlic-roasted lamb

SERVES 6

This recipe is as delicious as it is impressive, and your guests will have no idea just how simple it is to prepare. It makes for a beautiful centerpiece everyone will ooh and ah over, and we'll keep it our little secret that it only took 25 minutes to get it into the oven!

PREP: 25 MINUTES   ROAST: 1 HOUR 20 MINUTES
TOTAL: 1 HOUR 55 MINUTES

1 boneless leg of lamb roast
(3 to 4 pounds) (see Tip)

4 to 5 cloves garlic, peeled and cut into slivers

2 tablespoons fresh lemon juice

2 tablespoons extra-virgin olive oil

1½ teaspoons dried rosemary

½ teaspoon salt

½ teaspoon black pepper

LET the roast stand at room temperature for 30 minutes before you begin cooking.

PREHEAT the oven to 450°F. Line a large rimmed baking pan with parchment paper.

USING a sharp paring knife, make small holes ¼- to ½-inch deep and about 1 inch apart all over the fat side of the roast. Insert the garlic slivers into each cut.

IN a small bowl, whisk together the lemon juice and oil. Drizzle over the lamb and massage to coat. Sprinkle with rosemary, salt, and pepper.

PLACE the roast on the baking pan and roast for 10 minutes. Turn the heat down to 325°F and roast for an additional 1 hour and 10 minutes, or until 135°F (medium-rare) or 145°F (medium) when tested with a meat thermometer at the thickest part of the roast.

TRANSFER the lamb to a cutting board and tent with foil; let rest for at least 10 minutes. Slice and transfer to a serving platter.

tip: IF THE ROAST HAS NETTING, leave it on as it helps to keep the roast's shape. If not, you will need to tie the roast in 3 to 4 places with 100 percent-cotton kitchen string.

fingerling potatoes with parsley pesto

SERVES 4

Parboiling potatoes before roasting them is the key to getting them evenly cooked and crisp on the outside and fluffy on the inside—then fancy them up with a parsley pesto to add fresh, bright flavor.

....

PREP: 15 MINUTES   **COOK:** 8 MINUTES
ROAST: 12 MINUTES   **TOTAL:** 35 MINUTES

....

FOR THE POTATOES

1 pound fingerling potatoes, halved

¼ teaspoon plus ⅛ teaspoon salt

1 tablespoon extra-virgin olive oil or avocado oil

1 tablespoon Clarified Butter (page 241) or ghee, melted

¼ teaspoon black pepper

FOR THE PESTO

⅓ cup almonds

2 cloves garlic, roughly chopped

2 cups lightly packed chopped fresh parsley

2 tablespoons nutritional yeast

⅛ teaspoon salt

⅓ cup extra-virgin olive oil, plus 2 tablespoons

PREHEAT the oven to 400°F.

MAKE THE POTATOES: Bring enough water to cover the potatoes by 1 inch to boil in a medium pot. Add the potatoes and ¼ teaspoon of the salt. Reduce the heat to a simmer. Cook, covered, just until tender, 8 to 10 minutes. Drain. Transfer the potatoes to a large rimmed baking pan.

IN a small bowl, combine the olive oil, butter, ⅛ teaspoon salt, and the pepper. Drizzle oil mixture over the potatoes; toss to coat. Arrange the potatoes, cut sides down, on the baking pan. Bake for 12 to 15 minutes, turning once halfway through, until the potatoes are golden and fork tender.

MAKE THE PESTO: Meanwhile, place the almonds, garlic, parsley, yeast, and salt in a food processor. Cover and process until finely chopped. With the food processor running, add the olive oil and process until well combined and nearly smooth.

TO serve, transfer the pesto to a small serving dish or spoon over the potatoes.

tip: STORE LEFTOVER PESTO in an airtight container in the refrigerator for up to 3 days.

coconut ambrosia salad

SERVES 4

Typically, ambrosia salad is filled with canned cherries in syrup, mandarin oranges, and marshmallows. This version proves that no added sugar is needed to sweeten this beautiful array of fruit. This salad is easy to customize to your tastes by swapping the pineapple, kiwi, strawberries, and grapes for your favorites—such as apples, bananas, or blueberries. You can also opt for whatever type of nuts you have on hand—so feel free to use sliced almonds in place of the walnuts.

PREP: 25 MINUTES **TOTAL:** 25 MINUTES

1 cup diced pineapple

1 cup diced kiwi

1 cup quartered strawberries

1 cup grapes, halved

¼ cup unsweetened shredded coconut, plus more for garnish

¼ cup chopped walnuts, plus more for garnish

1 (14-ounce) can Whole30-compliant coconut milk, refrigerated overnight

¼ teaspoon ground cinnamon

1 vanilla bean, split lengthwise, seeds scraped

IN a large mixing bowl, combine the pineapple, kiwi, strawberries, grapes, shredded coconut, and walnuts.

OPEN the refrigerated can of coconut milk; drain off the liquid and reserve for smoothies. Spoon the coconut cream into a medium bowl. Add the cinnamon and vanilla bean seeds. Beat with an electric mixer on medium-high until fluffy, about 5 minutes.

FOLD the coconut cream into the fruit mixture until coated; do not overmix. Transfer the salad to a serving dish or spoon into individual bowls. Garnish with additional shredded coconut or walnuts.

mocktail mule

SERVES 4

This is the perfect drink for any festivity or get-together. It's light and refreshing, nonalcoholic, and it takes only a few minutes to create a beautiful presentation with fresh mint leaves and lime-slice garnishes.

PREP: 5 MINUTES **TOTAL:** 5 MINUTES

1 (16-ounce) bottle Whole30-compliant ginger kombucha, chilled

1 (12-ounce) can Whole30-compliant lime-flavored sparkling water, chilled

1 tablespoon fresh lime juice

Ice

Lime slices

Fresh mint leaves

IN a large pitcher, stir together the kombucha, sparkling water, and lime juice. Add ice to four 8-ounce glasses. Pour the mixture over the ice, and garnish with lime slices and mint leaves.

kid-friendly family dinner

Dinnertime with kids can easily fall into a rut, but add other kids (and grown-up friends) to the mix, and dinner becomes a fun social experience. Thinking back to my own childhood, some of my best memories were when my parents got together with friends from the neighborhood, and us kids had a blast playing games and running around outside. This tropical-themed menu offers up fun flavors and foods that adults will appreciate and that kids will love too. Bonus: The other parents will love this low-sugar menu for their littles—especially when it's time to take them home and put them to bed.

· ·

chili-lime roasted zucchini

jicama chips with guacamole

hawaiian chicken burgers

piña colada coleslaw

lemon butter–garlic sautéed kale

sweet potato–stuffed dates
wrapped in prosciutto

chilled coconut–almond
butter bananas

sparkling pineapple spritzer

Chrissa Benson
PHYSICALKITCHNESS.COM
Chrissa Benson is a self-proclaimed "kitchen ninja" with a mission to make healthy eating quicker and easier for busy women. Her recipes are focused on simple, family-friendly meals so you can make healthy living fun and sustainable.

party of six

IF YOUR FRIENDS AREN'T ON THE WHOLE30, their kids might be suspicious about some of these dishes. Mom Pro Tip #1: Serving a food with toothpicks makes any kid 87 percent more likely to try it.

ALMOST ALL OF THESE RECIPES lend themselves to being completely or partially made ahead. The stuffed dates, jicama chips and guac, and coleslaw can all be ready and waiting when guests arrive. Make the burgers and chill in the refrigerator; cut up the zucchini and mix up the marinade; and wash and tear up the kale.

IF YOUR KIDDOS ARE YOUNGER, separate out a portion of the zucchini dish and season without the chili powder, in case the spice of the original recipe is too much for budding palates.

FINALLY, if your friend's non-Whole30 kids are just not having some of these dishes (and their parents are pleading for backup), resort to Mom Pro Tip #2 and bust out some ketchup or ranch dressing for dipping—Whole30 versions or traditional. Just remember which condiments on the table are compliant for your own enjoyment.

chili-lime roasted zucchini

SERVES 8

It may look like a lot of chili powder, but if it's mild, everyone at the party—even the littlest ones—will enjoy this simple vegetable side dish.

PREP: 20 MINUTES   **ROAST:** 15 MINUTES
TOTAL: 35 MINUTES

6 medium zucchini, halved lengthwise and cut into ¾-inch slices

Grated zest and juice of 2 small limes

¼ cup extra-virgin olive oil

1 tablespoon Whole30-compliant chili powder

1½ teaspoons salt

½ teaspoon black pepper

PREHEAT the oven to 400°F. Line 2 large rimmed baking pans with parchment paper.

PLACE the zucchini in an extra-large bowl. In a small bowl, whisk together ¼ cup lime juice with the olive oil, chili powder, salt, and pepper. Drizzle over the zucchini and toss to coat.

ARRANGE the zucchini in a single layer in the two pans.

ROAST for about 15 minutes, until just tender, rotating pans halfway through.

TRANSFER the zucchini to a large serving bowl. Sprinkle with 2 teaspoons of the lime zest and gently stir to combine.

jicama chips with guacamole

SERVES 8

What's the best way to get kids to get veggies? Cut them into fun shapes! (And give them something yummy for dipping.)

PREP: 25 MINUTES **TOTAL:** 25 MINUTES

4 large ripe avocados, halved and pitted

2 tablespoons fresh lime juice

2 cloves garlic, minced

½ teaspoon salt

1 small jalapeño, seeded and minced

¼ cup finely chopped red onion

3 medium jicama (12 to 14 ounces each)

SCOOP the avocado flesh into a medium bowl. Add the lime juice, garlic, and salt. Mash with a fork until smooth. Stir in the jalapeño and onion.

PEEL the jicama. Use a mandoline set at $\frac{3}{16}$ inch to slice the jicama. (Alternatively, use a sharp knife to cut the jicama into ¼-inch slices.) Use small cookie cutters to cut the jicama into fun shapes.

SERVE the jicama chips with the guacamole.

hawaiian chicken burgers

SERVES 8

Be sure to use pineapple tidbits packed in 100 percent juice—not pineapple chunks—in these tropically themed burgers. If the bits of pineapple are too large, the burgers will break apart.

....

PREP: 15 MINUTES **FREEZE:** 15 MINUTES
COOK: 12 MINUTES **TOTAL:** 45 MINUTES

....

2 pounds ground chicken

1¼ cup drained canned pineapple tidbits (See Tip)

¼ cup coconut aminos

10 green onions, finely chopped

¼ cup plus 2 tablespoons almond flour

1 tablespoon coconut oil

½ teaspoon salt

1 tablespoon extra-virgin olive oil

8 Bibb lettuce leaves

½ cup Basic Mayonnaise (page 240) or Whole30-compliant mayonnaise

PREHEAT the oven to 200°F degrees. Line a large rimmed baking pan with parchment paper.

IN a large bowl, stir together the chicken, pineapple, coconut aminos, onions, almond flour, coconut oil, and salt. With wet hands, divide the mixture into 8 equal portions then shape into ¾-inch-thick patties. Place the patties on the baking pan. Place in the freezer for 15 minutes to firm up.

IN a large nonstick skillet, heat the olive oil over medium-high heat. When the skillet is hot, add 4 patties. Cook, turning once halfway through, until browned and cooked through (165°F). Transfer to a platter; cover with foil and place in the oven to keep warm. Repeat with the remaining patties, adding more oil to the pan if necessary.

TO serve, spread about 1 tablespoon mayonnaise on each lettuce leaf; top with the patties.

tip: USE CANNED PINEAPPLE FOR THIS RECIPE; the enzymes in fresh pineapple will break down the burgers and they will fall apart when cooking.

piña colada coleslaw

SERVES 8

While you may not be able to sip a piña colada on a Whole30, you can enjoy those same flavors (sans rum) in this coconutty coleslaw. Toasted macadamia nuts make a luxurious finishing touch.

PREP: 30 MINUTES **COOK:** 5 MINUTES
CHILL: 1 HOUR **TOTAL:** 1 HOUR 35 MINUTES

1 cup unsweetened shredded coconut

1 (14-ounce) package shredded cabbage and carrot coleslaw

½ cup sliced green onions

1 cup diced pineapple

½ cup Whole30-compliant coconut milk

¼ cup Basic Mayonnaise (page 240) or Whole30-compliant mayonnaise

½ cup 100% pineapple juice

1 teaspoon cider vinegar

½ teaspoon coarse salt

½ cup coarsely chopped macadamia nuts or almonds, toasted (see Tip)

IN a large skillet, toast the coconut over medium heat, stirring frequently, until golden brown, about 5 minutes. Set aside to cool.

IN a large bowl, combine the coleslaw mix, green onions, and pineapple; set aside.

IN a small bowl, whisk together the coconut milk, mayonnaise, pineapple juice, vinegar, and salt. Drizzle over the cabbage mixture; stir. Add ¾ cup of the toasted coconut; mix well. Cover and chill for at least 1 hour.

JUST before serving, stir in the nuts. Top with the remaining ¼ cup coconut.

tip: To TOAST THE NUTS, heat in a dry skillet over medium heat, stirring, until fragrant and lightly browned, about 2 minutes.

lemon butter–garlic sautéed kale

SERVES 8

A classic trifecta—lemon, butter, and garlic—gives these quick-cooked and nutrition-packed greens amazing flavor.

PREP: 10 MINUTES **COOK:** 5 MINUTES
TOTAL: 15 MINUTES

4 tablespoons Clarified Butter (page 241) or ghee

2½ bunches kale, stalks removed, leaves torn into bite-size pieces

3 tablespoons fresh lemon juice

3 cloves garlic, finely minced

½ teaspoon salt

¼ teaspoon black pepper

IN an extra-large skillet, melt the butter over medium-high heat. Add the kale; use tongs to turn to coat in the butter. Reduce the heat to medium. Add the lemon juice and garlic. Cook, stirring occasionally, until the kale is slightly wilted, 4 to 5 minutes. Season with the salt and pepper.

sweet potato–stuffed dates wrapped in prosciutto

SERVES 8

These sweet-and-salty bites are a Whole30-compliant twist on the classic cheese-stuffed, bacon-wrapped dates that are usually grilled or baked. They offer up similarly great flavor without the lava-hot cheese to contend with—especially when there are little ones grabbing for them.

·····································

PREP: 25 MINUTES   **COOK:** 5 MINUTES
TOTAL: 30 MINUTES

·····································

1 small sweet potato, scrubbed
16 Medjool dates with pits
1 tablespoon Whole30-compliant coconut milk
8 slices Whole30-compliant prosciutto, cut in half

PIERCE the sweet potato with a fork 4 or 5 times. Place on a microwave-safe plate and cook on high for 5 minutes, or until tender, rotating once halfway through. Set aside until cool enough to handle.

MEANWHILE, use a small sharp knife to make a slit lengthwise in the top of each date; use your fingers to remove the pits.

WHEN the potato is cool enough to handle, cut in half lengthwise and scoop the flesh into a medium bowl. Mash with a fork until roughly mashed. Add the coconut milk and mix with the fork until light and fluffy (you should have about ½ cup).

STUFF each date with a generous teaspoon of the sweet potato mixture. Wrap with a half slice of prosciutto and place on a serving platter. Spear with a toothpick to serve.

chilled coconut–almond butter bananas

SERVES 8

Don't freeze these any more than 20 minutes—they'll get too hard—and serve them right away. If they sit too long out of the freezer, the bananas start to turn brown and get mushy.

PREP: 15 MINUTES **TOTAL:** 35 MINUTES

4 bananas, peeled

⅓ cup Whole30-compliant almond butter

1 tablespoon unsweetened flaked coconut

LINE a large baking pan with parchment paper.

BIAS-SLICE each banana into four pieces. Place the almond butter in a small glass bowl; microwave for 10 to 15 seconds, or until spreadable. Spread about 1 teaspoon almond butter on a cut side of each piece of banana. Place on the prepared pan and sprinkle with coconut.

FREEZE for 20 minutes, then serve.

sparkling pineapple spritzer

SERVES 8

Although it's not a necessity, toasting the coconut for the decorative rim makes it prettier—and tastier too.

PREP: 10 MINUTES **COOK:** 5 MINUTES
TOTAL: 15 MINUTES

1 tablespoon coconut oil

½ cup unsweetened finely shredded coconut, toasted (see Tip)

Ice

8 (12-ounce) cans Whole30-compliant lime-flavored sparkling water, chilled

1 cup 100% pineapple juice, chilled

PLACE the coconut oil in a shallow glass dish; microwave until melted, about 20 seconds. Dip the rims of eight 16-ounce glasses into the melted coconut oil then the toasted coconut.

TO serve, add a few ice cubes to each glass. Pour 1 can of the sparkling water into each glass. Add 2 tablespoons of the pineapple juice; stir to mix.

tip: To TOAST THE COCONUT, heat in a dry skillet over medium heat, stirring, until fragrant and lightly browned, about 5 minutes.

game day

Getting together with friends to watch the big game is as much about the nosh as the play-by-play—and there's definitely an expectation of what a "game day" spread entails. This is not tea-sandwich territory! But while traditional poppers, hot wings, onion rings, and chips and dip are off the menu on a Whole30, our menu delivers compliant variations of the same hearty favorites. Enjoy bacon-wrapped jalapeños stuffed with ancho chile-spiced turkey sausage, crispy beet chips with a caramelized onion dip, hot wings flavored with lime and garlic, baked onion rings, and sausage-and-sauerkraut-loaded sweet potatoes. You'll score big with this menu—whether your team wins or not.

· ·

bacon-wrapped turkey jalapeño poppers

lime-garlic hot wings with green chile sauce

almond-crusted onion rings with green onion–cracked pepper aioli

oven-roasted beet chips with caramelized onion-chive dip

sausage-and-sauerkraut-loaded sweet potatoes

whole30 for the win!

IT HAS BEEN SCIENTIFICALLY PROVEN that beer is not physiologically required to enjoy watching a sporting event. Swap in a compliant kombucha, iced tea, coffee alternative, or sparkling water and wake up clear-headed and energetic—SCORE.

GOOD-NATURED RIBBING IS PART OF MOST COMPETITIONS, but if the roasting turns to your "weird" Whole30 diet, have a light but snappy comeback. "Well, I kicked your butt on the basketball court last weekend, so something I'm doing must be working." (Also effective: "Cool. No wings for you, then.")

MAXIMIZE VIEWING TIME BY PREPPING MOST OF THIS AHEAD. The wings have to marinate for 4 to 12 hours and the sauce can be made the day before. Stuff and wrap the jalapeños, make the dips for the beet chips and onion rings, and prep the sausage-sauerkraut mixture to reheat before serving.

IF YOU'RE LOOKING FOR MUNCHIE-STYLE PRE-SPREAD SNACKS, try roasted nuts and olives, veggies with compliant ranch dip and guacamole, and simple deviled eggs.

bacon-wrapped turkey jalapeño poppers

SERVES 8

In a competition between a cream cheese-stuffed, deep-fried jalapeño and these roasted chiles stuffed with savory seasoned turkey and wrapped in crispy bacon, there's no contest. It's bacon for the win!

....

PREP: 30 MINUTES **BAKE:** 25 MINUTES **TOTAL:** 1 HOUR

....

¾ cup almond flour

¼ cup chopped fresh cilantro

1 green onion, finely chopped

1 large egg

2 teaspoons ancho chile powder

1 teaspoon paprika

1 teaspoon cumin seeds, toasted (see Tip)

1 teaspoon oregano, crushed

1 teaspoon salt

½ teaspoon chipotle powder

1 pound ground turkey or lean beef

10 jalapeños, halved lengthwise and seeded

10 slices Whole30-compliant bacon, cut in half crosswise

PREHEAT the oven to 400°F. Line two large rimmed baking pans with parchment paper.

IN a medium bowl, combine the almond flour, cilantro, green onion, egg, ancho chile powder, paprika, cumin seeds, oregano, salt, and chipotle powder. Add the turkey and mix well.

SPOON 1 to 2 tablespoons filling into each jalapeño half; wrap each in a half piece of bacon. Secure with a toothpick.

ARRANGE the jalapeños, about 1 inch apart, on the baking pans. Bake for about 25 minutes, until the bacon is crisp and the filling is cooked through (175°F for turkey, 160°F for ground beef).

TRANSFER the poppers to a paper towel–lined platter. Let cool for 5 minutes before serving.

tip: To TOAST THE CUMIN SEEDS, heat in a dry skillet over medium heat, stirring, until fragrant and lightly browned, about 2 minutes.

lime-garlic hot wings with green chile sauce

SERVES 8

Sure, Buffalo wings are awesome—but for a change of pace, try these crispy wings infused with Mexican flavors next time friends gather to cheer on your favorite team.

....

PREP: 30 MINUTES   CHILL: 4 HOURS   ROAST: 50 MINUTES
TOTAL: 5 HOURS 20 MINUTES

....

16 chicken wings (about 5 pounds)

½ cup fresh lime juice

6 tablespoons extra-virgin olive oil

3 cloves garlic, minced

2½ teaspoons salt

1 tablespoon grated lime zest

1 tablespoon ground cumin

2½ teaspoons ground coriander

1 large poblano pepper, halved lengthwise and seeded

1 serrano chile, halved lengthwise and seeded (if desired)

½ cup lightly packed fresh cilantro

2 green onions, chopped

2 tablespoons 100% pineapple juice

USE kitchen shears or a very sharp chef's knife to remove the tips of the chicken wings (discard the tips or save them for making stock). Cut the rest of the wings at the joint to make two pieces each. Place the wings in a large resealable plastic bag.

IN a glass measuring bowl or small bowl, whisk together the lime juice, olive oil, garlic, salt, lime zest, cumin, and coriander. Pour ½ cup over the wings in the bag and reserve the remaining mixture. Seal the bag and refrigerate for 4 to 12 hours, turning the bag once or twice.

MEANWHILE, preheat the oven to 450°F. Line a large rimmed baking pan with foil. Place the peppers on the baking pan, skin sides up. Roast, about 15 minutes for the poblano and 10 minutes for the serrano, until the peppers are charred and crisp tender.

PEEL the loose skin from the peppers and roughly chop. Transfer the peppers to a blender. Add the reserved lime juice mixture, the cilantro, green onions, and pineapple juice. Cover and blend until smooth. Cover and chill the sauce for at least 1 hour or up to 24 hours.

PREHEAT the oven to 425°F. Line two large rimmed baking pans with foil. Place a wire rack on each baking pan.

DRAIN and discard the marinade from the chicken pieces. Arrange the pieces on the rack. Roast for 20 minutes. Turn each chicken piece and roast until cooked through and lightly browned, about 20 minutes. Brush the wings on both sides with some of the sauce and roast for 10 minutes more. Serve the wings with the remaining sauce.

almond-crusted onion rings with green onion–cracked pepper aioli

SERVES 8

Refrigerating the coated rings for between 1 and 4 hours helps the breading to adhere to the onion during baking and eating—so don't skip that step!

....

PREP: 30 MINUTES **CHILL:** 1 HOUR
BAKE: 20 MINUTES **TOTAL:** 1 HOUR 50 MINUTES

....

FOR THE ONION RINGS

1 cup almond flour

1 teaspoon paprika

1 teaspoon dried oregano, crushed

1 teaspoon coarse salt

½ teaspoon garlic powder

2 large eggs

2 medium yellow onions, sliced ½ inch thick

¼ cup extra-virgin olive oil

FOR THE AIOLI

2 green onions, chopped

1 egg, at room temperature

1 clove garlic

1 teaspoon Whole30-compliant Dijon mustard

1 tablespoon fresh lemon juice

1 to 1¼ cups light-tasting olive oil

1 teaspoon cracked black pepper

LINE two large rimmed baking pans with parchment paper.

MAKE THE ONION RINGS: In a large bowl, combine the almond flour, paprika, oregano, salt, and garlic powder. In another large bowl, whisk the 2 eggs. Stir ¼ cup of the flour mixture into the eggs.

SEPARATE the onion slices into rings. Add 3 to 4 onion rings at a time to the egg mixture and turn to coat. Use your hands or a slotted spoon to transfer the onions to the flour mixture; turn to coat.

TRANSFER the onions to the baking pans in a single layer. Refrigerate for at least 1 hour or up to 4 hours.

MAKE THE AIOLI: In a blender, combine the green onions, egg, garlic, mustard, and lemon juice. Cover and pulse to combine. With the blender running, slowly add the light olive oil until creamy. Add the pepper and pulse to combine. Transfer to a serving bowl; cover and refrigerate until ready to serve.

PREHEAT the oven to 450°F. Drizzle the onion rings with the extra-virgin olive oil. Bake until the onions are tender and the coating is golden and crisp, about 20 minutes. Transfer to a serving platter and serve with the aioli.

oven-roasted beet chips with caramelized onion-chive dip

SERVES 8

Although you can slice the beets with a good sharp knife, you will get the thinnest, crispiest chips if you use a mandoline.

....

PREP: 30 MINUTES   **CHILL:** 30 MINUTES
BAKE: 20 MINUTES   **TOTAL:** 1 HOUR 20 MINUTES

....

FOR THE DIP

1 tablespoon Clarified Butter (page 241) or ghee

1 medium onion, finely chopped

½ teaspoon coarse salt

½ teaspoon coarse black pepper

1 cup Basic Mayonnaise (page 240) or Whole30-compliant mayonnaise

1 tablespoon minced fresh chives

½ teaspoon onion powder

½ teaspoon ground Aleppo pepper or ¼ teaspoon red pepper flakes

FOR THE BEET CHIPS

4 medium beets, trimmed and peeled

2 tablespoons extra-virgin olive oil

1 teaspoon coarse salt

½ teaspoon coarse black pepper

MAKE THE DIP: In a medium skillet, melt the butter over medium-high heat. Add the onions, and sprinkle with ¼ teaspoon each salt and black pepper. Cook, stirring frequently, until the onions are softened, about 5 minutes. Reduce the heat to low. Cook, stirring occasionally, until the onions are tender and golden, about 10 minutes. Transfer the onions to a bowl to cool.

STIR in the mayonnaise, chives, onion powder, and Aleppo pepper into the cooled onions. Season with the remaining ¼ teaspoon each salt and black pepper. Cover and refrigerate for at least 30 minutes or up to 24 hours.

MAKE THE BEET CHIPS: Preheat the oven to 375°F. Line two large rimmed baking pans with parchment paper.

THINLY slice the beets with a mandoline on the thinnest setting or with a sharp knife. Place the slices in a large bowl; drizzle with olive oil and sprinkle with the salt and pepper; toss to coat. Arrange the slices in a single layer on the baking pans.

BAKE for 12 minutes. Turn the slices over and bake until lightly browned at the edges and the centers appear dry, 8 to 10 minutes more. Transfer to a wire rack to cool (the chips will continue to crisp as they cool). Serve the beet chips with the dip.

sausage-and-sauerkraut-loaded sweet potatoes

SERVES 8

Caraway, sauerkraut, and sausage give these piled-high sweet potatoes a German accent—perfect for watching World Cup soccer!

PREP: 25 MINUTES **BAKE:** 45 MINUTES
TOTAL: 1 HOUR 10 MINUTES

8 small (4 to 5 ounces each) sweet potatoes or russet potatoes, scrubbed

2 tablespoons extra-virgin olive oil

Coarse salt

1 tablespoon Clarified Butter (page 241) or ghee

1 large sweet onion, cut into thin wedges

1½ teaspoons caraway seeds

6 Whole30-compliant chicken and apple sausages, sliced (see Tip)

3 cups fresh sauerkraut, drained

¼ cup apple juice

2 teaspoons fresh thyme leaves

½ cup chopped fresh parsley

assorted toppings, such as sliced green onions, sliced roasted red peppers, Whole30 Sriracha (page 242), and/or sliced jalapeños

PREHEAT the oven to 425°F.

PLACE each potato on a square of aluminum foil; brush the potatoes with olive oil and lightly sprinkle with salt. Wrap the potatoes in foil. Bake for 45 to 60 minutes, until the potatoes are tender when tested with a fork.

MEANWHILE, in a large skillet, melt the butter over medium-high heat. Add the onion and caraway seeds. Cook, stirring occasionally, until the onion is browned in some spots, about 5 minutes. Add the sausage, cooking and stirring, until the sausage is lightly browned, 8 to 10 minutes. Stir in the sauerkraut, apple juice, and thyme. Bring to a boil and reduce the heat to low. Simmer, covered, for 5 minutes. Remove from the heat and stir in the parsley.

TO serve, unwrap each potato and use a knife to cut an X on top. Carefully press the ends of the potato to open. Spoon the sausage-sauerkraut mixture onto each potato. Top with green onions, roasted peppers, hot sauce, and/or jalapeños.

tip: FOR THE 6 SAUSAGES, you will need to purchase two (10- to 12-ounce) packages of Whole30-compliant chicken and apple sausages. Use the remaining two sausages for breakfast with eggs.

book club

Book clubs are about reading great books, getting together with friends, sharing your thoughts, and eating delicious food. This book club menu is simple enough that you can make every dish on it *and* still get your reading done. It features popular types of party fare perfect for nibbling while paging through a book—no messy ribs! We've got shrimp, meatballs, and yummy dips; something crunchy, but not potato chips . . . they're savory, crispy prosciutto strips! And the last word? A "shot" of berry puree topped with whipped coconut cream. And it's all Whole30-compliant, so you can skip asking, "Is there sugar in that?" and go straight to, "What did you think of the ending?"

....

**aleppo pepper–garlic
prosciutto crisps**

creole shrimp

muhammara dip

meatloaf meatballs

berry–coconut cream shots

coffee talk

FOR SOME, "book club" is synonymous with "wine club"—but that's not on the table here, literally. No one will miss it, though, if you serve a selection of sparkling mocktails, iced herbal teas, or decaf coffee with caramel Nutpods.

ALTHOUGH "THE MORE THE MERRIER" may apply to some types of parties, you should cap the number of book club members to avoid cross-talk and chaos in the conversation; that's why these recipes serve 6 (but the menu could stretch to 8).

BOOK CLUBS AREN'T JUST FOR WOMEN! I have a group of male friends who formed a club just for the guys: time set aside to open up, connect with each other, and talk about things that matter. (Warning: Serve this menu and you may find yourself named "permanent host.")

SET SOME GROUND RULES for the discussion, such as agreeing to disagree, making sure everyone has a chance to contribute, and politely deferring any Whole30 questions for after the book talk.

CHECK OUT litlovers.com for hundreds of book reviews, activities, and discussion guides and #melissaurbanreads on Instagram to see dozens of my favorite club-worthy books.

aleppo pepper–garlic prosciutto crisps

SERVES 6

Aleppo pepper is similar to crushed red pepper but about half as hot and much more complex in flavor. It has a subtlety—an earthiness and fruitiness—that crushed red pepper lacks. The marriage of the crispy, salty prosciutto; a little bit of mild heat from the chile; and the sweetness of the melon (if you choose to include it) makes a stimulating flavor combination—a perfect snack for encouraging stimulating conversation!

PREP: 5 MINUTES **BAKE:** 10 MINUTES
COOL: 5 MINUTES **TOTAL:** 20 MINUTES

2 (2-ounce) packages thinly sliced Whole30-compliant prosciutto

1 teaspoon ground Aleppo pepper

½ teaspoon garlic powder

Cut-up cantaloupe and/or honeydew melon (optional)

PLACE a rack in the center of the oven. Preheat the oven to 350°F. Line a large rimmed baking pan with parchment paper.

PLACE the prosciutto in a single layer on the baking pan. Bake for 10 to 15 minutes, until starting to crisp. Watch carefully to prevent burning. Transfer to a wire rack; the chips will crisp further as they cool.

IN a small bowl, stir together the Aleppo pepper and garlic powder. Sprinkle the chips with the seasoning.

IF desired, serve the crisps with cut-up melon for a sweet-salty appetizer.

creole shrimp

SERVES 6

The longer you marinate the shrimp, the more flavor they'll have—but don't go beyond 4 hours or the acid in the lemon juice will start to break down their delicate texture and turn them mushy.

••••••••••••••••••••••••••••••

PREP: 8 MINUTES **CHILL:** 1 HOUR **ROAST:** 7 MINUTES
TOTAL: 1 HOUR 15 MINUTES

••••••••••••••••••••••••••••••

¼ cup extra-virgin olive oil

1 tablespoon Whole30-compliant Creole seasoning

2 tablespoons fresh lemon juice

1 clove garlic, minced

1 tablespoon coconut aminos

1 tablespoon fresh orange juice

1 pound (16/20 count) peeled and deveined shrimp, thawed if frozen

2 tablespoons chopped fresh parsley

IN a 9 × 13-inch glass baking dish, combine the olive oil, seasoning, lemon juice, garlic, coconut aminos, and orange juice. Add the shrimp and turn to coat. Cover and marinate in the refrigerator for 1 hour or up to 4 hours, turning the shrimp every 30 minutes.

PREHEAT the oven to 450°F. Let the shrimp stand at room temperature while the oven preheats.

ROAST, uncovered, for 7 to 8 minutes, until the shrimp are opaque. Transfer to a serving platter and sprinkle with parsley.

tip: To make your own Creole seasoning, in a small bowl combine 1 tablespoon onion powder, 1 tablespoon garlic powder, 1 tablespoon dried oregano, 1 tablespoon dried basil, 1 teaspoon dried thyme, 2 teaspoons coarse black pepper, 2 teaspoons cayenne pepper, and 2 teaspoons coarse salt. Makes ½ cup. Store in an airtight container for up to 6 months.

muhammara dip

SERVES 6

Traditionally, this Syrian roasted red pepper and walnut dip calls for pomegranate molasses to add a hint of sweetness. This version calls for a single date to accomplish the same thing without any refined sugars. Toasting the walnuts enhances their flavor.

··································

PREP: 15 MINUTES   **TOTAL:** 15 MINUTES

··································

1 (12- to 15-ounce) jar roasted red peppers, drained

½ cup walnuts, toasted (see Tip)

2 tablespoons almond flour

1 tablespoon fresh lemon juice

1 clove garlic

1 Medjool date, pitted

1 teaspoon ground cumin

¼ teaspoon salt

¼ teaspoon black pepper

¼ teaspoon ground Aleppo pepper or ⅛ teaspoon cayenne pepper

¼ cup extra-virgin olive oil

1 tablespoon chopped fresh parsley

Assorted vegetables, such as jicama sticks, mini bell peppers, and radishes

IN a food processor, combine the peppers, walnuts, almond flour, lemon juice, garlic, date, cumin, salt, black pepper, and Aleppo pepper. Cover and process until well combined. While the food processor is running, slowly drizzle the olive oil through the tube until the dip is smooth.

TRANSFER the dip to a serving bowl. If desired, drizzle with additional olive oil. Sprinkle with parsley and serve with vegetables for dipping.

tip: To TOAST WALNUTS, heat in a skillet over medium heat, stirring, until fragrant and lightly browned, about 2 minutes.

meatloaf meatballs

SERVES 6

These meatballs studded with shallot, carrot, and celery provide the hearty element in a menu of nibbles so that guests will go home feeling full and satisfied.

....

PREP: 15 MINUTES **BAKE:** 12 MINUTES **TOTAL:** 30 MINUTES

....

¼ cup finely chopped fresh parsley

¼ cup almond flour

1 large egg, lightly beaten

3 tablespoons Whole30-compliant tomato paste

2 tablespoons coconut aminos

½ teaspoon salt

¼ teaspoon black pepper

1 large shallot, finely chopped

1 stalk celery, finely chopped

1 medium carrot, peeled and finely chopped

1 pound lean ground beef

1 (15.5-ounce) jar Whole30-compliant marinara sauce, warmed (optional)

PREHEAT the oven to 375°F. Line a rimmed baking pan with parchment paper or aluminum foil.

IN a large bowl, stir together the parsley, almond flour, egg, tomato paste, coconut aminos, salt, and pepper. Add the shallot, celery, carrot, and ground beef. Mix with your hands until just combined, then shape into 24 meatballs. Arrange the meatballs on the baking pan.

BAKE for 11 to 13 minutes, until cooked through. Serve the meatballs with warm marinara sauce for dipping, if desired.

tip: KEEP A BATCH OF MEATBALLS ON HAND so you're ready for guests any time! Cool the meatballs after baking; arrange on a rimmed baking pan lined with waxed paper. Freeze for 30 minutes or until firm. Transfer to resealable freezer bags. Seal; freeze for up to 2 months. Thaw in the refrigerator.

berry–coconut cream shots

SERVES 6

This berries-and-cream treat is a sweet way to wrap up an evening of food, friendship, and intellectual exploration.

....

PREP: 35 MINUTES **CHILL:** 8 HOURS
TOTAL: 8 HOURS 35 MINUTES

....

2 (14-ounce) cans Whole30-compliant coconut milk, refrigerated overnight (see Tip)

1 teaspoon Whole30-compliant vanilla bean powder (see Tip)

½ teaspoon grated lemon zest

2 cups strawberries, hulled (see Tip)

1 cup blueberries

OPEN the refrigerated cans of coconut milk; drain off the liquid and reserve for smoothies. Spoon the coconut cream into a large bowl. Add the vanilla bean powder to the coconut cream and beat with an electric mixer on medium-high until fluffy, about 5 minutes. Fold in the lemon zest. Refrigerate until needed.

RESERVE 6 small strawberries for garnish. Place the remaining strawberries and the blueberries in a blender or food processor. Cover and blend or process until smooth. To remove the seeds, press the puree through a fine-mesh strainer with a bowl underneath.

IN a small bowl, stir together ¼ cup of the puree and 1 cup of the whipped coconut cream.

DIVIDE the puree among six small juice glasses. Top with the puree-cream mixture. Spoon some of the coconut cream on top.

FOR the strawberry garnish, use a small sharp knife to make four or five cuts from just under the stem to the bottom. Gently fan the slices apart and place on top of the coconut cream.

tips: KEEP A COUPLE OF CANS OF COCONUT MILK in your refrigerator so you'll be ready whenever you want to make coconut cream.

IN PLACE OF THE VANILLA BEAN POWDER, you can scrape the seeds from ⅓ of a vanilla bean. One whole vanilla bean equals 3 teaspoons vanilla bean powder or extract.

TO REMOVE THE STEM AND HULL FROM A STRAWBERRY without a strawberry huller, use a sharp knife to cut around the stem. You can also use thawed-out frozen strawberries and blueberries for the puree.

camping

Stephanie Vanlochem

COOKBYCOLORNUTRITION.COM

Stephanie Vanlochem (BA, nutritional therapy practitioner, and Whole30 Certified Coach) is the founder of Cook by Color Nutrition, a practice that teaches the power of cooking real food as nourishment for both mind and body. Stephanie believes in eating for both health and pleasure, and helps clients create an individualized, sustainable, colorful lifestyle.

There's something about being in the great outdoors that really does build up an appetite. Setting up a campsite, hiking, swimming, canoeing, or rock climbing should be followed by a hearty, delicious meal eaten 'round the fire. (Fact: Sun, stars, and fresh air make food taste better too.) Every recipe in this menu is specially designed for camping—either prepping some of it at home and finishing or cooking it at camp, or easily making it from start to finish on-site with minimal mess. We've got you covered for every meal—breakfast, lunch, and dinner—so the only thing you need to stop and pick up is the firewood.

....

rainbow mango slaw with almond butter dressing and fresh herbs

japanese sweet potato hash

marinated chicken, pineapple, and vegetable foil packets

steak fajitas foil packets

sweet plantain, sausage, and broccoli breakfast skillet

sun-dried tomato and basil chicken salad with pepitas

turkey sausage scotch eggs

campfire grilled peaches

happy campers

YOU MAY HAVE A PORTABLE STOVE OR GRILL, but if you don't, you can cook "cowboy-style" using a large, well-seasoned cast-iron skillet and plenty of heavy-duty aluminum foil. Cast-iron can be placed directly on a campsite grill grate—or even in medium-hot coals—and foil is very handy for packet-cooking. (You can also ball it up and use it to clean a nasty grill grate!)

YOU'LL HAVE TO SKIP THE GORP (for the uninitiated, "good old raisins and peanuts"), but it's easy to make a Whole30 version: Toss together some compliant almonds, pecans, cashews, unsweetened coconut shreds, cacao nibs, and freeze-dried raspberries. (Or, be lazy and grab some compliant RXBARs.)

CAMP COFFEE IS EASY! Add a scoop of coffee to a coffee filter and tie it tightly with dental floss to make a tea bag-style coffee bundle. Just add hot water to make a single cup of coffee—and pack some Nutpods in the cooler.

YOU WON'T BE ROASTING MARSH-MALLOWS OVER THE FIRE, but that doesn't mean you have to miss out—just sharpen your sticks and pack some pineapple. Cut a fresh pineapple into chunks and roast it fireside—the outside gets toasty and caramelized, and it won't leave your kiddos on a sugar high right before bed.

rainbow mango slaw with almond butter dressing and fresh herbs

SERVES 6

This slaw is loaded with Asian-inspired flavor, vibrant color, and textures—perfect for accompanying your protein of choice. It is prepped entirely at home and mixed up at camp with no dishes! Add the dressing to a 2-gallon resealable plastic bag with the slaw, seal, and have enthusiastic little campers shake until well-combined.

....

PREP: 30 MINUTES   TOTAL: 30 MINUTES

....

FOR THE DRESSING

½ cup Whole30-compliant almond butter

½ cup rice vinegar

2 tablespoons sesame oil

2 tablespoons coconut aminos

1 piece (½ inch) fresh ginger, peeled and roughly chopped

1 green onion (white and green parts), roughly chopped

¼ teaspoon red pepper flakes

½ teaspoon coarse salt

½ teaspoon black pepper

FOR THE SLAW

½ napa cabbage, thinly sliced (about 8 cups)

1 cup thinly sliced purple cabbage

1 cup coarsely shredded carrots

1 cup matchstick-cut red bell pepper

2 green onions, chopped

1 large mango, chopped (about 1½ cups) (see Tip)

2 tablespoons chopped fresh mint,
plus more for garnish

¼ cup chopped fresh cilantro, plus more for garnish

¼ cup coarsely chopped cashews

at home

MAKE THE DRESSING: In a blender or food processor, combine the almond butter, vinegar, ¼ cup of water, sesame oil, coconut aminos, ginger, green onion, red pepper flakes, salt, and black pepper. Cover and blend until smooth. Store in an airtight container in a cooler or refrigerator until ready to serve.

MAKE THE SLAW: In a 2-gallon resealable plastic bag or 4-quart container with a lid, combine the cabbage, purple cabbage, carrots, bell pepper, and green onions. Store the mango, herbs, and cashews in separate airtight containers. Store the slaw ingredients in a cooler or refrigerator until ready to serve.

at camp

TO serve, add the mango, about two-thirds of the herbs, and 1 cup of the dressing to the vegetable mixture. Shake until combined. Add additional dressing, if desired. Top servings with cashews and the remaining herbs.

tip: TO CUT A MANGO, use a "Y" peeler to peel it, then use a sharp knife to trim the stem. Set the mango on one of its narrow sides and, holding it in one hand and a sharp knife in the other, slice through the flesh slightly off center to avoid the pit. Repeat with the other side. Dice or cut as desired.

japanese sweet potato hash

SERVES 6

This is a great side dish to serve for multiple meals at camp. Depending on how many people you are feeding, or how many meals this is supplementing, you can prepare more ingredients at home and cook in batches. This is excellent served with Turkey Sausage Scotch Eggs (page 115), a scattering of chopped fresh herbs, and hot sauce.

····················

PREP: 30 MINUTES   **COOK:** 15 MINUTES
TOTAL: 45 MINUTES

····················

1½ pounds Japanese sweet potatoes, peeled and chopped

3 small carrots, peeled, halved lengthwise, and chopped

1¼ teaspoons salt

1 small green bell pepper, chopped

1 small red bell pepper, chopped

1 small fennel bulb, trimmed and chopped (see Tip)

1 small yellow onion, chopped

3 cloves garlic, minced

1 serrano chile, seeded and minced

¼ cup extra-virgin olive oil, Clarified Butter (page 241), or ghee

½ teaspoon black pepper

2 teaspoons Whole30-compliant Italian seasoning

½ teaspoon garlic powder

½ teaspoon onion powder

at home

PRECOOK THE SWEET POTATOES AND CARROTS: Bring a large pot of water to a boil over medium-high heat. Add the sweet potatoes, carrots, and ½ teaspoon salt. Cook until the vegetables are crisp-tender, 3 to 4 minutes. Drain and let cool. Store in an airtight container in a cold place until ready to cook.

IN a large resealable plastic bag, combine the green pepper, red pepper, fennel, onion, garlic, and serrano. Store in a cold place until ready to cook.

at camp

PLACE an extra-large cast iron skillet on a grill grate over medium heat. Add the olive oil. Add the sweet potato, carrots, and bell pepper to the hot oil. Sprinkle with ¾ teaspoon salt and the pepper, Italian seasoning, garlic powder, and onion powder. Cook, stirring occasionally, until the vegetables are tender and lightly browned, 10 to 12 minutes.

tip: To TRIM A FENNEL BULB, cut off the stalks about 1 inch from the bulb. Cut a thin slice from the root end and discard. Remove any wilted outer layers with a vegetable peeler. Stand the bulb upright and cut in half. Cut away and discard the tough core from each half. Slice the fennel according to the recipe.

marinated chicken, pineapple, and vegetable foil packets

SERVES 6

This foil-packet dinner is sweet, spicy, and super-convenient! It's an ideal way to do the majority of the work at home, execute it at camp, and impress everyone with how delicious it is—and how little clean-up is involved. Use heavy-duty foil when creating the packets, and use two layers to prevent burning.

....

PREP: 25 MINUTES **MARINATE:** 1 HOUR
COOK: 10 MINUTES **TOTAL:** 1 HOUR 35 MINUTES

....

⅔ cup coconut aminos

½ cup orange juice

3 green onions, coarsely chopped

2 cloves garlic, coarsely chopped

1 piece (½ inch) fresh ginger, peeled and grated

1 teaspoon red pepper flakes

½ teaspoon coarse salt

½ teaspoon black pepper

2 pounds boneless, skinless chicken thighs, thinly sliced

½ cup Whole30-compliant diced pineapple

2 cups coarsely chopped carrots

2 cups sugar snap peas, trimmed

2½ cups broccoli florets

at home

IN a blender or food processor, combine the coconut aminos, orange juice, green onions, garlic, ginger, red pepper flakes, salt, and pepper. Cover and blend or process until almost smooth.

IN a large resealable plastic bag, combine the chicken, pineapple, carrot, snap peas, and broccoli. Add the marinade. Marinate in the refrigerator for 1 hour or up to 4 hours. Drain and discard the marinade. Store the chicken mixture in an airtight container in a cooler or refrigerator until ready to cook.

at camp

FOR each camper, make a foil packet with a double-thickness of heavy duty foil, about 18 inches long. Divide the chicken mixture between the foil packets. Bring the long sides of the foil together at the top and roll down tightly to seal before rolling up the sides, leaving room for steam to build.

PLACE the packet on a grill grate over medium heat. Cook for 10 minutes; carefully open the packets to stir and check for doneness. The vegetables should be crisp-tender, and the chicken cooked through (no longer pink). If the chicken is not done, cook for 2 to 5 minutes more. Serve in the foil packets.

steak fajitas foil packets

SERVES 6

Who doesn't want tender steak and flavorful fajita veggies without splattering oil or messy camp cleanup? If you'd like, serve these in lettuce boats topped with plenty of salsa, cilantro, and avocado—or enjoy straight from the foil packet.

PREP: 20 MINUTES **MARINATE:** 1 HOUR
COOK: 10 MINUTES **TOTAL:** 1 HOUR 30 MINUTES

⅓ cup fresh orange juice

½ cup fresh lime juice

¼ cup avocado oil

½ small white onion, coarsely chopped

1 tablespoon cider vinegar

1 tablespoon ground cumin

2 teaspoons dried oregano

2 teaspoons smoked paprika

2 teaspoons Whole30-compliant chili powder

1 cup coarsely chopped fresh cilantro, plus more for garnish

1½ teaspoons coarse salt

½ teaspoon black pepper

2 pounds flank steak, thinly sliced

3 cups thinly sliced bell peppers, any color

2 cups halved white or cremini mushrooms, stems trimmed

1 cup thinly sliced red onion

Avocado slices, Whole30-compliant salsa, and/or cilantro (optional)

at home

FOR the marinade, in a blender or food processor, combine the orange juice, lime juice, avocado oil, white onion, vinegar, cumin, oregano, paprika, chili powder, cilantro, salt, and pepper. Cover and blend or process until almost smooth.

PLACE the steak, peppers, mushrooms, and red onion in a large resealable plastic bag; add the marinade. Marinate for 1 hour or up to 4 hours. Drain and discard the marinade. Store the steak mixture in an airtight container in a cooler or refrigerator until ready to cook.

at camp

FOR each camper, make a foil packet with a double-thickness of heavy duty foil, about 18 inches long. Divide the steak mixture between the foil packets. Bring the long sides of the foil together at the top and roll down tightly to seal before sealing the ends, leaving room for steam to build.

PLACE the packet on a grill grate over medium heat. Cook for 10 minutes; carefully open the packets to stir and check for doneness. The vegetables should be crisp-tender, and the steak cooked to medium (slightly pink inside). If the steak is not done, cook for 2 to 5 minutes more.

SERVE in foil packets topped with avocado, salsa, and/or cilantro, if desired.

sweet plantain, sausage, and broccoli breakfast skillet

SERVES 6

This no-egg cast iron skillet breakfast is easily made at camp with minimal effort and no at-home prep required. It makes a hearty, energy-giving breakfast before a day of hiking, biking, canoeing, or kayaking.

PREP: 10 MINUTES   **COOK:** 10 MINUTES
TOTAL: 20 MINUTES

⅓ cup Whole30-compliant chicken, beef, or vegetable broth

3 cups bite-size broccoli florets

2 tablespoons coconut oil

1 (12-ounce) package Whole30-compliant chicken and apple sausages, cut into ½-inch slices on the bias

1 large ripe plantain, peeled and cut into ½-inch slices on the bias

2 teaspoons Whole30-compliant Italian seasoning

¼ teaspoon coarse salt

¼ teaspoon black pepper

⅓ cup chopped fresh cilantro (optional)

1 green onion, finely chopped (optional)

Whole30 Sriracha (page 242) or Whole30-compliant hot sauce (optional)

at camp

PLACE a large cast iron skillet on a grill grate over medium-high heat. Add the broth and heat until steaming. Add the broccoli. Cook, covered, until the broccoli is bright green, about 2 minutes. Transfer to a large plate.

LET any remaining broth in the skillet evaporate. Add 1 tablespoon coconut oil to the skillet. Turn the heat to medium (or move the skillet to a cooler area). Add the sausage and cook, stirring occasionally, until starting to brown, 4 to 5 minutes. Transfer to the plate with the broccoli.

ADD the remaining 1 tablespoon coconut oil to the skillet. Add the plantain and cook, turning occasionally, until golden on both sides, 4 to 5 minutes. Return the broccoli and sausage to the skillet. Add the Italian seasoning, salt, and pepper. Cook until heated through.

TO serve, top with cilantro, green onions, and Sriracha, if desired.

sun-dried tomato and basil chicken salad with pepitas

SERVES 6

This chicken salad makes a great lunch option when you're driving to your camping spot in the morning. It can sit in the cooler until after you're settled at your campsite—then just scoop it into the lettuce leaves, top with crunchy pepitas, and dig in!

PREP: 15 MINUTES **TOTAL:** 15 MINUTES

1 cup lightly packed basil leaves

⅓ cup Whole30-compliant oil-packed sun-dried tomatoes

¼ cup Basic Mayonnaise (page 240) or Whole30-compliant mayonnaise

3 tablespoons sun-dried tomato oil (from the jar)

2 teaspoons white wine vinegar

¼ teaspoon garlic powder

¼ teaspoon salt

¼ teaspoon black pepper

3 cups finely chopped cooked chicken

12 Bibb lettuce leaves

2 tablespoons roasted and salted pepitas

Thinly sliced fresh basil for garnish

at home

IN a blender or food processor, combine the basil, tomatoes, mayonnaise, oil, vinegar, garlic powder, salt, and pepper. Cover and blend or process until well combined.

IN a medium bowl, stir together the chicken and mayonnaise mixture. Transfer to an airtight container and store in a cooler or refrigerator until ready to serve.

STORE the lettuce leaves in a large resealable plastic bag in a cooler or refrigerator until ready to serve. Store the pepitas and basil for garnish in separate airtight containers in a cooler or refrigerator until ready to serve.

at camp

TO serve, scoop ¼ cup of chicken salad into each lettuce leaf. Top with pepitas and sliced basil.

turkey sausage scotch eggs

SERVES 6

These eggs are the ultimate camping food. All the work is done at home in your kitchen and you have a perfect, satiating protein-and-fat-packed snack to enjoy in so many ways. Nibble en route to the campsite, take along as a portable hiking snack, or serve with the Japanese Sweet Potato Hash (page 108) for breakfast.

PREP: 25 MINUTES **COOK:** 20 MINUTES **TOTAL:** 45 MINUTES

2 teaspoons extra-virgin olive oil

¼ cup minced yellow onion

2 pounds 85% lean ground turkey, chicken, or beef

½ cup minced apple

¼ cup finely chopped fresh sage

1 teaspoon dried marjoram leaves, crushed

1 teaspoon coarse salt

½ teaspoon black pepper

¼ teaspoon ground cinnamon

¼ teaspoon red pepper flakes (optional)

⅛ teaspoon ground ginger

12 large hard-cooked eggs, peeled (see Tip)

Avocado oil, Clarified Butter (page 241) or ghee (optional)

Whole30-compliant coarse-grain mustard, for serving

at home

PREHEAT the oven to 350°F. Line a large rimmed baking pan with parchment paper.

IN a small skillet, heat the olive oil over medium heat. Add the onion and cook until tender, 4 to 5 minutes. Transfer the onion to a large bowl. Add the turkey, apple, sage, marjoram, salt, black pepper, cinnamon, red pepper flakes (if using), and ginger. Gently mix until well combined.

DIVIDE the meat mixture into 12 equal portions. Form each portion into a ¼-inch-thick patty. For each Scotch egg, place the egg in the middle of the patty; enclose the egg in the meat, rolling to smooth the surface and seal any seams. Arrange the eggs on the pan at least 1 inch apart. Bake until the sausage is cooked through and lightly browned, 20 to 25 minutes.

LET cool completely. Store in an airtight container in a cooler or refrigerator until serving time.

at camp

IF desired, heat a cast iron skillet over medium heat. Add the Scotch eggs and drizzle each with a little avocado oil. Cook until heated through, about 5 minutes. Serve with mustard.

tip: PLACE THE EGGS IN A LARGE SAUCEPAN; add cold water to cover by 1 inch. Bring to a rolling boil. Remove from the heat. Let stand, covered, for about 15 minutes. Drain. Add cold water to the pan to cover the eggs. Add a few handfuls of ice cubes. Let stand until the eggs are cool enough to handle, about 15 minutes. Drain the eggs and peel.

campfire grilled peaches

SERVES 6

These grilled peaches will satisfy the tradition of gathering around and cooking over a campfire. To avoid burning, it's best to cook over coals, not flame. For safety and ease, use a campfire roasting fork or cook on a grill grate.

PREP: 10 MINUTES   **COOK:** 4 MINUTES   **TOTAL:** 14 MINUTES

6 8- or 10-inch wooden skewers

1 tablespoon Clarified Butter (page 241), ghee, or coconut oil, melted

½ teaspoon ground cinnamon

3 large ripe peaches, pitted and cut into large chunks

at home

SOAK the skewers in water for at least 30 minutes. In a large bowl, whisk together the butter and cinnamon. Add the peaches; toss to coat. Thread the peaches on the skewers. Store in an airtight container until ready to cook.

at camp

ARRANGE the skewers on a grill grate over medium heat. (Alternatively, skewer the peaches on toasting forks.) Cook until lightly charred, turning occasionally, 4 to 6 minutes.

office potluck

staff meeting 3pm !

Valerie Skinner

THYMEANDJOY.COM

Valerie Skinner is a profession-ally trained holistic chef who shares healthy recipes and easy cooking tips that make time in the kitchen approachable and fun. Valerie passionately shares her thoughts on attaining a balanced mindset around food, relationships, and lifestyle on her blog, and creates Whole30 Approved meals for her community through her personal chef services.

Most offices are dietary minefields any day of the week. Generous coworkers bring in doughnuts, bagels, and muffins while vending machines spit out candy bars and salty snacks. Office potlucks can be especially tricky: hot artichoke dip loaded with cheese, lil' smokies in a sugary barbecue sauce, lasagna, bean dip, and sweets of every stripe. You don't want to eat salad alone at your desk, but you also don't want to blow your Whole30, so bring something you can enjoy! Bonus: These offerings are so filling and delicious, your coworkers won't call your diet "restrictive" ever again.

························

sonoma chicken salad
hamburger skillet
pork chili verde
jalapeño popper chicken casserole
creamy buffalo dip

office space

BRINGING MORE THAN ONE DISH both ensures you have variety on your plate and makes you an office superstar. The Creamy Buffalo Dip served with raw veggies pairs terrifically with any of the hot or cold main dishes.

IF A COWORKER REALLY WANTS YOU TO TRY THEIR FAMILY FAVORITE but you know it's not compliant, be polite but firm. ("That looks so delicious, but I'm committed to my Whole30 right now, and I'm really loving it.") Then, engage them in a subject they like talking about, so if they're tempted to get pushy, they won't have an opportunity.

MAKE A POINT NOT TO TALK ABOUT YOUR WHOLE30 OVER FOOD; just seeing what you're doing can immediately make people feel defensive. Politely defer, then change the subject. "I'd love to tell you more about it after lunch. First, how is your vacation planning coming along?"

BRING A COPY OF YOUR WHOLE30 COOKBOOKS (including this one) into the office the week of the event. If anyone asks about your delicious dishes, offer to lend them your book. (You might end up with a Whole30 buddy out of it!)

sonoma chicken salad

SERVES 10

This is a classic chicken salad—cooked chicken in a rich mayo dressing, with celery for crunch—but with the addition of grapes for a touch of sweetness. Serve it in lettuce wraps or on top of salad greens.

PREP: 15 MINUTES **TOTAL:** 15 MINUTES

4 cups shredded or chopped cooked chicken

1½ cups Basic Mayonnaise (page 240) or Whole30-compliant mayonnaise

3 stalks celery, finely chopped

1 small red onion, finely chopped

½ cup chopped pecans

2 tablespoons chopped fresh parsley

1½ teaspoons celery seeds

1 teaspoon garlic powder

¼ teaspoon salt

¼ teaspoon black pepper

1 cup seedless red grapes, halved

IN a large bowl, combine the chicken, mayonnaise, celery, onion, pecans, parsley, celery seeds, garlic powder, salt, and pepper and toss to coat. Fold in the grapes.

hamburger skillet

SERVES 8 TO 10

It may taste like your favorite fast-food burger, but it's a whole lot healthier. The homemade Thousand Island Dressing makes it!

••••••••••••••••••••••••••••

PREP: 20 MINUTES **COOK:** 20 MINUTES
TOTAL: 40 MINUTES

••••••••••••••••••••••••••••

1 tablespoon extra-virgin olive oil

1 medium red onion, finely chopped

1½ pounds ground beef

2 tablespoons Whole30-compliant tomato paste

1 tablespoon Whole30-compliant yellow mustard

3 tablespoons coconut aminos

1 teaspoon garlic powder

½ teaspoon salt

¼ teaspoon black pepper

2 (16-ounce) packages cauliflower crumbles or rice, prepared according to package directions

1 tomato, thinly sliced

½ cup Whole30-compliant dill pickle slices

1 cup Thousand Island Dressing (right)

1 head romaine lettuce, chopped

IN a large skillet, heat the olive oil over medium heat. Add half of the onion and cook, stirring until tender, 5 to 8 minutes. Add the ground beef, breaking it up with a wooden spoon, until browned, about 10 minutes. Add the tomato paste, mustard, coconut aminos, garlic powder, salt, and pepper. Cook until heated through, 2 minutes more.

SPOON the hamburger mixture on top of the cauliflower; top with the sliced tomato, dill pickles, and remaining onion, and drizzle with the dressing. Garnish with the lettuce.

thousand island dressing

IN a medium bowl, stir together 1 cup Basic Mayonnaise (page 240) or Whole30-compliant mayonnaise, 2 tablespoons Whole30-compliant tomato paste, 2 tablespoons coconut aminos, 2 tablespoons finely chopped Whole30-compliant dill pickles, 2 tablespoons minced shallot, 1 teaspoon dried parsley, ½ teaspoon garlic powder, ⅛ teaspoon salt, and ⅛ teaspoon black pepper. Store in an airtight container in the refrigerator for up to 1 week. Makes 1½ cups.

pork chili verde

SERVES 10

Next time there's an office chili cook-off, bring this beauty. You'll stand apart from the ground-beef-and-tomato crowd with this hearty green chili made with pork tenderloin, tomatillos, jalapeños, green chilies, and Yukon Gold potatoes.

....

PREP: 25 MINUTES   **BROIL/COOK:** 50 MINUTES
TOTAL: 1 HOUR 15 MINUTES

....

FOR THE VERDE SAUCE

2 jalapeños

6 tomatillos, husks removed and chopped (about 2 cups)

1 (16-ounce) can roasted green chilies

¼ cup fresh cilantro leaves, plus more for garnish

FOR THE CHILI BASE

1 tablespoon extra-virgin olive oil or avocado oil

2 pounds Whole30-compliant pork tenderloin, cut into ½-inch cubes

4 cloves garlic, minced

1 medium yellow onion, chopped

1 pound Yukon Gold potatoes, chopped

1 green bell pepper, chopped

1 tablespoon ground cumin

½ teaspoon salt

1½ teaspoons Whole30-compliant chili powder

1 teaspoon black pepper

1 teaspoon dried oregano

6 cups Whole30-compliant chicken broth

¾ cup Whole30-compliant coconut milk

ADJUST the oven racks so one is about 6 inches from the broiler heat. Preheat the broiler. Line a small baking pan with foil.

MAKE THE VERDE SAUCE: Cut the jalapeños in half; remove the seeds, if desired. Place the jalapeños, cut sides down, on the baking pan. Broil until charred, about 4 minutes.

PLACE the jalapeños, tomatillos, green chilies, and cilantro in a blender. Cover and pulse until combined yet chunky.

MAKE THE CHILI BASE: In a large pot over medium-high heat, heat the olive oil. Add the pork and cook until opaque, 5 to 7 minutes. Add the garlic, onion, potatoes, bell pepper, cumin, salt (if desired), chili powder, black pepper, and oregano. Cook, stirring, until the vegetables begin to soften, 6 to 7 minutes.

ADD the verde sauce and chicken broth to the pork mixture. Turn the heat to medium-high and bring to a gentle boil for 5 minutes. Turn the heat to low and simmer until the pork is cooked through and the potatoes are tender, about 30 minutes. Stir in the coconut milk.

TOP servings with cilantro.

jalapeño popper chicken casserole

SERVES 8 TO 10

This spaghetti-squash casserole has the perfect amount of heat from jalapeños, a crunchy and salty kick from bacon, and a creamy texture contributed by a sauce made from mayo, chives, parsley, garlic powder, and dill.

·····················

PREP: 20 MINUTES   **BAKE:** 35 MINUTES
TOTAL: 55 MINUTES

·····················

FOR THE CREAM SAUCE

½ cup Basic Mayonnaise (page 240) or Whole30-compliant mayonnaise

1 tablespoon dried chives

1 tablespoon dried parsley

1 teaspoon garlic powder

½ teaspoon dried dill

¼ teaspoon salt

⅛ teaspoon black pepper

FOR THE CASSEROLE

8 slices Whole30-compliant bacon

6 cups cooked spaghetti squash (from a 4-pound squash) (see Tip)

2 cups shredded or chopped cooked chicken breast

2 medium jalapeños, seeded and chopped

2 large eggs, lightly beaten

1 jalapeño, sliced into rings (optional)

PREHEAT the oven to 350°F. Lightly grease a 9 × 13-inch baking pan.

MAKE THE CREAM SAUCE: In a medium bowl, stir together the mayonnaise, chives, parsley, garlic powder, dill, salt, and pepper. Set aside.

MAKE THE CASSEROLE: In a large skillet, cook the bacon over medium heat until crisp, about 10 minutes. Let cool then roughly chop.

IN a large bowl, stir together the cooked squash, chicken, chopped jalapeños, eggs, bacon, and cream sauce. Spoon into the baking pan; top with jalapeño rings, if desired.

BAKE about 35 minutes, until heated through and bubbly around the edges (160°F).

tip: To cook the spaghetti squash, heat the oven to 400°F. Slice the squash in half lengthwise and scoop out the seeds. Lightly drizzle with olive oil. Place the squash, cut sides down, on the baking pan and roast until tender, 45 to 50 minutes. Use a fork to scrape out the flesh.

creamy buffalo dip

SERVES 10

This creamy Buffalo dip is a crowd pleaser for office parties or game day. Made with clean ingredients like cashews, tahini, hot sauce, clarified butter, and coconut aminos, it's a great vehicle for vegetable dippers.

PREP: 15 MINUTES **STAND:** 4 HOURS
TOTAL: 4 HOURS 15 MINUTES

2 cups raw cashews

⅓ cup Whole30-compliant tahini

½ cup Whole30-compliant hot sauce

2 tablespoons Clarified Butter (page 241) or ghee

1 tablespoon coconut aminos

1 clove garlic, minced

¼ teaspoon salt

⅛ teaspoon black pepper

Cut-up vegetables, such as cucumbers, carrots, and/or bell peppers

PLACE the cashews in a large bowl and add water to cover by 1 inch. Cover the bowl and let stand for 4 hours or up to overnight. Drain the cashews and rinse under cold water. Place the cashews, tahini, hot sauce, butter, 2 tablespoons of water, coconut aminos, salt, and pepper in a high-speed blender or food processor. Cover and blend or process until smooth, about 5 minutes. Transfer to a serving bowl.

SERVE the dip with the vegetables. Store leftovers in an airtight container in the refrigerator for up to 5 days.

family movie night

After a long week, there's nothing better than snuggling with your favorite people, sharing the experience of a good movie, and eating yummy food. The familiar plan of action for movie night is to order a pizza, make some popcorn, and scoop up some ice cream, but we're offering a Whole30-compliant menu that feels just as special, and may help your family create new, healthier traditions. Bonus: Each dish can be eaten completely utensil-free (except for maybe those last few bites of Walking Tacos). You'll stick to your Whole30, the kids will love eating their dinner out of a bag, and no one will miss the same old pizza, I promise.

• •

bacon-wrapped sweet potato bites

zucchini coins with whole30 ranch dressing

sweet and savory snack mix

walking tacos

orange juliet

five-star foods

IF YOUR MOVIE NIGHT IS A FRIDAY, it's easy to get most of the menu made the night before. Prep the sweet potato bites up to the point of baking, then make the zucchini coins, dressing, and snack mix. You can also cook up the plantain coins and the meat for the Walking Tacos and reheat before serving.

IF ZUCCHINI ISN'T THEIR THING, you can swap the coins out for baked sweet potato fries, extra fried plantain coins, or any raw veggie they enjoy. You can also omit the chili powder from the snack mix for younger palates.

IF YOUR KIDS COMPLAIN ABOUT THE MENU CHANGE-UP, remind them the whole point of movie night is spending time together, not what's on your plate. Plus, this menu is fun *and* delicious, with small touches (like the paper bag "bowl" and toothpicks) that kids will love.

THE ORANGE JULIUS–STYLE DRINK IS MEANT AS A FINISHER, so offer up flavored fizzy water, unsweetened iced tea, or RETHINK juice box-style waters with the meal.

bacon-wrapped sweet potato bites

SERVES 4

Warmly spiced cubes of tender sweet potato are swathed in crisp, smoky bacon in these one-bite treats.

••••••••••••••••••••••••••••

PREP: 15 MINUTES **COOK:** 3 MINUTES
BAKE: 25 MINUTES **TOTAL:** 45 MINUTES

••••••••••••••••••••••••••••

½ large sweet potato, peeled (4 ounces)

¼ teaspoon ground cinnamon

¼ teaspoon ground cumin

¼ teaspoon paprika

1 tablespoon Clarified Butter (page 241) or ghee, melted

9 slices Whole30-compliant bacon

PREHEAT the oven to 400°F. Line a large rimmed baking pan with parchment paper or aluminum foil.

CUT the sweet potato into 1-inch pieces. Place the pieces in a medium saucepan, add water to cover and bring to a boil. Cook the potatoes for 3 to 4 minutes, until just fork-tender; drain.

MEANWHILE, in a small bowl, stir together the cinnamon, cumin, and paprika. Transfer the potatoes to a medium bowl and drizzle with the butter. Sprinkle with the spice mixture and stir to coat.

CUT the bacon strips into thirds. Wrap each potato piece with a piece of bacon, securing it with a toothpick. Arrange the bites on the baking pan. Bake for 15 minutes. Turn the bites over and bake 10 minutes more, until the potatoes are tender and the bacon is crisp.

zucchini coins with whole30 ranch dressing

SERVES 4

After almost 2 hours in a low-heat oven, slices of zucchini turn into paper-thin, super-crisp rounds that are just perfect for dipping in ranch dressing. Because these take some time to make (although they're completely hands-off), start them first before you make whatever else you're serving.

PREP: 10 MINUTES   **BAKE:** 1 HOUR 45 MINUTES
TOTAL: 1 HOUR 55 MINUTES

1 medium zucchini

1 to 1 ½ teaspoons avocado oil
or extra-virgin olive oil

½ teaspoon coarse salt

1 to 2 tablespoons finely chopped fresh
dill or 1 to 2 teaspoons dried dill

Whole30 Ranch Dressing (page 133) or
bottled Whole30-compliant ranch dressing

PREHEAT the oven to 200°F. Line a large rimmed baking pan with parchment paper.

THINLY slice the zucchini with a mandoline on the thinnest setting or with a sharp knife. Place the slices in a medium bowl and drizzle with the oil; gently toss to coat.

ARRANGE the slices in a single layer on the baking pan. Sprinkle the zucchini with the salt and dill. Bake 1¾ hours to 2 hours, until crisp. Serve with ranch dressing for dipping.

tip: IF YOU HAVE A DEHYDRATOR, arrange the zucchini in an even layer on the dehydrator shelves; sprinkle with the salt and dill. Cover and dehydrate at 135°F until crisp, 8 to 9 hours.

whole30 ranch dressing

IN a medium bowl, whisk together 1 cup Basic Mayonnaise (page 240) or Whole30-compliant mayonnaise; ½ cup Whole30-compliant coconut milk; 1 small clove garlic, minced; ½ teaspoon onion powder; ¼ teaspoon black pepper; 1 tablespoon finely chopped fresh dill; 1 tablespoon finely chopped chives; and 2 teaspoons fresh lemon juice. Use immediately or store in an airtight container in the refrigerator for up to 1 week.

sweet and savory snack mix

MAKES 3 CUPS

Everyone knows part of the fun of watching a movie together is the communal munching that accompanies the happenings on screen! This crunchy snack mix satisfies that urge with a healthful blend of spiced nuts, coconut, sunflower seeds, and cacao nibs. The nibs add a bit of chocolate flavor with just a hint of bitterness. If your family isn't into that, simply leave them out.

··

PREP: 10 MINUTES **BAKE:** 8 MINUTES
COOL: 20 MINUTES **TOTAL:** 40 MINUTES

··

1 cup macadamia nuts

½ cup pecans

½ cup almonds

1 teaspoon Whole30-compliant chili powder

½ teaspoon garlic powder

¼ teaspoon salt

¼ teaspoon ground cumin

⅛ teaspoon cayenne pepper (optional)

1 teaspoon avocado oil or extra-virgin olive oil

⅓ cup unsweetened flaked coconut

¼ cup roasted pepitas

¼ cup sunflower seeds

2 tablespoons cacao nibs

PREHEAT the oven to 350°F. Line a large rimmed baking pan with parchment paper.

ARRANGE the the macadamia nuts, pecans, and almonds in a single layer on the baking pan. Bake for 8 to 10 minutes, stirring once halfway through, until the nuts are lightly toasted. Remove from the oven and cool in the pan on a wire rack.

MEANWHILE, in a small bowl, stir together the chili powder, garlic powder, salt, cumin, and cayenne (if desired).

TRANSFER the cool nuts to a bowl and drizzle with the oil; stir to coat. Sprinkle with the spice mixture and stir to combine. Gently stir in the coconut, pepitas, sunflower seeds, and cacao nibs.

TRANSFER to a serving bowl. Store leftovers in an airtight container for up to 2 weeks.

walking tacos

SERVES 4

These hearty snacks-in-a-bag are every
bit as much fun to eat as the concession-
stand version but are a lot better for
you. Crispy plantain coins stand in for
the fried corn chips and they're packed
with fresh veggies. Build them in waxed-
paper sandwich bags and you're ready
to snuggle up on the sofa and dig in!

· ·

PREP: 30 MINUTES **BAKE:** 20 MINUTES
COOK: 15 MINUTES **TOTAL:** 1 HOUR 5 MINUTES

· ·

Cashew Cream (page 242)

½ teaspoon grated lime zest

1 light green plantain, peeled

1 teaspoon avocado oil or
extra-virgin olive oil

½ teaspoon salt

1 pound lean ground beef

¼ cup onion, finely chopped

½ cup Whole30-compliant tomato sauce

4 teaspoons Whole30-compliant
taco seasoning (see Tip)

2 teaspoons nutritional yeast

½ cup lightly packed shredded
kale, spinach, or lettuce

½ cup halved cherry tomatoes

¼ cup sliced pitted Whole30-compliant olives

½ cup Whole30-compliant salsa

¼ cup chopped fresh cilantro

PLACE 1 cup of the cashew cream in a small serving bowl; stir in the lime zest. Cover and refrigerate until serving.

PREHEAT the oven to 350°F. Line a rimmed baking pan with parchment paper.

THINLY slice the plantain with a mandoline on the thinnest setting or with a sharp knife. Arrange the plantain slices in a single layer on the baking pan; brush with the oil. Sprinkle lightly with the salt. Bake for 20 to 25 minutes, until crispy and golden brown around the edges.

MEANWHILE, in a large skillet, cook the ground beef and onion over medium-high heat, stirring with a wooden spoon to break up the meat, until browned, about 10 minutes. Stir in the tomato sauce, taco seasoning, and nutritional yeast. Simmer until heated through, stirring occasionally, about 5 minutes.

TO serve, in four waxed-paper sandwich bags, layer the plantain coins, taco meat, kale, tomatoes, olives, and salsa. Top with a little cashew cream and sprinkle with cilantro. Fold down the top of the bag.

tip: IF YOU CAN'T FIND a Whole30-compliant taco seasoning, it's easy to make your own. In a container with an airtight lid, combine 2 tablespoons chili powder, 2 teaspoons ground cumin, 1 teaspoon salt, 1 teaspoon each garlic and onion powder, 1 teaspoon paprika, ½ teaspoon black pepper, ½ teaspoon crushed red pepper flakes (optional), and ½ teaspoon dried oregano. Store in a cool, dark place for up to 6 months. Stir or shake well before using.

orange juliet

SERVES 4

This creamy concoction is kind of like a cross between a drink and a dessert. It tastes similar to the fast-food favorite the kids might beg for at the mall, but without all of the processed ingredients and sugar!

PREP: 10 MINUTES **TOTAL:** 10 MINUTES

1 orange

1 (14-ounce) can Whole30-compliant coconut milk

½ frozen banana

2 teaspoons Whole30-compliant vanilla bean powder (see Tip)

½ teaspoon ground nutmeg

REMOVE 2 teaspoons grated zest from the orange. Remove and discard the peel, then segment the orange. Place the orange zest, segments, coconut milk, banana, vanilla bean powder, and nutmeg in a blender. Cover and blend on high until smooth. Pour into four 4-ounce glasses.

tip: YOU CAN ALSO SCRAPE THE SEEDS from two-thirds of a vanilla bean to equal 2 teaspoons vanilla bean powder.

kids' birthday party

You don't have to serve a truckload of sugar, gluten, and food coloring for kids to have fun at a party. Our Whole30 menu is a bonanza of favorite kid foods—hot dogs, hamburgers (in the form of meatballs on a skewer, because kids love eating things on sticks), chicken tenders, and pizza. Plus we've got stuff the grown-ups will like too, like orange sweet pepper dip and bacon-wrapped broccoli "trees." (I've passed on too many pieces of cold pizza at birthday parties to leave that out.) And the finale—a bright pink fizzy punch and watermelon "shortcakes"—add festive flair without the post-party sugar crash.

....

zoodle sausage-pepper pizza bites

bacon-wrapped trees with roasted
red pepper–almond dip

mile-high hamburger meatball
kabobs with special sauce

hot dog bites in ginger-
pineapple barbecue sauce

sub-lime chicken tenders
with confetti ranch

mexican-style dino kale chips

raspberry-lime sparkling punch

citrusy watermelon
strawberry shortcakes

happy birthday to you!

I'VE BEEN TO A LOT OF KIDS' BIRTHDAY PARTIES at this point, so I know a formula that works: lots of activities, two hours tops, and food as an afterthought, not the start of the show. Rent out a trampoline gym, bowling alley, or local park and no kid will be sad there aren't neon blue-frosted cupcakes.

ON THE INVITA-TION, indicate whether or not parents are invited to stay. (At the parties I've been to, parents staying is greatly appreciated, especially if the whole class is involved.)

RECRUIT THE BIRTHDAY KID TO SET A THEME FOR THE EVENT, choose the decorations and napkins, and help in the kitchen pre-party.

SHARING THE MENU (or our photo of the menu) in the invitation will help set expectations for the event, and is also a great way to suss out guests' food allergies so you can make sure no kid feels left out (or goes home sick). You can add, "The menu will be gluten-free, dairy-free, and low-sugar. If your child has allergies, please let me know ahead of time."

zoodle sausage-pepper pizza bites

SERVES 10

What's a kids' party without pizza? It shows up here in these pizza bites made in muffin cups. A generous dose of nutritional yeast brings great cheesy flavor to the party.

PREP: 25 MINUTES **STAND:** 30 MINUTES
BAKE: 30 MINUTES **TOTAL:** 1 HOUR 25 MINUTES

4 (10.7-ounce) packages zucchini noodles, or 6 medium zucchini, spiralized

1 tablespoon salt

4 large eggs, lightly beaten

1½ cups almond flour

2 teaspoons Whole30-compliant Italian seasoning

1 (8-ounce) can Whole30-compliant tomato sauce

1 tablespoon nutritional yeast

¾ teaspoon dried oregano, crushed

½ teaspoon garlic powder

1 (12-ounce) package Whole30-compliant Italian sausage, sliced and quartered

1 small green bell pepper, finely chopped

USE kitchen shears to cut the zucchini noodles into short strands. In a large bowl, combine the noodles and salt; toss to combine. Transfer to a colander set over the bowl. Let stand 30 minutes. Transfer the zucchini to paper towels and lightly press to remove excess moisture. Discard any liquid in the bowl. Add the eggs, almond flour, and Italian seasoning to the bowl. Stir well. Add the zucchini and stir to combine.

PREHEAT the oven to 400°F. Grease twenty-four 2½-inch muffin cups.

SPOON about ¼ cup of the zucchini mixture into each muffin cup; press lightly to create a bottom crust. Bake for 12 to 15 minutes, until set.

MEANWHILE, in a medium bowl, stir together the tomato sauce, nutritional yeast, oregano, and garlic powder. Spoon 1 tablespoon sauce on top of each zucchini crust. Top with the sausage and bell pepper.

BAKE for 18 to 20 minutes more, until the sauce is bubbly at the edges and the sausage is lightly browned. Let cool for 10 minutes before removing the pizza bites from the pans.

bacon-wrapped trees with roasted red pepper–almond dip

SERVES 10

Kids will clamor to eat broccoli when it takes the form of tiny trees wrapped in bacon. This recipe is a cinch to make. While the bacon-wrapped broccolini bakes, whiz the dip in the blender and you're ready to go.

....

PREP: 10 MINUTES **BAKE:** 15 MINUTES
TOTAL: 25 MINUTES

....

1 (10-ounce) package Whole30-compliant bacon

3 bunches broccolini or 2 bunches baby broccoli, trimmed (you will need 20 pieces)

1 cup drained and chopped roasted red peppers

½ cup slivered blanched almonds

¼ cup extra-virgin olive oil

1 tablespoon fresh lemon juice

1 teaspoon paprika

1 clove garlic, chopped

½ teaspoon salt

PREHEAT the oven to 425°F. Line two large rimmed baking pans with parchment paper.

CUT each slice of bacon in half crosswise. Wrap a half slice of bacon around each piece of Broccolini, stretching the bacon slightly as you wrap. Arrange the wrapped broccolini on the baking pans.

BAKE for 15 to 20 minutes, until the bacon is browned and the broccolini is tender. Transfer to a paper towel–lined plate to drain.

MEANWHILE, in a blender, combine the roasted red peppers, almonds, olive oil, lemon juice, paprika, garlic, and salt. Blend until smooth. Transfer to a serving bowl.

ARRANGE the broccolini on a platter. Serve with the dip.

tip: STORE LEFTOVER DIP in an airtight container in the refrigerator for up to 1 week.

mile-high hamburger meatball kabobs with special sauce

SERVES 10

Skip the bun—dipping is just plain fun and will encourage kids to eat not only the meatballs but the skewered salad too.

·····································

PREP: 20 MINUTES **BAKE:** 15 MINUTES
TOTAL: 35 MINUTES

·····································

FOR THE MEATBALLS

1½ pounds ground beef

⅓ cup almond flour

1 large egg

2 teaspoons onion powder

1 teaspoon salt

1 teaspoon garlic powder

½ teaspoon black pepper

FOR THE SAUCE

½ cup Basic Mayonnaise (page 240) or Whole30-compliant mayonnaise

½ cup Whole30-compliant ketchup

¼ cup finely chopped drained roasted red peppers

2 teaspoons Whole30-compliant yellow mustard

FOR THE SKEWERS

20 Whole30-compliant dill pickle slices

20 cherry or grape tomatoes

1 small head iceberg lettuce, cut into about twenty 1-inch portions

20 6-inch wooden skewers

PREHEAT the oven to 425°F. Line a large baking pan with parchment paper.

MAKE THE MEATBALLS: In a large bowl, combine the ground beef, almond flour, egg, onion powder, salt, garlic powder, and pepper. Shape into 20 meatballs; arrange on the pan. Bake until cooked through (160°F), 15 to 20 minutes.

MAKE THE SAUCE: Meanwhile, in a serving bowl, stir together the mayonnaise, ketchup, roasted red peppers, and mustard.

THREAD each skewer with a pickle, cherry tomato, piece of iceberg lettuce, and a meatball. Serve kabobs with the sauce.

hot dog bites in ginger-pineapple barbecue sauce

SERVES 10

Yes, there are Whole30-compliant hot dogs, and they are so much better than the ones made with preservatives and other unsavory things. These frankfurter bites swimming in a tasty tomato sauce are so yummy, the adults in the room might want to sneak a few, too.

·····················

PREP: 10 MINUTES   **COOK:** 15 MINUTES   **TOTAL:** 25 MINUTES

·····················

1 (15-ounce) can Whole30-compliant tomato sauce

1½ cups finely chopped fresh pineapple

2 tablespoons balsamic vinegar

1 piece (¾ inch) fresh ginger, peeled and grated

2 cloves garlic, minced

1 teaspoon onion powder

¼ teaspoon smoked paprika

2 (10-ounce) packages Whole30-compliant hot dogs, cut into 1-inch pieces

IN a medium saucepan, combine the tomato sauce, pineapple, vinegar, ginger, garlic, onion powder, and smoked paprika. Stir in the hot dogs. Cook, covered, over medium heat until hot and bubbly, 15 to 20 minutes.

TRANSFER the hog dog bites and sauce to a warm serving dish.

sub-lime chicken tenders with confetti ranch

SERVES 10

All you have to say to most kids is "ranch dressing" and they are on board with whatever you put in front of them. This yummy version is packed with the usual herbs, and has a bit of red bell pepper for color.

....

PREP: 20 MINUTES   **CHILL:** 30 MINUTES
BAKE: 10 MINUTES   **TOTAL:** 1 HOUR

....

3 tablespoons extra-virgin olive oil

3 tablespoons fresh lime juice

2 tablespoons chopped fresh dill

2 teaspoons grated lime zest

1 teaspoon salt

1 teaspoon black pepper

1 teaspoon paprika

2½ pounds chicken breast tenderloins (20 pieces)

FOR THE DIP

1¼ cups Basic Mayonnaise (page 240) or Whole30-compliant mayonnaise

⅓ cup red bell pepper, finely chopped

1 tablespoon chopped fresh cilantro

1 tablespoon chopped fresh parsley

2 teaspoons chopped fresh chives

1 clove garlic, minced

20 6-inch wooden skewers, if grilling

IN a medium bowl, combine the olive oil, 2 tablespoons lime juice, 1 tablespoon dill, lime zest, salt, pepper, and paprika. Add the chicken; toss to coat. Refrigerate, covered, for 30 minutes or up to 2 hours.

MEANWHILE, in a blender or food processor, combine the mayonnaise, bell pepper, remaining 1 tablespoon lime juice, remaining 1 tablespoon dill, cilantro, parsley, chives, and garlic. Cover and blend or process until smooth. Transfer to a serving bowl; cover and chill until needed.

PREHEAT the oven to 450°F. Line a two large rimmed baking pans with parchment paper. Or, if grilling the chicken, soak the skewers for 30 minutes.

REMOVE the chicken from the marinade; discard the marinade. Thread each chicken tender onto a skewer; arrange on the pan. Bake for about 10 minutes, until cooked through (165°F). (Or grill over direct heat for 10 minutes, turning once.)

ARRANGE the chicken kabobs on a platter and serve with the ranch dip.

mexican-style dino kale chips

SERVES 10

Kids—and grownups—can't get enough of these crunchy chips coated in a cheesy-tasting, taco-inspired spice mixture. Dinosaur kale gets its name from its dark green color and nubby-looking texture. If you can't find it, regular kale will work too.

PREP: 10 MINUTES **BAKE:** 25 MINUTES **TOTAL:** 35 MINUTES

¼ cup almond flour

1 tablespoon nutritional yeast

2 teaspoons Whole30-compliant mild chili powder

1 teaspoon ground cumin

1 teaspoon dried oregano, crushed

3 bunches dinosaur (lacinato) kale, stemmed and torn into 2-inch pieces

¼ cup extra-virgin olive oil

1½ teaspoons coarse salt

PREHEAT the oven to 300°F. Line two large baking pans with parchment paper.

IN a small bowl, stir together the almond flour, nutritional yeast, chili powder, cumin, and oregano. Set aside.

PLACE the kale in a large bowl. Drizzle with the olive oil and sprinkle with salt. Massage the kale to soften and coat. Sprinkle with about ¼ cup of the seasoning; toss to coat. Arrange the kale in a single layer on the pans.

BAKE for 15 minutes. Turn and rearrange the kale on the pans. Bake 10 to 15 minutes more, until the kale is dry and crisp. Sprinkle with the remaining seasoning. Let cool completely, then transfer to a serving bowl.

raspberry-lime sparkling punch

SERVES 10

No one will miss the sugary "juice" or soda when they're served this fizzy drink made from fresh raspberries, lime, pineapple juice, and sparkling water.

PREP: 15 MINUTES **TOTAL:** 15 MINUTES

2 pints fresh raspberries or 1 (16-ounce) package frozen raspberries, thawed

⅓ cup fresh lime juice

2 teaspoons grated lime zest

4 cups 100% pineapple juice, chilled

2 bottles (25 ounces each) Whole30-compliant sparkling water, chilled

Fresh raspberries and/or mint leaves for garnish

IN a blender, combine the raspberries, 1 cup water, lime juice, and zest. Cover and blend until smooth. Place a fine-mesh strainer over a large measuring cup or bowl; pour the fruit mixture into the sieve. Press the fruit with a large spoon to remove the seeds. Discard the seeds.

ADD the fruit puree to a 4-quart pitcher or a punch bowl, then whisk in the pineapple juice. Add the sparkling water; stir gently to combine. Pour or ladle into 10- to 12-ounce glasses. Garnish with fresh raspberries and/or mint leaves.

citrusy watermelon strawberry shortcakes

SERVES 10

A biscuit cutter is used to cut perfectly round "shortcakes" from slices of watermelon that are topped with strawberries, orange-and-vanilla-infused whipped coconut cream, and toasted almonds.

....

PREP: 20 MINUTES   **CHILL:** 8 HOURS
TOTAL: 8 HOURS 20 MINUTES

....

1 (14-ounce) can Whole30-compliant coconut milk, refrigerated overnight

½ vanilla bean, split lengthwise and seeds scraped, or 1½ teaspoons Whole30-compliant vanilla bean powder

3 tablespoons fresh orange juice

1 teaspoon grated orange zest

2 cups sliced fresh strawberries or unsweetened frozen sliced strawberries, thawed

1 medium seedless watermelon, cut into 1½-inch slices

½ cup sliced almonds, toasted (optional) (see Tip)

OPEN the refrigerated can of coconut milk; drain off the liquid and reserve for smoothies. Spoon the coconut cream into a medium bowl. Add the vanilla bean seeds and beat with an electric mixer on medium-high until fluffy, about 5 minutes. Beat in 1 tablespoon orange juice, and ½ teaspoon orange zest. Cover and refrigerate until serving.

IN a medium bowl, combine the strawberries, the remaining 2 tablespoons orange juice, and ½ teaspoon of the orange zest. Cover and let stand at room temperature, stirring and slightly mashing the strawberries occasionally, 30 to 45 minutes.

USING a 2½-inch round biscuit cutter, cut circles from the watermelon slices. Cover and chill until serving.

PLACE 1 watermelon round on each serving plate. Spoon ¼ cup of the strawberries and about 2 tablespoons of the coconut cream onto each watermelon round. If desired, sprinkle with sliced almonds.

tip: To toast the sliced almonds, heat in a dry skillet over medium heat, stirring, until fragrant and lightly browned, about 2 minutes.

adult party time

Carmen Sturdy
EVERYLASTBITE.COM

Carmen Sturdy is a passionate foodie who created her blog, Every Last Bite, after achieving remission from an autoimmune disease through dietary changes. She is now a passionate advocate for healthy eating and showing others that regardless of your dietary restrictions, you can still make delicious meals that won't leave you feeling deprived.

Being a grown-up is hard work. Between work and kids, housework and volunteering, shopping, cooking, running errands, paying bills, and sleep, it's easy to let socializing take a backseat. But it's important! Friends keep you grounded, support you, make you laugh, and offer help when you need it. You don't need a special occasion to invite friends over for good conversation and great food. This Mexican-themed menu offers up mix-and-match options for putting together a fantastic spread without having to spend your entire Saturday in the kitchen.

....

tomato gazpacho shots

shrimp and avocado cucumber bites

**saucy chicken collard
green enchiladas**

tuna ceviche with plantain crisps

mexican cauliflower rice

**spicy mexican slaw with
lime-cilantro dressing**

**orange and cumin pork carnitas
in celery root tortillas**

**mango con chile y limon
(mango with chile and lime)**

**melon ball salad with
lime, mint, and chile**

**watermelon and lime
sparkling refresher**

let's get together

YOU'D HAVE TO BE REALLY AMBITIOUS to make everything on this menu. Choose one of the mains—the enchiladas or pork carnitas—and pair it with an appetizer and a salad. Or, focus on the small plates and dine family-style—chile-lime bites of ripe mango, tomato gazpacho shots topped with crab, tuna ceviche, and smoky shrimp and avocado on slices of cucumber.

SAVE SOME EFFORT and make the carnitas in the slow cooker instead of the oven. Combine all of the ingredients in a 3½- to 4-quart slow cooker. Cover and cook on high for 4 to 5 hours or on low for 8 to 10 hours.

TELL YOUR FRIENDS AHEAD OF TIME that you are serving a delicious Whole30 menu so they don't show up with plates of cheese and crackers or a bottle of that fantastic new wine they want you to try.

CLEAN-UP CAN BE QUITE FESTIVE when you let your guests help! Start the party with an empty sink, dishwasher, and trash can. Assign a few people kitchen tasks, someone to post-dinner decaf or tea duty, and another to choosing a relaxing playlist for post-meal conversation.

tomato gazpacho shots

SERVES 6

Whether they're sipped and savored or enjoyed in one big delicious gulp, these shots of chilled soup are sure to be a hit—something a little different among the usual dips, spreads, and nibbles.

PREP: 20 MINUTES **CHILL:** 4 HOURS
TOTAL: 4 HOURS 20 MINUTES

3 large very ripe tomatoes, cut into large chunks (about 1½ pounds)

½ cucumber, peeled and coarsely chopped

¼ red bell pepper, coarsely chopped

¼ cup chopped red onion

1 small red chile (such as Fresno), seeded and coarsely chopped

½ teaspoon ground cumin

1 clove garlic

1 tablespoon extra-virgin olive oil

1 teaspoon balsamic vinegar

¾ teaspoon salt

3 tablespoons flaked crabmeat

Finely chopped fresh basil

Finely chopped fresh parsley

IN a blender, combine the tomatoes, cucumber, bell pepper, onion, chile pepper, cumin, garlic, olive oil, vinegar, and salt. Cover and blend until smooth. (Blend in batches if necessary.)

TRANSFER the gazpacho to a glass container. Cover and chill for at least 4 hours or up to overnight.

TO serve, divide the gazpacho among 18 shot glasses. Top each with ½ teaspoon of the crabmeat. Sprinkle with basil and parsley.

shrimp and avocado cucumber bites

SERVES 6

Leave the tails on the shrimp as a "handle" should these delicious but slightly-messy-to-eat bites have to be disassembled in the process of eating.

······························

PREP: 23 MINUTES COOK: 2 MINUTES
TOTAL: 25 MINUTES

······························

12 large peeled and deveined shrimp, tails on

1 tablespoon extra-virgin olive oil

1 teaspoon ground cumin

½ teaspoon smoked paprika

½ teaspoon salt

1 small ripe avocado, halved and pitted

1 teaspoon fresh lime juice

1 large ripe mango

12 ¼-inch cucumber slices (2 cucumbers)

2 tablespoons finely chopped fresh cilantro

IN a medium bowl, toss together the shrimp, olive oil, cumin, smoked paprika, and ¼ teaspoon salt. Heat a large nonstick skillet over medium-high heat. Add the shrimp and cook, turning once, until opaque, 2 to 4 minutes.

SCOOP the avocado flesh into a small bowl. Add the lime juice and the remaining ¼ teaspoon salt. Mash with a fork until almost smooth.

USE a "Y" peeler to peel the mango, then use a sharp knife to trim the stem. Set the mango on one of its narrow sides and, holding the mango in one hand and a knife in the other, slice through the flesh slightly off center to avoid the pit, then cut into ¼-inch slices. Repeat with the other side. Cut the slices into pieces about the same size as the cucumber slices.

TO serve, arrange the cucumber slices on a serving platter. Top each cucumber slice with a piece of mango and a spoonful of the avocado. Top with the shrimp. Sprinkle with cilantro.

saucy chicken collard green enchiladas

SERVES 4

The homemade enchilada sauce for this dish is absolutely delicious—so much fresher-tasting and piquant than the canned stuff—and has no sugar, food coloring, or "modified" anything.

PREP: 20 MINUTES **COOK:** 20 MINUTES **TOTAL:** 40 MINUTES

8 collard green leaves, stems removed

FOR THE SAUCE

3 tablespoons extra-virgin olive oil

⅓ cup finely chopped onion

2 cloves garlic, minced

1 (6-ounce) can Whole30-compliant tomato paste

2 tablespoons ancho chile powder

1 teaspoon dried oregano

1 teaspoon ground cumin

½ teaspoon salt

2 cups Whole30-compliant chicken broth

½ cup carrot juice

2 tablespoons fresh lemon juice

FOR THE FILLING

3 cups cooked shredded chicken

1 cup chopped fresh cilantro, plus more for garnish

¾ cup Cashew Cream (page 242), plus more for garnish

½ cup chopped green onions

2 teaspoons Whole30-compliant taco seasoning

BRING a large pot of water to a boil. Prepare a large bowl of ice water. Place the collard green leaves in the boiling water to cook for 1 minute. Transfer to the ice water and let stand 2 minutes. Drain well and pat the leaves dry with a paper towel.

MAKE THE SAUCE: Heat the olive oil over medium-high heat in an extra-large skillet. Add the onion and cook until tender, 5 minutes. Add the garlic; cook 30 seconds. Stir in the tomato paste, ancho chile powder, oregano, cumin, and salt; cook for 1 minute. Gradually whisk in the broth, carrot juice, and lemon juice. Bring to a simmer, stirring occasionally.

MAKE THE FILLING: In a large bowl, combine the chicken, cilantro, cashew cream, green onions, and taco seasoning. Spoon about ½ cup of the filling on each collard green leaf. Roll up the leaves.

PLACE the filled leaves in the sauce. Cover and simmer, gently shaking the skillet occasionally to prevent sticking, until heated through, about 10 minutes. If desired, top the enchiladas with additional cilantro and drizzle with additional cashew cream.

tuna ceviche with plantain crisps

SERVES 6

Be sure to get sushi-grade tuna because although the lime juice appears to "cook" the fish as it marinates, it's still raw.

....

PREP: 30 MINUTES   CHILL: 1 HOUR
COOK: 10 MINUTES   TOTAL: 1 HOUR 40 MINUTES

....

FOR THE CEVICHE

1 pound sushi-grade Ahi tuna, cut into ¼-inch-thick strips

¼ teaspoon salt

½ cup fresh lime juice

3 tablespoons fresh orange juice

2 tablespoons fresh lemon juice

⅓ cup finely diced red onion

1 avocado, halved, pitted, peeled, and finely diced

⅓ cup finely chopped fresh cilantro

1 jalapeño, finely diced

1 large tomato, seeded and finely diced

Lime wedges

FOR THE PLANTAIN CRISPS

2 light green plantains, peeled (see Tip)

2 tablespoons Clarified Butter (page 239) or ghee

½ teaspoon salt

MAKE THE CEVICHE: Line a large rimmed baking pan with plastic wrap. Arrange the tuna slices in a single layer on the baking pan and freeze until fairly firm, about 15 minutes.

STACK the slices of tuna. Use a very sharp knife to cut the tuna into ¼-inch cubes. In a large glass or ceramic serving bowl, combine the tuna, salt, lime juice, orange juice, lemon juice, and onion. Toss to coat. Cover and chill for 1 hour, carefully stirring every 15 minutes.

MAKE THE PLANTAIN CRISPS: Meanwhile, slice the plantains with a mandoline on the ¼-inch setting or with a sharp knife. In a large nonstick skillet, heat the butter over medium-high heat. Add half of the plantain slices (do not crowd the pan). Cook until golden and crisp, turning once halfway through, 3 to 4 minutes. Transfer to a paper towel–lined baking pan. Sprinkle with ¼ teaspoon of the salt. Repeat with remaining plantains, adding more butter to the skillet if necessary. Sprinkle with the remaining ¼ teaspoon salt.

TO serve, carefully stir the avocado, cilantro, jalapeño, and tomato into the tuna mixture. Serve the ceviche with lime wedges and the plantain crisps for scooping.

tip: IT'S IMPORTANT TO USE LIGHT GREEN, not ripe, plantains. Ripe plantains are softer and will not crisp as nicely.

mexican cauliflower rice

SERVES 6

This well-seasoned cauliflower rice makes a perfect side to the Orange and Cumin Pork Carnitas (page 160) for a party, but it's simple enough to stir up any night of the week to be served alongside grilled steak or chicken.

PREP: 20 MINUTES **COOK:** 15 MINUTES **TOTAL:** 35 MINUTES

1 medium head cauliflower, cut into large florets

1 tablespoon extra-virgin olive oil

1 medium onion, finely chopped

2 cloves garlic, minced

½ teaspoon salt

2 cups seeded and chopped tomatoes

2 tablespoons ground cumin

2 tablespoons fresh lime juice

1 tablespoon smoked paprika

⅛ teaspoon cayenne pepper

½ cup chopped fresh cilantro

IN batches, place the cauliflower in a food processor (don't fill more than three-quarters full). Pulse the florets until they're in rice-size pieces.

IN a large skillet, heat the olive oil over medium-high heat. Add the onion and garlic. Cook, until the onion softens, about 5 minutes. Add the cauliflower, salt, and tomatoes; stir to combine. Reduce the heat to medium. Cook, covered, until the cauliflower softens, 5 to 7 minutes.

ADD the cumin, lime juice, paprika, and cayenne. Continue to cook, stirring occasionally, until the cauliflower is tender, 5 to 7 minutes more. Stir in the cilantro just before serving.

spicy mexican slaw with lime-cilantro dressing

SERVES 6

This vinaigrette-dressed slaw adds crunch and vibrant color to any Mexican-themed meal. The jalapeños look pretty thinly sliced on the round, but if you want just a little bit of jalapeño flavor, seed and mince them instead.

PREP: 15 MINUTES **CHILL:** 1 HOUR
TOTAL: 1 HOUR 15 MINUTES

FOR THE SLAW

5 cups shredded red cabbage

8 small radishes, trimmed and thinly sliced

2 medium carrots, peeled and shredded

⅓ cup chopped fresh cilantro

2 small jalapeños, thinly sliced

¾ cup thinly sliced red onion

FOR THE DRESSING

⅓ cup chopped fresh cilantro

¼ cup extra-virgin olive oil

2 tablespoons fresh lime juice

1 clove garlic

1 teaspoon ground cumin

½ teaspoon salt

MAKE THE SLAW: In a large bowl, toss together the cabbage, radishes, carrots, cilantro, jalapeños, and onion. Set aside.

MAKE THE DRESSING: In a blender, combine the cilantro, olive oil, lime juice, garlic, cumin, and salt. Cover and blend until smooth.

DRIZZLE the dressing over the slaw. Toss to combine. Chill for 1 hour before serving.

orange and cumin pork carnitas in celery root tortillas

SERVES 6 (3 TACOS EACH)

If you have never tried making celery root tortillas, you must. As they're grilled or griddled, they sweeten slightly, soften up enough for easy wrapping, and take on a beautiful golden color with lightly charred edges. They are an ideal vehicle for the intensely flavored carnitas.

PREP: 20 MINUTES BAKE: 2 HOURS 30 MINUTES
COOK: 20 MINUTES TOTAL: 3 HOURS 10 MINUTES

FOR THE CARNITAS

1½ cups fresh orange juice

¼ cup fresh lime juice

2 tablespoons ground cumin

1 teaspoon smoked paprika

1 teaspoon ground coriander

2 cloves garlic, crushed, skins removed

½ teaspoon salt

2 to 2½ pounds boneless pork shoulder, trimmed and cut into 2-inch chunks

FOR THE TORTILLAS

2 large celery roots (about 1 pound each), ends trimmed, peeled

FOR SERVING

Guacamole

Whole30-compliant fresh salsa or pico de gallo

Whole30 Sriracha (page 242) or Whole30-compliant hot sauce (optional)

PREHEAT the oven to 350°F.

MAKE THE CARNITAS: In a Dutch oven or large oven-proof pot, combine the orange juice, lime juice, cumin, paprika, coriander, garlic, and salt. Add the pork and stir to combine. Bake, covered, until very tender, about 2½ hours.

USING a slotted spoon, transfer the pork to a cutting board. Use two forks to shred the pork into small pieces and return it to the pot. Simmer uncovered, over medium-low heat, until almost all of the liquid is gone, about 20 minutes.

MAKE THE TORTILLAS: Meanwhile, thinly slice the celery roots with a mandoline on the ⅛-inch setting or with a sharp knife. Choose the 18 largest slices for tortillas. (Store any leftover slices in an airtight container in the refrigerator for another use.)

HEAT a grill pan over medium heat. Cook, turning occasionally, until grill marks form and the tortillas are tender and pliable, about 5 minutes. (You may need to press gently on the tortillas with a spatula.)

TO serve, spoon about 1 tablespoon of the meat into each tortilla. Top with guacamole, salsa, and Sriracha, if desired.

tip: THIS RECIPE MAKES about 4 cups of carnitas, so you will have leftovers. Store the meat in an airtight container in the refrigerator for up to 3 days.

mango con chile y limon (mango with chile and lime)

SERVES 6

Seasoned mango is a popular street snack in Mexico. The sweetness of the mango, spiciness of the chile, and tartness of the lime—with a flavor-enhancing sprinkle of salt—is dynamite for the taste buds. In Mexico, it's often served as a whole mango on a stick. We thought cubes speared on toothpicks were a little easier to eat at a grown-up party.

....

PREP: 10 MINUTES **TOTAL:** 10 MINUTES

....

2 ripe mangoes (about 1 pound each)

2 tablespoons fresh lime juice

½ teaspoon ancho chile powder

¼ teaspoon coarse salt

FOR each mango, use a "Y" peeler to peel it, then use a sharp knife to trim the stem. Set the mango on one of its narrow sides and, holding the mango in one hand and a knife in the other, slice through the flesh slightly off center to avoid the pit. Repeat with the other side. Cut into cubes.

ARRANGE the mango cubes on a serving platter. Sprinkle with the lime juice, chile powder, and salt. Serve with toothpicks.

melon ball salad with lime, mint, and chile

This salad is the ultimate in light and fresh. If you don't have a melon baller, you can cut the melons into cubes—but a bowl of pink, peach, and pale green balls with speckles of red chile and chopped fresh mint does make for a pretty presentation.

PREP: 25 MINUTES   TOTAL: 25 MINUTES

1½ cups chilled cantaloupe balls or cubes

1½ cups chilled honeydew melon balls or cubes

1½ cups chilled watermelon balls or cubes

1 teaspoon grated lime zest

2 tablespoons fresh lime juice

1 small red chile (such as a Fresno), seeded and minced

⅓ cup coarsely chopped fresh mint

PLACE the fruit in a large bowl. Add the lime zest, lime juice, chile pepper, and mint. Toss gently to combine.

watermelon and lime sparkling refresher

SERVES 6

Not straining the watermelon puree—simply combining it with lime juice and sparkling water—gives this drink nice body.

PREP: 15 MINUTES   TOTAL: 15 MINUTES

6 cups cubed watermelon

½ cup fresh lime juice

¼ cup mint leaves, plus more for garnish

1 (12-ounce) can Whole30-compliant sparkling water, chilled

Ice

Thinly sliced watermelon wedges, for garnish

IN a blender, combine the watermelon, lime juice, and mint leaves. Cover and blend until smooth (in batches if necessary). Pour the watermelon mixture into a large pitcher. Stir in the sparkling water.

TO serve, pour the watermelon mixture over ice-filled glasses. Garnish with a wedge of watermelon and fresh mint leaves

study group

There is no magic to getting good grades—it's all about your study habits. Research has demonstrated that studying in groups speeds learning and improves understanding of material. You can't put off doing the reading or the assignment if you know you need to be prepared for study group. (You want to look smart, right?) You also get fresh perspectives from other people and may learn new study skills from them, too. Of course, another piece of successful learning is a diet that fuels energy, focus, and a good mood. This menu skips the sugar and processed carbs and offers up snacks that really will boost your brain power.

· ·

spicy tuna lettuce wraps
crisp prosciutto-topped deviled eggs
**olive- and pesto-stuffed
mini bell peppers**
cinnamon-orange dip
cucumber-lime infused water

smart choices

ALL OF THESE RECIPES CAN BE MADE AHEAD OF TIME and stored in the refrigerator until serving time (and the Cinnamon-Orange Dip doesn't even need to be refrigerated). Get an easy A by having your menu ready when guests arrive, so you can get right down to business.

IF YOU'RE NOT HOSTING THE STUDY GROUP, bring a portable, snackable dish (or two) the group can share, like the Deviled Eggs and the Cinnamon Orange Dip, so you don't go home hungry.

FOOD PREP LIKE CHOPPING AND COOKING can be a very stress-relieving task. Plus, it feels good going into the big exam knowing your self-care practices are on-point. The self-confidence boost you'll get from sticking to your Whole30 even during a stressful time will translate into confident answers come test time.

spicy tuna lettuce wraps

SERVES 6

Asian flavors—coconut aminos, sesame, ginger, rice vinegar, red pepper flakes, green onions, and cilantro—make plain tuna a lot more interesting for these crunchy wraps.

....

PREP: 20 MINUTES **TOTAL:** 20 MINUTES

....

3 tablespoons coconut aminos

1 tablespoon toasted sesame oil

1 piece (¾ inch) fresh ginger, peeled and finely chopped

2 teaspoons rice vinegar

½ teaspoon red pepper flakes

3 (5-ounce) pouches light tuna

2 green onions, green tops only, finely chopped

2 tablespoons chopped fresh cilantro

12 small Bibb lettuce leaves (see Tip)

2 teaspoons sesame seeds, toasted (optional, see Tip)

IN a medium bowl, whisk together the coconut aminos, sesame oil, ginger, vinegar, and red pepper flakes. Add the tuna, green onion tops, and cilantro. Stir until combined.

TO serve, arrange the lettuce leaves on a large serving platter. Divide the tuna mixture among the leaves. Sprinkle with sesame seeds, if desired.

tips: USE 2 HEADS OF BIBB LETTUCE to get the 12 small leaves. Use the innermost leaves because they are the smallest. Use any leftover lettuce for salads or other lettuce wraps throughout the week.

TO TOAST THE SESAME SEEDS, heat in a dry skillet over medium heat, stirring, until fragrant and lightly browned, about 2 minutes.

crisp prosciutto-topped deviled eggs

SERVES 6

Protein-rich eggs help fuel the brain and the healthy fat in avocado promotes blood flow—and more blood flow means a better-functioning brain—so eat up!

PREP: 15 MINUTES   **STAND:** 15 MINUTES
COOL: 15 MINUTES   **TOTAL:** 45 MINUTES

6 large eggs

1 teaspoon extra-virgin olive oil

1 very thin slice Whole30-compliant prosciutto, cut lengthwise into three strips

½ ripe avocado, peeled and pitted

1 tablespoon fresh lemon juice

1 clove garlic, minced

1 tablespoon finely chopped fresh chives

⅛ teaspoon salt

⅛ teaspoon black pepper

PLACE the eggs in a large saucepan; add cold water to cover by 1 inch. Bring the water to a rolling boil. Remove from the heat. Let stand, covered, for 15 minutes. Drain the eggs. Add cold water to the pan to cover the eggs. Add a few handfuls of ice cubes. Let stand until the eggs are cool enough to handle, about 15 minutes. Drain the eggs and peel.

MEANWHILE, in a small skillet, heat the olive oil over medium heat. Add the prosciutto and cook, turning once, until browned and crisp, about 2 minutes. Transfer the prosciutto to a paper towel-lined plate to cool. Coarsely chop the strips.

CUT the eggs in half lengthwise and place the yolks in a medium bowl; reserve the whites. Add the avocado, lemon juice, and garlic. Use a fork to mash the yolks and avocado until almost smooth. Stir in the chives, salt, and pepper. Use a small spoon to fill the reserved egg whites with the filling. Top the filling with the prosciutto.

tip: To PIPE THE FILLING into the reserved egg whites, spoon the filling into a quart-size resealable plastic bag. Snip a corner off the bag and pipe.

olive- and pesto-stuffed mini bell peppers

SERVES 6

Watercress has the same mildly peppery bite as arugula. If you can find it, definitely try it—but if you can't, no worries. Arugula works equally well in the pesto for these stuffed peppers.

···

PREP: 20 MINUTES   TOTAL: 20 MINUTES

···

FOR THE PESTO

1½ cups lightly packed stemmed watercress or arugula

¾ cup lightly packed fresh basil leaves

¼ cup chopped walnuts, toasted (see Tip)

2 cloves garlic, chopped

¼ teaspoon salt

⅛ teaspoon black pepper

⅓ cup extra-virgin olive oil

FOR THE PEPPERS

6 mini bell peppers

2 tablespoons Basic Mayonnaise (page 240) or Whole30-compliant mayonnaise

¼ cup seeded and chopped tomato

2 tablespoons chopped pitted Whole30-compliant olives, plus sliced olives for garnish

MAKE THE PESTO: Place the watercress, basil, walnuts, garlic, salt, and pepper in a food processor. Cover and pulse until finely chopped. While the food processor is running, slowly drizzle in the olive oil until almost smooth. Set aside.

MAKE THE PEPPERS: Cut a thin slice across the top of each pepper to remove the stem; cut the peppers in half. Use a small sharp knife to cut out the seeds and membranes, keeping the pepper intact. Set the peppers, cut sides up, on a serving platter.

IN a small bowl, stir together ¼ cup of the pesto and the mayonnaise until smooth. Stir in the tomato and chopped olives. Spoon the mixture into the peppers. If desired, garnish with sliced olives.

tips: To TOAST THE NUTS, heat in a dry skillet over medium heat, stirring, until fragrant and lightly browned, about 2 minutes.

THE RECIPE FOR THE PESTO WILL MAKE 1 CUP. Store any unused pesto in an airtight container in the refrigerator for up to 3 days.

cinnamon-orange dip

SERVES 6

This elevates the classic apples and peanut butter combo to new heights with a blend of sunflower butter, orange, cinnamon, and vanilla.

....

PREP: 10 MINUTES   **TOTAL:** 10 MINUTES

....

⅔ cup Whole30-compliant sunflower seed butter

2 tablespoons Clarified Butter (page 241) or ghee, softened

½ teaspoon grated orange zest

1 tablespoon fresh orange juice

¼ teaspoon ground cinnamon

⅛ teaspoon Whole30-compliant vanilla bean powder (optional)

4 apples, quartered, cored, and sliced

IN a medium bowl, stir together the sunflower butter and butter. Stir in orange zest and juice, cinnamon, and vanilla bean powder (if using) until well combined. Serve with apple slices for dipping.

cucumber-lime infused water

SERVES 6

Help students stay hydrated with this not-boring water. Plan ahead—it has to chill at least 8 hours (or up to 24 hours) to get infused with the flavors of lime, cucumber, ginger, and mint.

....

PREP: 10 MINUTES   **CHILL:** 8 HOURS
TOTAL: 8 HOURS 10 MINUTES

....

2 limes, peeled and thinly sliced

1 medium cucumber, peeled and thinly sliced

1¼ cups lightly packed fresh mint

1 piece (4 inches) fresh ginger, peeled and thinly sliced

Ice

DIVIDE the lime slices, cucumber, mint, and ginger between two large pitchers. Add 6 cups water to each pitcher; cover. Chill at least 8 hours or up to 24 hours. Strain the solids.

TO serve, pour the infused water into ice-filled glasses.

weekend houseguests

There are two simple ways to make overnight houseguests feel welcome: Provide a comfy bed, and make them tasty food. This menu is designed with both you and your guests in mind, with dinner, snacks, and breakfast that have great appeal to adults and kids alike. For pre-dinner nibbles, set out the Veggies with Herb-Garlic Dip before serving the fajita bowls and melon-berry lemonade. Finish up with fresh fruit dolloped with vanilla coconut cream (or save that for breakfast). If you're up late catching up, offer the Pumpkin-Spiced Sweet Potatoes. For breakfast the next day, muffin-cup eggs with potatoes and sausage will send them off with full and happy bellies.

....

veggies with herb-garlic dip
potato-sausage breakfast bites
peppered beef fajita bowls
pumpkin-spiced sweet potatoes
fizzy melon-berry lemonade
fruit with vanilla coconut cream

comforts of home

HAVE PLENTY OF HEALTHY SNACKS and beverages on hand that both you and your guests can indulge in, like spiced nuts, compliant prosciutto and olives, fruit, fresh veggies, and compliant guacamole and salsa. Brew a big pitcher of iced black or herbal tea and keep it in the fridge and stock up on flavored sparkling waters. Offer a selection of herbal tea bags so guests can enjoy a cup before bed.

PROVIDE A FEW MAGAZINES, novels, or your copy of *The Whole30* in the guest room—along with a sticky note with your Wi-Fi password. It's a thoughtful touch and will give them something to do if they're night owls or early risers.

IF SOME OF YOUR GUESTS ARE CHILDREN (and you don't have any or they're no longer in the house), borrow some toys or games like Uno, coloring books and crayons, or an age-appropriate puzzle.

veggies with herb-garlic dip

SERVES 4

This colorful array of veggies served with a simple dip gives everyone something to nibble on while you put the finishing touches on dinner.

····················

PREP: 15 MINUTES **STAND:** 4 HOURS
ROAST: 25 MINUTES **TOTAL:** 4 HOURS 40 MINUTES

····················

⅔ cup cashews

1 small head garlic

1 tablespoon extra-virgin olive oil

¼ teaspoon coarse salt

⅛ teaspoon black pepper

4 teaspoons nutritional yeast

2 tablespoons chopped fresh chives

1 teaspoon chopped fresh thyme or oregano

Assorted vegetables, such as bell peppers, snap peas, carrots, celery, broccoli, and/or cauliflower

PLACE the cashews in a medium bowl and add water to cover by 1 inch. Cover the bowl and let stand for 4 hours or up to overnight. Drain the cashews and rinse under cold water. Set aside.

PREHEAT the oven to 400°F.

CUT about ¼ inch from the top of the garlic to expose the cloves, keeping the head intact. Place the garlic on a 4-inch piece of foil; drizzle with olive oil. Fold and seal the foil. Bake for 25 to 30 minutes, until the garlic is tender.

WHEN cool enough to handle, squeeze the roasted garlic cloves into a blender. Add the cashews, ⅓ cup water, salt, pepper, and nutritional yeast. Cover and blend until smooth.

TRANSFER to a serving bowl. Stir in the chives and thyme, then serve with vegetables for dipping.

potato-sausage breakfast bites

SERVES 4

These muffin-cup bites incorporate all of the elements of a hearty breakfast—bacon, homemade turkey sausage, eggs, and shredded potatoes—in one dish.

PREP: 15 MINUTES   **COOK:** 10 MINUTES
BAKE: 20 MINUTES   **TOTAL:** 45 MINUTES

2 slices Whole30-compliant bacon, chopped

4 ounces ground turkey

⅓ cup chopped red or green bell pepper

¼ cup chopped onion

1⅓ cups coarsely shredded Yukon Gold potatoes (about 10 ounces)

½ teaspoon dried sage

¼ teaspoon dried thyme

¼ teaspoon garlic powder

¼ teaspoon salt

⅛ teaspoon black pepper

5 large eggs, beaten

PREHEAT the oven to 375°F. Lightly grease eight 2½-inch muffin cups.

IN a large skillet, partially cook the bacon over medium heat, stirring occasionally, about 5 minutes. Add the turkey, bell pepper, and onion. Cook, stirring occasionally, until the turkey is cooked through and the bacon is crisp, 5 to 7 minutes. Transfer to a large bowl.

ADD the potatoes, sage, thyme, garlic powder, salt, and pepper to the meat; stir to combine. Spoon the filling into the muffin cups. Pour the eggs over the filling until the cups are full.

BAKE for about 20 minutes, until a knife inserted in the center comes out clean. Run the knife around the edges of the muffin cups to release the muffins. Serve warm.

175

peppered beef fajita bowls

SERVES 4

These can be part of the evening entertainment if you let your guests build their own bowls from the meat mixture, sautéed pepper and onion, cauliflower rice, guacamole, salsa, and cilantro. Set out all of the ingredients and let them go for it!

....

PREP: 20 MINUTES   **COOK:** 10 MINUTES   **TOTAL:** 30 MINUTES

....

FOR THE BEEF

1 pound flank steak or skirt steak, thinly sliced

1 teaspoon paprika

½ teaspoon salt

½ teaspoon dried oregano

½ teaspoon garlic powder

½ teaspoon ground cumin

¼ teaspoon black pepper

⅛ teaspoon cayenne pepper

1 tablespoon extra-virgin olive oil

FOR THE VEGETABLES

1 tablespoon extra-virgin olive oil

2 small red, green, and/or yellow bell peppers, cut into ½-inch strips

1 small red onion, halved and cut into ¼-inch slices

1 clove garlic, minced

1 (12-ounce) package frozen riced cauliflower or 4 cups raw riced cauliflower

¼ teaspoon salt

⅛ teaspoon black pepper

1 cup Whole30-compliant guacamole

½ cup Whole30-compliant salsa

¼ cup chopped fresh cilantro (optional)

Lime wedges (optional)

MAKE THE BEEF: Place the beef in a medium bowl. In a small bowl, combine the paprika, salt, oregano, garlic powder, cumin, black pepper, and cayenne. Sprinkle the spice mixture over the beef and toss to coat. Let stand while cooking the vegetables.

MAKE THE VEGETABLES: In a large skillet, heat 1 tablespoon olive oil over medium heat. Add the bell peppers and onion. Cook, stirring frequently, until the vegetables are crisp-tender, 7 to 8 minutes. Stir in the garlic. Transfer the vegetables to a serving dish; cover to keep warm.

MEANWHILE, prepare the cauliflower rice according to the package directions. Add the salt and pepper; stir to combine. Cover to keep warm.

IN the same large skillet, heat 1 tablespoon olive oil over medium heat; add the beef. Cook, stirring frequently, 3 to 4 minutes or to desired doneness.

SPOON the cauliflower into four shallow serving bowls. Top with the vegetables, beef, guacamole, and salsa. If desired, sprinkle with cilantro and serve with lime wedges.

pumpkin-spiced sweet potatoes

SERVES 4

Toss the potato-chip bag! These simple sweet potato chips baked in clarified butter and seasoned with pumpkin spice are a super-satisfying snack with health benefits. They're loaded with fiber, vitamins, minerals, and antioxidants.

PREP: 10 MINUTES **BAKE:** 15 MINUTES
TOTAL: 25 MINUTES

1 sweet potato (10 ounces)

3 tablespoons Clarified Butter (page 241) or ghee, melted

¾ teaspoon pumpkin pie spice

PREHEAT the oven to 375°F. Place a wire rack on each of two large rimmed baking pans.

USE a mandoline set at $1/16$ or $1/8$ inch or a sharp knife to thinly slice the potatoes. Place the potato slices in a bowl and drizzle with the butter. Sprinkle with the pumpkin pie spice; toss to coat. Arrange the slices in a single layer on the wire racks.

BAKE for 12 to 15 minutes, until the potatoes are lightly browned and crisp around the edges.

fizzy melon-berry lemonade

SERVES 4

This fruit-based beverage is the perfect thing to serve to both adults who are avoiding alcohol as well as kids. It's a little bit sweet and bubbly, too, so it feels very festive!

PREP: 10 MINUTES **CHILL:** 1 HOUR
TOTAL: 1 HOUR 10 MINUTES

¾ cup chopped seedless watermelon

¾ cup coarsely chopped, hulled fresh strawberries

½ cup frozen unsweetened dark sweet cherries, thawed

1 bottle (25-ounces) Whole30-compliant lemon-flavored sparkling water, chilled

Ice

IN a blender, combine the watermelon, strawberries, cherries, and ¼ cup water. Cover and blend until smooth.

PLACE a fine-mesh strainer over a large measuring cup or bowl; line with cheesecloth. Pour the fruit mixture into the sieve. Press the fruit with a large spoon to squeeze out the juice, discard the seeds and pulp.

POUR the fruit juice into a 2-quart pitcher. Cover and chill for 1 hour or up to 24 hours.

SLOWLY pour the sparkling water into the pitcher with the fruit juice; stir gently to combine. Pour into ice-filled glasses.

fruit with vanilla coconut cream

SERVES 4

This simple strawberry-and-banana fruit salad can be served as a nighttime sweet or as morning fruit alongside the Potato-Sausage Breakfast Bites (page 175).

••••••••••••••••••••••••••••••

PREP: 15 MINUTES   **TOTAL:** 8 HOURS 15 MINUTES

••••••••••••••••••••••••••••••

1 (14-ounce) can Whole30-compliant coconut milk, refrigerated overnight

¼ teaspoon Whole30-compliant vanilla bean powder

12 large strawberries, hulled

1 medium banana, peeled and sliced crosswise into 8 slices

2 tablespoons finely chopped pecans, toasted (see Tip)

OPEN the refrigerated can of coconut milk; drain off the liquid and reserve for smoothies. Spoon ½ cup of the coconut cream into a medium bowl (reserve the remaining coconut cream for another use). Beat the coconut cream and vanilla bean powder with an electric mixer on medium speed until fluffy, about 5 minutes. Transfer to a small resealable plastic bag; cut off one corner of the bag.

TO serve, place the strawberries and banana slices on a serving platter. Pipe the cream into the center of the strawberries and on top of the banana slices. Sprinkle with pecans.

tip: To TOAST THE PECANS, heat in a dry skillet over medium heat, stirring, until fragrant and lightly browned, about 2 minutes.

backyard bbq

Ashley McCrary

HEALTHYLITTLEPEACH.COM

In 2014, the Whole30 program completely transformed Ashley's life and allowed her to successfully fight polyscystic ovarian syndrome (PCOS) and to take back her health. Now she is passionate about sharing her success story and budget-friendly recipes that the whole family will love. Today, she is a Whole30 Certified Coach and loves supporting and encouraging the Whole30 community with tips, tricks, and free resources.

The classic American cookout already includes Whole30-friendly fare like salads, fruit, and grilled meats, chicken, and seafood, but we're not sending anyone into the summer with a plain burger and garden salad. This elevated BBQ menu was contributed by *Healthy Little Peach* blogger Ashley McCrary, so naturally, peaches figure prominently in the Grilled Steak and Peach Salad and the peach-infused iced tea. But it also offers cilantro chicken and shrimp, barbecue-sauced meatballs, Buffalo chicken burgers, and itty-bitty hamburgers served on crispy fried plantain buns with jalapeño relish, plus options for fresh and crunchy salads.

•••••••••••••••••••••••••

bacon-wrapped stuffed peppers
barbecue meatballs
creamy cauliflower and broccoli salad
buffalo chicken patties
grilled cilantro chicken and shrimp
grilled steak and peach salad
tostones hamburger sliders
ranch coleslaw
fruit and rxbar kabobs
peach tea

fire up the grill

IF YOU'RE A GUEST, you'll obviously be asking, "What can I bring?" But as the host usually takes care of the meat and beverages, let them know you're doing the Whole30 up front, in case they can set aside some unsauced chicken or shrimp for you.

THIS MENU OFFERS LOTS OF OPPORTUNITIES FOR MIX-AND-MATCH MEALS. Pair the Buffalo Chicken Patties or Grilled Cilantro Chicken and Shrimp with the Ranch Coleslaw. Try the Bacon-Wrapped Stuffed Peppers and Tostones Hamburger Sliders with the Creamy Cauliflower and Broccoli Salad. Or keep things simple with the Grilled Steak and Peach Salad—a main course and side in one.

IF YOU'RE HOSTING, provide at least one special non-alcoholic option so non-drinkers aren't stuck drinking plain tap water out of a Solo cup. Make the peach iced tea and provide an ice-filled cooler with sparkling waters, infused still waters, and compliant coconut water.

BRING OR OFFER A VARIETY OF COMPLIANT CONDIMENTS, like classic dill pickles, sauerkraut, pickled veggies, Whole30 ketchup, and your favorite compliant barbecue sauce.

bacon-wrapped stuffed peppers

SERVES 8

These sausage-stuffed mini bell peppers are a nice option for those who love the idea of jalapeño poppers but don't necessarily want the heat of them.

·····

PREP: 20 MINUTES   **COOK:** 15 MINUTES
BAKE: 20 MINUTES   **TOTAL:** 1 HOUR

·····

FOR THE SAUCE

1 cup Basic Mayonnaise (page 240) or Whole30-compliant mayonnaise

1 tablespoon finely chopped onion

2 teaspoons coconut aminos

½ teaspoon salt

1 teaspoon black pepper

FOR THE PEPPERS

1 tablespoon extra-virgin olive oil

1 clove garlic, minced

½ cup finely diced yellow onion

1 pound Whole30-compliant bulk pork sausage (see Tip)

8 mini bell peppers, halved lengthwise and seeded

8 slices Whole30-compliant bacon, cut in half crosswise

PREHEAT the oven to 400°F. Line a large rimmed baking pan with parchment paper.

MAKE THE SAUCE: In a small bowl, combine the mayonnaise, onion, coconut aminos, salt, and pepper. Stir to combine and set aside.

MAKE THE PEPPERS: Heat the olive oil in a skillet over medium heat. Add the garlic and onions. Cook until the onions are translucent, 8 to 10 minutes. Add the sausage and cook, stirring frequently, until cooked through, 7 to 8 minutes. Drain any fat. Add ⅓ cup of the mayonnaise sauce; stir to combine. Refrigerate the remaining sauce until serving.

ARRANGE the peppers, cut sides up, on the pan. Spoon the sausage filling into the peppers; wrap with a ½ slice of bacon. Bake until the peppers are crisp-tender and the bacon is fully cooked, about 20 minutes. Carefully transfer the peppers to a paper towel–lined pan to drain.

ARRANGE the peppers on a serving platter. Serve with the remaining mayonnaise sauce for dipping.

tip: IF YOU CAN'T FIND compliant bulk pork sausage, it's easy to make your own. In a medium bowl, combine 1 teaspoon dried sage, crushed; ¾ teaspoon coarse salt; ¾ teaspoon black pepper; ½ teaspoon dried thyme, crushed; ½ teaspoon garlic powder; ½ teaspoon onion powder; ¼ teaspoon cayenne pepper; and 1 teaspoon fennel seeds. Stir to combine. Add 1 pound ground pork and gently mix well.

barbecue meatballs

SERVES 8

Bottled compliant barbecue sauce serves as the base of the barbecue sauce in this recipe—you just jazz it up a bit with garlic powder, coconut aminos, and smoked paprika.

....

PREP: 25 MINUTES   **ROAST:** 20 MINUTES
COOK: 5 MINUTES   **TOTAL:** 50 MINUTES

....

FOR THE MEATBALLS

1½ pounds ground beef

1 large egg, lightly beaten

3 tablespoons finely chopped yellow onion

2 tablespoons tapioca flour

1 tablespoon plus 1½ teaspoons coconut aminos

¾ teaspoon garlic powder

¾ teaspoon salt

¾ teaspoon black pepper

FOR THE BARBECUE SAUCE

1 cup Whole30-compliant barbecue sauce

¼ teaspoon garlic powder

1 tablespoon coconut aminos

1 teaspoon smoked paprika

PREHEAT the oven to 400°F. Line a large rimmed baking pan with parchment paper.

MAKE THE MEATBALLS: In a large bowl, combine the beef, egg, onion, tapioca flour, coconut aminos, garlic powder, salt, and pepper. Gently mix until combined. Shape into 24 meatballs. Arrange the meatballs on the pan. Roast for 20 to 25 minutes, until cooked through (160°F).

MAKE THE BARBECUE SAUCE: In a large skillet, whisk together the barbecue sauce, garlic powder, coconut aminos, and paprika over medium heat. Add the meatballs; stir to coat. Simmer until the sauce thickens slightly, stirring occasionally, about 5 minutes. Transfer to a serving platter.

creamy cauliflower and broccoli salad

SERVES 8

You can make your own ranch dressing for this crunchy salad, but if you're short on time, bottled compliant dressing works too. The coating on the vegetables will be a little thinner than with homemade dressing, but the flavor will be fine.

....

PREP: 15 MINUTES   **ROAST:** 10 MINUTES   **CHILL:** 1 HOUR
TOTAL: 1 HOUR 25 MINUTES

....

3 slices Whole30-compliant bacon

3 cups small broccoli florets

3 cups small cauliflower florets

⅓ cup finely chopped red onion

1 cup Whole30 Ranch Dressing (page 133) or Whole30-compliant ranch dressing

3 tablespoons sliced green onions

PREHEAT the oven to 400°F. Line a rimmed baking pan with parchment paper.

ARRANGE the bacon on the pan. Roast for about 10 minutes, until crisp. Transfer to a paper towel–lined plate to drain. Crumble when cool. Refrigerate in an airtight container until serving.

MEANWHILE, in a large bowl, mix together the broccoli, cauliflower, red onion, and dressing until combined. Cover and chill for at least 1 hour or up to overnight.

TO serve, top the salad with the bacon and green onions.

buffalo chicken patties

SERVES 8

Whether it's on wings or in patties, the Buffalo sauce flavor is almost universally popular. These grilled patties are for super-fans of the stuff—there's hot sauce in both the ground chicken mixture and the spicy ranch dressing.

....

PREP: 15 MINUTES **FREEZE:** 14 MINUTES
COOK: 6 MINUTES **TOTAL:** 35 MINUTES

....

FOR THE PATTIES

2 pounds ground chicken

1½ teaspoons garlic powder

½ teaspoon salt

1 teaspoon black pepper

3 tablespoons Whole30-compliant hot sauce

1 large egg, beaten

1 teaspoon Basic Mayonnaise (page 240) or Whole30-compliant mayonnaise

3 tablespoons tapioca flour

½ cup chopped green onions

Extra-virgin olive oil

FOR THE SPICY RANCH

1 cup Basic Mayonnaise (page 240) or Whole30-compliant mayonnaise

2 tablespoons Whole30-compliant hot sauce

2 tablespoons Whole30-compliant coconut milk (see Tip)

1 tablespoon chopped fresh parsley

1 tablespoon dried chives

2 teaspoons dried dill

1 teaspoon salt

1 teaspoon cider vinegar

1 teaspoon white wine vinegar

1 teaspoon garlic powder

1 teaspoon cracked black pepper

1 teaspoon fresh lime juice

½ teaspoon onion powder

FOR SERVING

¼ cup chopped green onions (optional)

LINE a large rimmed baking pan with parchment paper.

MAKE THE PATTIES: In a large bowl, combine the chicken, garlic powder, salt, pepper, hot sauce, egg, mayonnaise, tapioca flour, and green onions. Gently mix until well combined. Divide into 8 portions. With wet hands, shape into 8 ½-inch-thick patties. Place in the freezer for 14 to 16 minutes to firm them.

MAKE THE SPICY RANCH: Meanwhile, in a medium bowl, stir together the mayonnaise, hot sauce, coconut milk, parsley, chives, dill, salt, vinegars, garlic powder, pepper, lime juice, and onion powder. Cover and refrigerate until ready to serve.

PREHEAT a grill to medium-high heat. Generously oil the grate with olive oil. Grill, turning once halfway through, until cooked through (165°F), 6 to 8 minutes.

TO serve, top the patties with some of the dressing and sprinkle with green onions, if using.

tip: CANNED COCONUT MILK separates in the can, with the cream rising to the top. Be sure to whisk the coconut milk well before measuring.

grilled cilantro chicken and shrimp

SERVES 8

Tajín seasoning is a shortcut to great flavor in this recipe. It's a popular seasoning blend in Mexico and is often sprinkled on mango or melon. The only ingredients are dried and ground chiles, salt, and dehydrated lime juice—so it's totally compliant.

....

PREP: 25 MINUTES   MARINATE: 1 HOUR
COOK: 15 MINUTES   TOTAL: 1 HOUR 40 MINUTES

....

FOR THE CILANTRO MARINADE
1 cup coarsely chopped fresh cilantro

1 teaspoon black pepper

1 teaspoon coarse salt

1 cup extra-virgin olive oil

¼ cup fresh lime juice

¼ cup fresh lemon juice

4 cloves garlic, crushed and peeled

8 boneless, skinless chicken breasts (6 to 8 ounces each)

FOR THE GUACAMOLE
3 ripe medium avocados, halved and pitted

1 medium tomato, cored, seeded, and chopped

¼ cup finely chopped red onion

1 teaspoon garlic powder

¾ teaspoon coarse salt

½ teaspoon black pepper

2 tablespoons fresh lime juice

FOR THE CHICKEN AND SHRIMP
24 large shrimp, peeled and deveined

3 tablespoons fresh lime juice

1 tablespoon Tajín seasoning

Coarsely chopped fresh cilantro, for garnish

Lime wedges

MAKE THE CILANTRO MARINADE: For the marinade, in a blender or food processor, combine the cilantro, pepper, salt, olive oil, lime juice, lemon juice, and garlic. Cover and blend or process until smooth. Place the chicken breasts in 2 large resealable plastic bags; add half of the marinade to each bag. Marinate in the refrigerator at least 1 hour but no more than 2 hours.

MAKE THE GUACAMOLE: Meanwhile, scoop the avocado flesh into a medium bowl. Mash with a fork. Stir in the tomato, onion, garlic powder, salt, pepper, and lime juice. Cover and refrigerate until ready to serve.

MAKE THE CHICKEN AND SHRIMP: Preheat the grill to high. Remove the chicken from the marinade; discard the marinade. Arrange the chicken on a grill rack. Grill, turning once halfway through, until cooked (165°F), 14 to 15 minutes.

MEANWHILE, place the shrimp in a large bowl. Drizzle the lime juice over the shrimp and toss to coat. Sprinkle the Tajín seasoning over the shrimp and toss to coat.

TRANSFER the chicken to a large platter; tent with foil to keep warm. Add the shrimp to the grill. Cook, turning once halfway through, until translucent and pink, 2 to 3 minutes.

SERVE the chicken with the shrimp and guacamole. Top with cilantro and serve with lime wedges.

grilled steak and peach salad

SERVES 8

This is a composed salad in that the elements are arranged on individual serving plates, not tossed. If you do it assembly-line style, it's not a problem to make for even a crowd.

....

PREP: 30 MINUTES   **MARINATE:** 1 HOUR
COOK: 20 MINUTES   **TOTAL:** 1 HOUR 50 MINUTES

....

FOR THE PEACH VINAIGRETTE

1 large ripe peach, pitted and coarsely chopped

2 cloves garlic, minced

½ cup extra-virgin olive oil

⅓ cup white wine vinegar

1 teaspoon coarse salt

½ teaspoon black pepper

1 tablespoon Whole30-compliant coarse-grain Dijon mustard

1 tablespoon coconut aminos

FOR THE STEAK

½ cup coconut aminos

1 teaspoon coarse salt

1 teaspoon black pepper

1 teaspoon garlic powder

2 pounds flank steak

FOR THE SALAD

4 large ripe peaches, pitted and quartered

2 tablespoons avocado oil

3 (5-ounce) containers spinach and arugula salad blend

2 medium ripe avocados, halved, pitted, peeled, and sliced

4 slices Whole30-compliant bacon, crisp-cooked and crumbled

1 medium red onion, thinly sliced and rings separated

½ cup coarsely chopped pecans

MAKE THE PEACH VINAIGRETTE: In a blender or food processor, combine the peach, garlic, olive oil, vinegar, 1 teaspoon salt, pepper, mustard, and 1 tablespoon coconut aminos. Cover and blend or process until well combined. Store in an airtight container in the refrigerator until ready to serve.

MAKE THE SALAD: In a small bowl, combine the ½ cup coconut aminos, 1 teaspoon salt, pepper, and garlic powder. Place the steak in a large resealable plastic bag; add the marinade. Seal and turn to coat the steak. Marinate in the refrigerator, turning occasionally, at least 1 hour or up to overnight.

PREHEAT the grill to medium-high heat. Remove the steak from the marinade and discard the marinade. Arrange the steak on the grill rack. Grill, turning once halfway through, until cooked to desired doneness, 12 to 15 minutes for medium (145°F). Transfer the steak to a cutting board; tent loosely with foil to rest, 5 minutes. Thinly slice the steak against the grain.

MEANWHILE, brush the peaches with the avocado oil; arrange on the grill rack, cut sides down. Grill until the peaches have grill marks, rotating once halfway through, 5 to 6 minutes.

TO serve, divide the salad blend among 8 serving plates. Top with the steak, avocado, peaches, bacon, onion, and pecans. Drizzle with the vinaigrette.

tip: STORE ANY LEFTOVER VINAIGRETTE in an airtight container in the refrigerator for up to 1 week.

tostones hamburger sliders

SERVES 8

Tostones (*tohs-TOH-nays*) are green plantain slices that fried in hot oil, smashed into thin disks, and then fried again until crisp. They're a popular side dish in Puerto Rico and the Dominican Republic. Here, they serve as "buns" for these tasty sliders.

PREP: 40 MINUTES **COOK:** 30 MINUTES
TOTAL: 1 HOUR 10 MINUTES

FOR THE JALAPEÑO RELISH

¼ cup Whole30-compliant dill pickle relish or ½ Whole30-compliant dill pickle, chopped

1 small jalapeño, seeded and roughly chopped

1 mini red bell pepper, roughly chopped

1 pitted date, roughly chopped

1 clove garlic, roughly chopped

1½ teaspoons white wine vinegar

¼ teaspoon salt

½ teaspoon black pepper

FOR THE TOSTONES

1 cup coconut oil

4 large light green plantains, peeled and cut into 1-inch slices (see Tip)

¾ teaspoon coarse salt

FOR THE SLIDERS

1 large egg, beaten

¼ cup very finely chopped onion

½ teaspoon salt

½ teaspoon black pepper

½ teaspoon garlic powder

1⅓ pounds ground beef

1 tablespoon coconut aminos

1 tablespoon tapioca flour

Whole30-compliant mustard (optional)

MAKE THE JALAPEÑO RELISH: In a blender or food processor, combine the dill relish, jalapeño, bell pepper, date, garlic, vinegar, salt, and pepper. Cover and pulse until finely chopped. Transfer the relish to a serving bowl. Cover and refrigerate until ready to serve.

MAKE THE TOSTONES: In a large skillet, heat ½ cup coconut oil over medium heat. Cook the plantain slices, half at a time and turning once halfway through, until lightly browned, 3 to 4 minutes. Transfer to a paper towel–lined baking pan to drain.

USE the bottom of a glass to smash each slice until about ¼ inch thick. If necessary, add the remaining ½ cup of coconut oil to the skillet. Cook, half at a time and turning once halfway through, until golden brown, 3 to 4 minutes. Transfer to a paper towel–lined baking pan to drain. Sprinkle with salt. Set aside.

MAKE THE SLIDERS: Preheat the grill to medium heat. In a large bowl, combine the egg, onion, salt, pepper, and garlic powder. Add the beef, coconut aminos, and tapioca flour. Mix with your hands until just combined. Shape into sixteen ½-inch-thick patties. Use your thumb to make a slight indentation in the center of each patty. Grill, turning once, until cooked through (160°F), 8 to 10 minutes.

TO serve, place one patty on a tostone. Add mustard, if using, and jalapeño relish. Top with another tostone.

tip: USE 32 OF THE LARGEST PLANTAIN SLICES for this recipe to accommodate the meat patties.

ranch coleslaw

SERVES 8

Start with a package of shredded coleslaw mix, add a few fresh ingredients and seasonings, toss with ranch dressing—homemade or bottled—and you've got a creamy, crunchy refreshing slaw in minutes. Chilling for 1 hour before serving helps the flavors to blend.

PREP: 10 MINUTES   **CHILL:** 1 HOUR
TOTAL: 1 HOUR 10 MINUTES

1 (14-ounce) package shredded cabbage and carrot coleslaw

⅓ cup finely chopped red onion

¼ cup chopped fresh parsley

½ teaspoon black pepper

¼ teaspoon garlic powder

1 cup Whole30 Ranch Dressing (page 133) or Whole30-compliant ranch dressing

IN a medium bowl, toss together the coleslaw mix, onion, parsley, pepper, and garlic powder. Drizzle the dressing over the cabbage mixture; toss to coat. Cover and chill for 1 hour.

fruit and rxbar kabobs

SERVES 8

These super-simple kabobs feature little bites of Blueberry RXBARs. The ingredients are listed right on the front of the package of each bar: "3 Egg Whites, 6 Almonds, 4 Cashews, 2 Dates, No B.S."

PREP: 20 MINUTES TOTAL: 20 MINUTES

1 (14-ounce) can Whole30-compliant coconut milk, refrigerated overnight

1 teaspoon grated lemon zest

16 (10-inch) metal skewers

6 blueberry RXBARs, each cut into 8 pieces

16 large green grapes

16 thick banana slices

16 small strawberries

16 fresh pineapple chunks

2 tablespoons fresh lemon juice

OPEN the refrigerated can of coconut milk; drain off the liquid and reserve for smoothies. Spoon the coconut cream into a medium bowl. Beat with an electric mixer on medium-high until fluffy, about 5 minutes. Stir in the lemon zest; cover and chill until ready to serve.

ON each skewer, thread 1 piece RXBAR, 1 grape, 1 banana slice, a second RXBAR piece, 1 strawberry, 1 pineapple chunk, and a third RXBAR piece. Brush the bananas with a little lemon juice to prevent browning.

SERVE the kabobs with the coconut cream.

peach tea

SERVES 8

Sure, you can buy tea—black or herbal—that comes already infused with peach essence, but the flavor is so much fresher when you coax it out of fresh, ripe peaches.

PREP: 10 MINUTES CHILL: 1 HOUR
TOTAL: 1 HOUR 10 MINUTES

6 black tea bags

2 ripe peaches, pitted and sliced

1 sprig fresh mint, leaves bruised

Ice

Fresh mint leaves, for garnish

IN a large saucepan, bring 4 cups of water to a boil. Remove from the heat; add the tea bags.

COVER and steep for 5 to 6 minutes. Remove and discard the tea bags. Add 8 cups water, the peaches, and the mint sprig. Cover and chill for 1 to 2 hours.

USING a slotted spoon, remove the mint and peach slices, reserving the peach slices for garnish.

TO serve, pour the tea into ice-filled glasses. Garnish with fresh mint leaves and a reserved peach slice.

friendsgiving

On a November 1994 episode of the TV show *Friends*, no one could go home for Thanksgiving, so they ate together in Monica's apartment. Though the word "Friendsgiving" was never actually used, the idea of celebrating a second Thanksgiving with friends caught on. We created a casual approach to this very traditional meal to keep it relaxed and fun. This menu features a turkey breast stuffed with mildly spicy chorizo filling, a creamy sweet potato soup, a fresh citrus and arugula salad, and awesome sides like bacon-herb mushrooms.

. . . .

smoky pecans

warm spiced olives

bacon-herb mushrooms

arugula, fennel, and citrus salad

roasted sweet potato soup

**roasted turkey breast
with chorizo filling**

**smashed potatoes with
herb-garlic butter**

**warm spiced apples with
nutty coconut topping**

cardamom-ginger poached pears

fall sangria

giving thanks

WE CELEBRATE FRIENDSGIVING at my sister's house in San Diego on the first Saturday of November. It's not so close to Thanksgiving that we're turkeyed out, but there's still the crisp of fall in the air.

IF NOT ALL YOUR GUESTS ARE ON THE WHOLE30, have them bring more traditional sides for those who want a dinner roll, brown sugar–topped sweet potatoes, or apple pie. Have small menu cards for each dish, alerting guests to ingredients and allergens.

MY FAVORITE FRIENDSGIVING tradition is to go around the table and say one or two things you've been grateful for in the past year. You can toast with sparkling water or cider; it will be just as festive and meaningful as with wine.

AFTER DINNER, we bust out a huge easel with paper and play Pictionary, boys versus girls. (The girls always win.) Catch Phrase is another fun game with large groups.

ONE LAST THOUGHTFUL TOUCH is to pick up some extra plastic storage containers, so you can send guests home with leftovers.

smoky pecans

SERVES 10

While you're putting the finishing touches on the main event and sides, guests can nibble on these nicely spiced roasted nuts.

....

PREP: 5 MINUTES   **BAKE:** 10 MINUTES   **TOTAL:** 15 MINUTES

....

3 tablespoons melted Clarified Butter (page 241), melted ghee, or extra-virgin olive oil

1½ teaspoons smoked paprika

1 teaspoon coarse salt

½ teaspoon black pepper

½ teaspoon garlic powder

⅛ to ¼ teaspoon cayenne pepper

3 cups whole pecans

PREHEAT the oven to 350°F. Line a large rimmed baking pan with parchment paper.

IN a medium bowl, stir together the butter, smoked paprika, salt, black pepper, garlic powder, and cayenne. Add the pecans and stir to coat.

ARRANGE the pecans on the baking pan in a single layer. Bake for about 10 minutes, stirring once halfway through, until the pecans are lightly browned. Cool completely.

tips: MAKE THESE MOUTHWATERING PECANS up to 1 week ahead. Store in an airtight container in the refrigerator.

THERE ARE THREE TYPES OF PAPRIKA—sweet, hot, and smoked. Sweet paprika adds vibrant color to a dish and has a sweet pepper flavor without any heat. Hot paprika is the Hungarian variety and adds peppery, spicy heat to food. Smoked paprika is often called pimento, and is made from peppers that are smoked and dried over an oak fire. The rich red color and smoky flavor of smoked paprika is available mild, medium-hot, and hot.

warm spiced olives

SERVES 10

Marinated olives are delicious, but serving them warm heightens and enhances their flavor in truly unexpected ways. They're more tender, juicier, and meatier, too.

....

PREP: 5 MINUTES   **COOK:** 10 MINUTES
TOTAL: 15 MINUTES

....

2 teaspoons fennel seeds

¾ cup extra-virgin olive oil

1 lemon

4 large cloves garlic, smashed

1 tablespoon ground Aleppo pepper

4 cups assorted Whole30-compliant olives with pits, such as Castelvetrano, Cerignola, and/or Kalamata

Fresh thyme or rosemary sprigs

IN a large skillet, heat the fennel seeds over medium heat, stirring occasionally, until toasted and fragrant, 2 to 3 minutes. Add the olive oil.

USE a vegetable peeler to remove wide strips of peel from the lemon (be sure to not remove the bitter pith). Add the peel to the fennel seeds.

ADD the garlic and Aleppo pepper; stir to combine. Add the olives and thyme or rosemary sprigs. Simmer over medium-low heat, 5 to 10 minutes. Do not let boil.

SERVE the olives warm.

bacon-herb mushrooms

SERVES 10

While these meaty herbed mushrooms make a superb side to the Thanksgiving turkey, they're equally awesome alongside a summer burger.

....

PREP: 15 MINUTES   **COOK:** 20 MINUTES
TOTAL: 35 MINUTES

....

15 slices Whole30-compliant bacon, chopped

2 large shallots, sliced

3½ to 4 pounds fresh assorted mushrooms (such as cremini and shiitake), stems removed and sliced

3 tablespoons chopped fresh thyme

1½ tablespoons chopped fresh rosemary

2 tablespoons coconut aminos

1 tablespoon fresh lemon juice

¾ teaspoon coarse salt

¾ teaspoon coarse black pepper

IN an extra-large skillet, cook the bacon and shallots over medium heat until the shallots are tender and the bacon is partially cooked but not crisp, about 5 minutes.

ADD the mushrooms to the skillet and cook over medium-high heat, stirring occasionally, until their liquid is released and the mushrooms have softened, 10 to 15 minutes. Add the thyme, rosemary, coconut aminos, lemon juice, salt, and pepper; cook for 5 minutes.

arugula, fennel, and citrus salad

SERVES 10

This salad offers up a beautiful balance to the rich dishes on this celebration menu. The combination of peppery arugula, anise-y fennel, and the sweet-but-astringent flavors of grapefruit and orange offers brightness in every bite.

....

PREP: 20 MINUTES **TOTAL:** 20 MINUTES

....

2 red grapefruit, supremed (see Tip)

1 navel orange, supremed (see Tip)

3 tablespoons extra-virgin olive oil

⅛ teaspoon salt

⅛ teaspoon black pepper

1 fennel bulb, trimmed, halved, and cored (see Tip)

1 package (5 ounces) arugula

Fresh mint leaves

IN a small bowl, whisk together 3 tablespoons of the citrus juices with the olive oil, salt, and pepper. Set aside.

USE a mandoline set at ⅛ inch or a sharp knife to thinly slice the fennel. In a large serving bowl, combine the fennel, arugula, and citrus segments. Drizzle with the vinaigrette and toss gently to combine. Sprinkle with mint leaves.

tips: TO SUPREME THE GRAPEFRUIT AND ORANGES (remove the membranes so the fruit can be easily served in segments), use a sharp knife to trim the ends of each fruit. Set one end flat on a cutting board and slice off the peel and pith in sections. Holding the fruit over a bowl to catch the juices, carefully cut toward the center, along a membrane. Then slice along the adjacent membrane until the cuts meet, releasing the segment. Repeat with the remaining segments. Squeeze the juice from the membranes, then discard the squeezed membranes.

TO TRIM A FENNEL BULB, cut off the stalk about 1 inch from the bulb. Cut a thin slice from the root end and discard. Remove any wilted outer layers with a vegetable peeler. Stand the bulb upright and cut in half. Cut away and discard the tough core from each half. Slice the fennel according to the recipe.

roasted sweet potato soup

SERVES 10

Instead of the more familiar starter soup made with butternut squash, try this creamy first course of pureed sweet potatoes and coconut milk flavored with cumin, garlic, ginger, jalapeño, lemon juice, and coriander.

PREP: 20 MINUTES **BAKE:** 20 MINUTES
COOK: 5 MINUTES **TOTAL:** 45 MINUTES

1½ pounds sweet potatoes, peeled
and cut into ½-inch pieces

1 medium yellow onion, coarsely chopped

2 medium carrots, peeled and cut into 1-inch pieces

4 tablespoons extra-virgin olive oil

1 teaspoon coarse salt

½ teaspoon black pepper

2 teaspoons cumin seeds, crushed

3 cloves garlic, minced

1 piece (2 inches) fresh ginger, peeled and chopped

1 jalapeño, seeded and chopped

4 cups Whole30-compliant chicken broth

1 (14-ounce) can Whole30-compliant coconut milk

2 tablespoons fresh lemon juice

1 teaspoon ground coriander

¼ cup toasted pepitas

PREHEAT the oven to 450°F. Line a large rimmed baking pan with parchment paper.

IN a large bowl, combine the sweet potatoes, onion, and carrots. Drizzle with 3 tablespoons of the olive oil; toss to coat. Sprinkle with the salt, pepper, and cumin seeds; toss to combine. Transfer to the baking pan. Bake for 20 to 25 minutes, until tender and beginning to brown.

IN a large pot over medium heat, heat the remaining olive oil. Add the garlic, ginger, and jalapeño; cook for 1 minute. Stir in the broth, coconut milk, lemon juice, and coriander; bring to a boil. Carefully add the roasted vegetables. Remove from the heat.

USE an immersion blender to blend the soup in the pot. (Or let the soup cool briefly, then carefully transfer to a blender in batches. Cover and pulse a few times, then blend until smooth.)

TOP each serving with some pepitas.

roasted turkey breast with chorizo filling

SERVES 10

The savory filling of ground pork spiced with ancho chile, paprika, oregano, cumin, pepper, cinnamon, and cloves packs a flavor wallop.

....

PREP: 30 MINUTES COOK: 10 MINUTES ROAST: 1½ HOURS
STAND: 20 MINUTES TOTAL: 2 HOURS 30 MINUTES

....

1 (5-ounce) package baby spinach or baby kale

2 tablespoons ancho chile powder

1 tablespoon paprika

1 teaspoon dried oregano

1 teaspoon ground cumin

3 teaspoons coarse salt

½ teaspoon black pepper

¼ teaspoon ground cinnamon

¼ teaspoon ground cloves

1 pound ground pork

1 large clove garlic, minced

3 tablespoons sherry vinegar or cider vinegar

2 medium yellow onions, finely chopped (see Tip)

2 medium carrots, peeled and finely chopped

2 boneless skin-on turkey breast halves
(3 pounds each, see Tip)

1 lemon, sliced

1 medium yellow onion, sliced

Extra-virgin olive oil

2 tablespoons smoked paprika

PREHEAT the oven to 425°F.

PLACE the spinach in a microwave-safe bowl. Cover with plastic wrap, venting one corner. Microwave on high power until the leaves are wilted, about 2 minutes. Pour off any liquid. When cool enough to handle, place the spinach in a tea towel or cheesecloth and squeeze the spinach until dry. Set aside.

FOR the chorizo, in a small bowl, stir together the ancho chile powder, paprika, oregano, cumin, 1 teaspoon salt, black pepper, cinnamon, and cloves. Place the pork in a large bowl; add the garlic and vinegar, and sprinkle with the spice mixture. Gently mix until well combined.

IN a large skillet, cook the chorizo and chopped onions and carrots over medium heat, stirring, until the meat is cooked and onions and carrots are tender, about 10 minutes. Add the wilted spinach. Let cool 20 minutes.

MEANWHILE, cut ten 12-inch pieces of 100-percent-cotton kitchen string. Place each breast, length-wise, skin side down, on a cutting board. In the thick side, opposite the tenderloin, cut a pocket with a small sharp knife, leaving about a 1-inch opening.

STUFF about a quarter of the filling under the tenderloin of each, and a quarter in the pocket. Slide a piece of string under the center of a breast and tie fairly tightly, securing the filling. Repeat with 4 more pieces of string at 1-inch intervals.

PLACE the lemon and sliced onion in the center of a roasting pan. Place the breasts on the onion and lemon. Brush the turkey skin with olive oil; sprinkle the top and sides with the remaining 2 teaspoons salt and the smoked paprika.

ROAST for 1 hour 30 minutes to 1 hour 45 minutes, basting occasionally with any pan juices, until an instant-read thermometer inserted in the thickest part of the turkey registers 160°F. Tent the turkey with foil if it browns too quickly.

TRANSFER the turkey to a cutting board and let rest 20 minutes. Slice crosswise to serve.

tips: A FOOD PROCESSOR makes quick work of finely chopping the onions and carrots.

ASK A BUTCHER TO DEBONE the turkey breasts for you. Be sure to plan this a few days ahead of the day you are cooking.

smashed potatoes with herb-garlic butter

SERVES 10

Baby potatoes are cooked until tender, flattened with a glass, brushed with clarified butter, and seasoned well, then baked to fabulous crispiness. A sprinkle of fresh chives is the crowning touch.

....

PREP: 10 MINUTES **COOK:** 15 MINUTES
ROAST/BROIL: 20 MINUTES **TOTAL:** 45 MINUTES

....

10 baby Yukon Gold potatoes

½ cup Clarified Butter (page 241) or ghee

4 cloves garlic, minced

1 teaspoon dried thyme

1 teaspoon dried rosemary

¾ teaspoon salt

½ teaspoon coarse black pepper

¼ teaspoon smoked paprika

3 tablespoons chopped fresh chives
or parsley

PREHEAT the oven to 400°F. Line a large rimmed baking pan with parchment paper.

PLACE the potatoes in a large pot; add water to cover. Bring to a boil over high heat; cook until just tender, about 15 minutes. Drain. Let cool slightly while making the herbed butter.

MELT the butter in a small saucepan over medium heat. Add the garlic, thyme, rosemary, salt, pepper, and smoked paprika. Cook, stirring constantly, 1 minute. Remove from the heat.

PLACE the potatoes on the baking pan. Use the bottom of a glass to smash each potato until about ½ inch thick. Drizzle with herbed butter. Roast for 17 to 20 minutes, until tender. Turn the oven to broil. Broil for about 3 minutes, until the potatoes are crisp on top. Sprinkle with chives.

warm spiced apples with nutty coconut topping

SERVES 10

This fruit and nut dessert is a delightful combination of textures and temperatures. Warm, cinnamon-spiced, and tender apples are topped with cold whipped coconut cream and a crunchy nut crumble.

....

PREP: 20 MINUTES   COOK: 20 MINUTES   TOTAL: 40 MINUTES

....

FOR THE COCONUT CREAM

1 (14-ounce) can Whole30-compliant coconut milk, refrigerated overnight (see Tip)

½ teaspoon Whole30-compliant vanilla bean powder

1 teaspoon grated orange zest

FOR THE APPLES

3 tablespoons Clarified Butter (page 241) or ghee

5 apples (such as Braeburn, Granny Smith, Honeycrisp, Pink Lady, and/or Jonagold), peeled, cored, and diced

2 teaspoons ground cinnamon

½ teaspoon ground nutmeg

2 star anise (optional)

1 tablespoon cider vinegar

½ teaspoon Whole30-compliant vanilla bean powder

½ teaspoon coarse salt

FOR THE NUTTY COCONUT TOPPING

2 tablespoons Clarified Butter (page 241) or ghee

⅔ cup chopped almonds, walnuts, and/or pecans

⅓ cup pepitas

⅓ cup unsweetened flaked or shredded coconut

¼ teaspoon ground nutmeg or cinnamon

¼ teaspoon coarse salt

MAKE THE COCONUT CREAM: Open the refrigerated can of coconut milk; drain off the liquid and reserve for smoothies. Spoon the coconut cream into a large bowl. Add the vanilla bean powder and beat with an electric mixer on medium-high until fluffy, about 10 minutes. Fold in the orange zest. Transfer to a serving dish. Cover and refrigerate until needed.

MAKE THE APPLES: In a large skillet, melt the butter over medium heat. Add the apples, cinnamon, nutmeg, and star anise (if using). Cook, stirring occasionally, until the apples are tender, 13 to 15 minutes. Add the vinegar, vanilla bean powder, and salt. Stir to combine.

MAKE THE NUTTY COCONUT TOPPING: Meanwhile, in a medium skillet, melt the butter over medium heat. Add the nuts and pepitas. Cook, stirring occasionally, until the nuts are lightly browned, 5 to 7 minutes. Stir in the coconut, nutmeg, and salt. Cook until the coconut is lightly browned, about 2 minutes.

SPOON the apples into shallow bowls; sprinkle with the nut crumble. Top with coconut cream.

tip: KEEP A COUPLE OF CANS OF COCONUT MILK in your refrigerator so you'll be ready whenever you want to make coconut cream.

cardamom-ginger poached pears

SERVES 10

This lovely dessert can be made up to 24 hours in advance. Just refrigerate the pears and coconut cream in separate airtight containers. Let the pears stand at room temperature for an hour before serving.

....

PREP: 20 MINUTES **COOK:** 10 MINUTES **TOTAL:** 30 MINUTES

....

FOR THE COCONUT CREAM

1 (14-ounce) can Whole30-compliant coconut milk, refrigerated overnight

½ teaspoon Whole30-compliant vanilla bean powder

⅛ teaspoon ground cardamom

FOR THE PEARS

2 cups apple cider

2 chai tea bags

2 green cardamom pods, crushed to release seeds

1 piece (2 inches) fresh ginger, peeled and thinly sliced

2 teaspoons grated orange zest

5 Bosc pears, halved lengthwise and cored

⅓ cup chopped raw pistachios

MAKE THE COCONUT CREAM: Open the refrigerated can of coconut milk; drain off the liquid and reserve for smoothies. Spoon the coconut cream into a large bowl. Add the vanilla bean powder and cardamom; beat with an electric mixer on medium-high until fluffy, about 10 minutes. Transfer to a serving dish. Cover and refrigerate until needed.

MAKE THE PEARS: Combine 2 cups of water and the cider in a large saucepan. Bring to a boil; remove from heat. Add the tea bags; let steep for 5 minutes. Remove and discard the tea bags. Add the

cardamom pods, ginger, orange zest, and pears. Return to a boil, then reduce the heat. Simmer, uncovered, until the pears are tender, about 10 minutes. Use a slotted spoon to remove the pears and let cool to room temperature.

TO serve, top each pear with some of the coconut cream and sprinkle with pistachios.

tip: KEEP A COUPLE OF CANS OF COCONUT MILK in your refrigerator so you'll be ready whenever you want to make coconut cream.

fall sangria

SERVES 10

This sparkling, spice-infused sipper is loaded with good stuff, including antioxidant-rich black tea, a splash of fresh juices, and fruit.

....

PREP: 15 MINUTES **CHILL:** 4 HOURS
TOTAL: 4 HOURS 15 MINUTES

....

3 Earl Grey tea bags

2 cups 100% pomegranate juice

3 cups fresh orange juice

2 cinnamon sticks

2 star anise

2 apples, cored and diced

2 lemons, halved, seeded, and thinly sliced

1 orange, halved, seeded, and thinly sliced

4 cups Whole30-compliant sparkling water

IN a large pot, bring 3 cups water to a boil over high heat. Add the tea bags; remove from the heat. Let steep for 5 minutes; discard the tea bags. Stir in the juices, cinnamon sticks, star anise, and fruit. Refrigerate for 4 to 24 hours. Just before serving, stir in the sparkling water.

church picnic

On a warm spring or summer Sunday, there isn't a more wholesome activity than the after-church picnic. Everybody spills out onto the lawn and puts their potluck contribution on the proper table—appetizers, main dishes, salads and sides, or desserts. There are a few staple dishes that pop up at almost any potluck—pulled pork swathed in sugary barbecue sauce, cheesy potatoes bubbling away in a slow cooker, and sour cream-based dip served with potato chips—but there isn't always much for a Whole30er to choose from . . . until now. This menu is specifically designed to echo some of those favorite dishes. Each one is yummy, meant to be shared, and fits perfectly into your Whole30 plan. Pick a dish (or two) to contribute and wait for the recipe requests to come in!

. . . .

**tiny tomato salad with
champagne vinaigrette
smoky roasted cauliflower–garlic dip
green chile pulled pork
grilled apricots, peaches, and plums
with charred green onion vinaigrette
crunchy asian noodle salad**

rejoice and give thanks

IF YOU HAVE THE TIME AND ENERGY, bring two dishes—a main like the Green Chile Pulled Pork, and a side or salad to round out your plate. That way, you won't have to take a chance on a dressing or hidden ingredient that may not be compliant.

IT'S HARD TO GET MUCH DONE BEFORE CHURCH ON SUNDAY MORNING, so do as much prep as you can ahead of time. The pulled pork, cauliflower dip, veggies, fruit, and salads can be made a day ahead. Just reheat the meat in a slow cooker set it on low, and toss the salads right before serving.

TAKING DELICIOUS, Whole30-compliant foods to a potluck is a great conversation starter and opportunity to share the program and its benefits in a no-pressure way. And what better place than church to spread our Good Food word!

PLAN SOME FUN GAMES for the littler kids to reinforce the idea that events like this aren't about the sweets and treats, they're about the friendships and community. Googling "fun games for church picnics" yields a wealth of ideas.

tiny tomato salad with champagne vinaigrette

SERVES 6

This salad is as simple as it gets—a jumble of colorful tomatoes with crunchy cucumber and fresh herbs in a lemony vinaigrette. It's a refreshing side to richer, heartier foods.

....

PREP: 15 MINUTES   **CHILL:** 1 HOUR
TOTAL: 1 HOUR 15 MINUTES

....

FOR THE VINAIGRETTE

¼ cup extra-virgin olive oil

2 tablespoons champagne vinegar, rice vinegar, or white wine vinegar

½ teaspoon grated lemon zest

¼ teaspoon coarse salt

⅛ teaspoon coarse black pepper

FOR THE SALAD

3 cups yellow pear tomatoes, orange cherry tomatoes, and/or red grape tomatoes, halved

1 medium English cucumber, sliced

3 tablespoons chopped fresh chives, cilantro, or parsley

MAKE THE VINAIGRETTE: In a small bowl, whisk together the olive oil, vinegar, lemon zest, salt, and pepper.

MAKE THE SALAD: In a large bowl, combine the tomatoes, cucumber, and chives. Drizzle with the vinaigrette and gently toss. Cover and chill for 1 hour. Gently stir before serving.

smoky roasted cauliflower– garlic dip

SERVES 6

Similar in flavor and texture to traditional hummus, this smoky dip calls for sumac as an optional ingredient. Ground sumac is a made from the dried red berries of the sumac bush, which is native to the Middle East. The dip will still be delicious without it, but sumac does give it a nice balancing touch of tangy citrus flavor.

....

PREP: 15 MINUTES **BAKE:** 20 MINUTES
COOL: 10 MINUTES **TOTAL:** 45 MINUTES

....

4 cups small cauliflower florets

6 tablespoons extra-virgin olive oil

2 teaspoons smoked paprika

1 teaspoon coarse salt

1 teaspoon ground cumin

1 teaspoon ground sumac (optional)

1 head garlic

2 tablespoons Whole30-compliant tahini

2 tablespoons fresh lemon juice

2 tablespoons roasted pepitas

1 tablespoon finely chopped fresh parsley

Assorted vegetables such as radishes, carrots, and/or endive

PREHEAT the oven to 425°F. Line a large rimmed baking pan with parchment paper.

PLACE the cauliflower on the baking pan and drizzle with 2 tablespoons olive oil. In a small bowl, combine the smoked paprika, salt, cumin, and sumac (if using). Sprinkle over the cauliflower and toss to coat.

CUT about ¼ inch from the top of the garlic to expose the cloves, keeping the head intact. Place the garlic on a 4-inch piece of foil; drizzle with 1 tablespoon olive oil. Fold and seal the foil; place on the baking pan with the cauliflower.

BAKE for 20 to 25 minutes, until the cauliflower and garlic are tender. Cool for about 10 minutes. Squeeze the roasted garlic cloves out of their skins.

IN a food processor, combine the cauliflower, garlic, 3 tablespoons olive oil, tahini, and lemon juice. Cover and process until smooth.

TRANSFER to a serving bowl and top with the pepitas and parsley. Serve with the vegetables.

green chile pulled pork

SERVES 6

Pulled pork is a potluck staple, usually swathed in barbecue sauce. This Mexican-style pulled pork is a nice change of pace. Slow cooked with poblanos and jalapeños, garlic, chili powder, cumin, oregano, and coriander, it is positively packed with flavor.

....

PREP: 20 MINUTES BAKE: 2 HOURS 30 MINUTES
TOTAL: 2 HOURS 50 MINUTES

....

2 tablespoons coconut oil or extra-virgin olive oil

3 to 3½ pounds boneless pork shoulder, trimmed

1 teaspoon salt

½ teaspoon black pepper

1 medium yellow onion, chopped

1 (16-ounce) jar Whole30-compliant salsa verde

2 poblano chile peppers, seeded and chopped

1 jalapeño, seeded and chopped (optional)

2 cloves garlic, minced

1 tablespoon Whole30-compliant chili powder

2 teaspoons ground cumin

1 teaspoon dried oregano, crushed

1 teaspoon ground coriander

PREHEAT the oven to 325°F.

IN a large Dutch oven over medium-high heat, heat the oil. Rub the pork with salt and pepper on all sides. Add the pork and cook until all sides are browned, about 3 minutes per side. Remove the pork. Add the onion and bring to a simmer, scraping the browned bits with a wooden spoon. Add the salsa verde, poblanos, jalapeño (if using), garlic, chili powder, cumin, oregano, and coriander. Mix together.

RETURN the pork to the Dutch oven; cover and place in the oven. Bake until the meat is very tender and the internal temperature is 145°F, 2½ to 3 hours. Transfer the meat to a cutting board. Use two forks to pull the meat apart into large shreds and place the shreds in a serving bowl. Skim the fat from the cooking liquid. Drizzle about 2 cups cooking liquid over the meat to moisten. Discard the remaining cooking liquid.

tip: STORE LEFTOVERS in an airtight container in the freezer for up to 3 months. Thaw 8 hours in the refrigerator.

grilled apricots, peaches, and plums with charred green onion vinaigrette

SERVES 6

This is the perfect salad for a summer potluck, when stone fruits are at their sweetest and juiciest.

·····································

PREP: 15 MINUTES   **COOK:** 5 MINUTES
COOL: 10 MINUTES   **TOTAL:** 35 MINUTES

·····································

3 ripe apricots, halved and pitted

2 ripe peaches, halved and pitted

2 ripe plums, halved and pitted

5 tablespoons plus 1 teaspoon extra-virgin olive oil

½ teaspoon coarse black pepper

¼ teaspoon smoked paprika

2 green onions, ends trimmed

2 tablespoons plus 1 teaspoon fresh orange juice

1 tablespoon fresh lemon juice

⅛ teaspoon salt

PREHEAT the grill to medium heat.

ARRANGE the apricots, peaches, and plums in a single layer, cut sides up, on a large rimmed baking pan.

IN a small bowl, stir together 2 tablespoons of the olive oil and the pepper and smoked paprika. Drizzle over the fruit. Arrange the fruit, cut sides down, on the grill rack. Grill, rotating once halfway through to create grill marks, 5 to 6 minutes total for the cut side. Turn the fruit over and grill until slightly softened, about 3 minutes more. Lightly coat the green onions with 1 teaspoon of the olive oil. Place the green onions on the grill rack. Grill until slightly wilted, turning once halfway through, 2 to 4 minutes.

TRANSFER the fruit and green onions to a cutting board. When cool enough to handle, coarsely chop the fruit and chop the green onions. Transfer to a serving bowl.

MEANWHILE, in a small bowl, whisk together the remaining 3 tablespoons olive oil and the orange juice, lemon juice, and salt. Drizzle over the fruit. Serve warm or at room temperature.

crunchy asian noodle salad

SERVES 6

At nearly any potluck you go to, there is a big bowl of a crunchy ramen noodle salad. This version forgoes the wheat noodles, sugar, vegetable oil, and MSG-infused seasoning packets. It has the same satisfying crunch but is more flavorful and—better yet—is totally clean.

....

PREP: 20 MINUTES   **TOTAL:** 20 MINUTES

....

2 (10.7-ounce) packages zucchini noodles; or 3 medium zucchini, spiralized and snipped into 2- to 3-inch pieces

½ (10-ounce) package shredded red cabbage or 2 cups thinly sliced red cabbage

2 medium carrots, peeled and coarsely grated or cut into matchsticks

½ cup slivered almonds, toasted (see Tip)

½ cup chopped fresh cilantro

¼ cup chopped green onions

3 tablespoons extra-virgin olive oil

2 tablespoons rice vinegar

2 tablespoons coconut aminos

1 tablespoon toasted sesame oil

1 piece (1 inch) fresh ginger, peeled and grated (see Tip)

1 large clove garlic, minced

¼ teaspoon red pepper flakes

¼ teaspoon salt

¼ teaspoon coarse black pepper

2 tablespoons sesame seeds, toasted (see Tip)

IN a large bowl, combine the zucchini, cabbage, carrots, almonds, cilantro, and green onions.

IN a small bowl, whisk together the olive oil, vinegar, coconut aminos, sesame oil, ginger, garlic, red pepper flakes, salt, and pepper. Drizzle over the salad and gently toss to coat. Sprinkle with sesame seeds.

SERVE immediately or store in an airtight container in the refrigerator for up to 2 hours.

tip: TO TOAST SLIVERED ALMONDS AND SESAME SEEDS, heat in a skillet over medium heat, stirring, until fragrant and lightly browned, about 2 minutes.

STEER CLEAR OF STORE-BOUGHT JARS OF MINCED GINGER, as they almost always contain added sugar and/or soybean oil.

tailgating

Marissa Allen

FIRSTANDFULL.COM

Marissa Allen believes in the power of good food to connect people. She creates delicious, approachable recipes using real ingredients to bring family and friends to the dinner table.

Tailgating is a time-honored tradition, and in some groups, an essential step in getting pumped up to root for your team. Unless you're one of those super-dedicated fans towing an RV into the stadium, tailgating can present some logistical challenges. This menu of popular tailgate foods like wings, potato skins, and brisket doesn't require a full kitchen or any fancy cooking apparatus—just a cooler and a grill. Every recipe is prepped at home and finished on-site, and most don't even require silverware. (Just pack some wet-wipes to avoid Cajun-spiced high-fives.)

••••••••••••••••••••••••

cajun-rubbed chicken wings

crispy pulled pork potato skins with chipotle slaw

grilled pineapple

roasted garlic–ranch chicken kabobs

smoky barbecue brisket

win the points!

MUCH LIKE "GAME DAY," good-natured ribbing and trash-talking is all part of the pre-game fun, but be prepared to stand your ground if you're peer-pressured to have "just one" beer, nacho, or slice of pizza. A simple, "No thanks, I'm good" (said with direct eye contact) then changing the subject to something game-related is always a winning strategy.

PACK A LARGE PLASTIC BIN with all of the tailgating essentials—grilling tools, sunscreen, bug spray, hand sanitizer, wipes, paper towels, first-aid kit, and extension cords.

IF YOU USE PLASTIC OR MELAMINE DISHES and cups and metal flatware, pack everything in a large plastic bin with a lid so you can load the dirty dishes into the same bin for the ride home.

IF YOU WON'T BE IN CLOSE PROXIMITY to a bathroom with running water (or just in case), bring an empty liquid laundry detergent bottle filled with water and a small bottle of liquid hand soap to use as hand-washing station.

cajun-rubbed chicken wings

SERVES 12

These Cajun-Rubbed Chicken Wings are always a crowd pleaser. Prepare the rub at home and toss them on the grill when you get to the game. They're a great start to a long day of food, friends, and football!

PREP: 20 MINUTES MARINATE: 1 HOUR
COOK: 10 MINUTES TOTAL: 1 HOUR 30 MINUTES

4 pounds chicken wings
½ cup avocado oil
1 teaspoon cayenne pepper
2 teaspoons white pepper
2 teaspoons black pepper
1½ teaspoons coarse salt
2 teaspoons onion powder
2 teaspoons garlic powder
2 teaspoons smoked paprika
1 teaspoon ancho chile powder

at home

USE kitchen shears or a very sharp chef's knife to remove the tips of the chicken wings. (Discard the tips or save them for making stock.) Cut the rest of the wings at the joint to make two pieces each. Place the wings in a large resealable plastic bag.

IN a small bowl, stir together the avocado oil, cayenne, white pepper, black pepper, salt, onion powder, garlic powder, smoked paprika, and ancho chile powder. Pour over the chicken and massage to coat. Marinate at least 1 hour or up to overnight. Store in a cooler or refrigerator until ready to cook.

at the tailgate

GRILL the chicken, covered, over medium heat, until cooked through, turning occasionally, 10 to 15 minutes.

crispy pulled pork potato skins with chipotle slaw

SERVES 12

Potato skins are often underutilized. They have the capacity to be stuffed with so many delicious Whole30 fillings that it makes them a no-brainer on game day!

....

PREP: 30 MINUTES   ROAST: 35 MINUTES
COOK: 20 MINUTES   TOTAL: 1 HOUR 30 MINUTES

....

FOR THE POTATO SKINS

6 medium russet potatoes, scrubbed

2 tablespoons avocado oil

½ teaspoon coarse salt

3 tablespoons Clarified Butter
(page 241) or ghee, melted

FOR THE PULLED PORK

4 cups leftover pulled pork (see Tip)

½ cup Whole30-compliant barbecue sauce

1 teaspoon ground cumin

½ teaspoon onion powder

¼ teaspoon coarse salt

¼ teaspoon chipotle powder

½ teaspoon dried oregano, crushed

¼ teaspoon black pepper

¼ teaspoon ground coriander

¼ teaspoon Whole30-compliant chili powder

FOR THE CHIPOTLE SLAW

1 large clove garlic, minced

2 pitted dates, softened in hot water and chopped

⅓ cup avocado oil

2 tablespoons red wine vinegar

1 tablespoon fresh lime juice

1½ teaspoons chipotle powder

½ teaspoon coarse salt

¼ teaspoon black pepper

4 cups shredded cabbage and carrot coleslaw mix

at home

PREHEAT the oven to 425°F. Line a large rimmed baking pan with foil.

MAKE THE POTATO SKINS: Place the potatoes on the pan; drizzle with the oil and rub all over to coat. Sprinkle with the salt. Roast for 35 to 40 minutes, until the potatoes are tender when pierced with a fork. Cool slightly. Cut in half lengthwise and scoop out the flesh (reserve for another use). Cool completely. Store in an airtight container in a cooler or refrigerator until ready to cook.

MAKE THE PULLED PORK: In a large bowl, combine the pork, barbecue sauce, cumin, onion powder, salt, chipotle powder, oregano, pepper, coriander, and chili powder. Mix well and transfer to an airtight container. Store in a cooler or refrigerator.

MAKE THE CHIPOTLE SLAW: For the dressing, in a blender or food processor, combine the garlic, dates, avocado oil, vinegar, lime juice, chipotle powder, salt, and pepper. Cover and blend or process until smooth. In a large bowl, stir together the coleslaw mix and dressing. Store in an airtight container in a cooler or refrigerator until ready to serve.

at the tailgate

PREHEAT a grill to medium heat. Place the pork in a large cast iron skillet or Dutch oven. Cook until heated through, about 10 minutes. Generously brush the inside of the potato skins with melted butter. Fill with the pork. Grill until the potato skins are crisp, about 10 minutes. Top with the slaw.

tip: Cut a 2¼ pound pork shoulder into large chunks; add to a slow cooker with ½ cup water. Cover; slow cook on high for 4 to 5 hours or until fork tender.

grilled pineapple

SERVES 12

This is the perfect end to a hot and sweaty tailgate. The pineapple is just sweet enough with the tang from the lime juice and a little zing from the salt added at the end. It's refreshing and satisfying at the same time!

....

PREP: 15 MINUTES   **COOK:** 5 MINUTES   **TOTAL:** 20 MINUTES

....

2 ripe pineapples

2 tablespoons avocado oil

¼ cup fresh lime juice

Pinch coarse salt (optional)

at home

CUT off the top and bottom of the pineapple. Trim off the rind in strips; cut deep enough to remove the "eyes" but save as much flesh as possible. Slice the pineapple in half lengthwise. Slice the pineapple into 6 wedges. Trim the core from each wedge and discard. Store the pineapple in an airtight container in a cooler or refrigerator until ready to cook.

at the tailgate

PREHEAT the grill to medium-high heat. Brush the pineapple wedges with the avocado oil and lime juice. Grill the pineapple until lightly charred, turning occasionally, about 5 minutes. Sprinkle the wedges with a pinch of salt, if desired.

roasted garlic–ranch chicken kabobs

SERVES 12

Homemade ranch does double-duty as both a marinade and dipping sauce in this winning recipe. The roasted garlic adds a touch of mellow garlic flavor as well as a bit of sweetness.

....

PREP: 25 MINUTES   **MARINATE:** 1 HOUR
COOK: 5 MINUTES   **TOTAL:** 1 HOUR 30 MINUTES

....

½ cup avocado oil, plus more for greasing the grill

½ cup Whole30-compliant coconut milk (see Tip)

⅔ cup Basic Mayonnaise (page 240) or Whole30-compliant mayonnaise

1 small head garlic, roasted (see Tip)

1 tablespoon dried parsley

2 teaspoons red wine vinegar

½ teaspoon dried dill

½ teaspoon onion powder

¼ teaspoon dried thyme, crushed

½ teaspoon black pepper

½ teaspoon coarse salt

1 tablespoon fresh lemon juice

2 pounds boneless, skinless chicken breast, cut into 1- to 1⅛-inch pieces

12 (8-inch) wooden skewers

at home

IN a blender, combine the avocado oil, coconut milk, mayonnaise, roasted garlic, parsley, vinegar, dill, onion powder, thyme, pepper, salt, and lemon juice. Cover and blend until smooth.

SOAK the skewers in water for 30 minutes. Thread 4 to 5 pieces of chicken onto each skewer. Place the kabobs in a large airtight container or 9 × 13-inch baking pan. Pour 1¼ cups of the dressing over the chicken. Turn the skewers to coat. Marinate in the refrigerator for 1 hour or up to 4 hours. Drain and discard the marinade. Store the kabobs and the ¾ cup reserved dressing separately in airtight containers in a cooler or refrigerator until ready to cook.

at the tailgate

PREHEAT the grill to medium-high heat. Oil the grate with avocado oil or olive oil. Grill the kabobs, turning occasionally, until the chicken is cooked through, 5 to 8 minutes.

SERVE the kabobs with the reserved dressing for dipping.

tips: CANNED COCONUT MILK separates in the can, with the cream rising to the top. Make sure to whisk the coconut milk well before measuring.

TO ROAST GARLIC, cut about ¼ inch from the top of the garlic to expose the cloves, keeping the head intact. Place the garlic on a 4-inch piece of foil; drizzle with 1 teaspoon olive oil. Fold and seal the foil; place on a small baking pan. Roast in a 425°F oven for 20 to 25 minutes, until tender.

smoky barbecue brisket

SERVES 12

This is one of my favorite Whole30 recipes! Almost all conventional rubs and marinades contain sugar of some sort, making it hard to enjoy smoked meats on a Whole30. This spice rub adds tons of flavor to a brisket, pork shoulder, tenderloin, or rack of ribs.

· ·

PREP: 10 MINUTES **COOK:** 3 HOURS
STAND: 10 MINUTES **TOTAL:** 3 HOURS 20 MINUTES

· ·

1 tablespoon smoked paprika

1 tablespoon coarse salt

1½ teaspoons black pepper

1½ teaspoons garlic powder

1½ teaspoons onion powder

1½ teaspoons ground cumin

1½ teaspoons chipotle powder

½ teaspoon dried oregano, crushed

1 teaspoon dried parsley, crushed

¼ teaspoon ground coriander

¼ teaspoon cayenne pepper

1 3-pound beef brisket

¼ cup Whole30-compliant barbecue sauce, plus more for serving (optional)

SPECIAL EQUIPMENT

2 cups hickory wood chips

2 12×10×2-inch grill-safe foil pans

at home

IN a small bowl, stir together the paprika, salt, pepper, garlic powder, onion powder, cumin, chipotle powder, oregano, parsley, coriander, and cayenne. Rub 3 tablespoons of the seasoning all over the brisket. (Store the remaining rub in an airtight container for up to 6 months.) Tightly wrap the brisket in plastic wrap and store in a cooler or refrigerator until ready to cook.

at the tailgate

POUR the wood chips into one of the foil pans and add enough water to cover. Cover tightly with foil. Cut 10 to 12 slits in the foil to allow smoke to escape.

HEAT a grill to low (300°F). Place the brisket on the grill, fat side up, and grill for 5 minutes. Turn and grill 5 minutes more. Transfer the brisket to the remaining foil pan, fat side up. Place the pan on one side of the grill and the wood chips pan on the other side. Cook, covered, maintaining a grill temperature of 300°F, 2½ hours.

TURN the brisket so the fat side is down and brush with some of the barbecue sauce. Cook for 30 minutes more, brushing with barbecue sauce every 10 minutes.

REMOVE the brisket from the heat. Let the brisket rest 10 minutes before slicing. Serve with additional barbecue sauce, if desired.

sunday brunch

Christina Shoemaker
THEWHOLECOOK.COM

Christina Shoemaker is the creator of The Whole Cook, a blog dedicated to real food recipes made from wholesome ingredients. She credits the Whole30 program with setting her down the path of eating and serving nutrient-dense food to her family. Now she creates easy-to-prepare recipes your whole family can love too!

Sunday brunch is perfect for entertaining when you're doing the Whole30. It's usually a late-morning affair, and though mimosas are a common brunch beverage, it's not unusual to pass on alcohol at 11 a.m. (The bubbly Pink Sunrise Mocktail is more fun than a tired old mimosa anyway.) Eggs can creatively be made into all kinds of delicious veggie-packed, Whole30-compliant dishes. But the best part about a Whole30 brunch? You leave clear-eyed, full of energy, and with a happy belly, ready to make the most of the rest of your weekend.

· ·

buffalo chicken frittata

spinach-arugula breakfast hash

skillet breakfast potatoes

balsamic peach-arugula salad

salmon–sweet potato stacks
with lemon-dill sauce

taco breakfast casserole

sheet pan sweet potato
hash and eggs

pink sunrise mocktail

brunch so hard

BONUS POINTS FOR SCHEDULING YOUR BRUNCH AFTER A FUN ACTIVITY, like a short hike, bike ride, rock climbing session, or yoga class. Shifting the social scene away from late-night bars to health-conscious daytime pursuits is a great way to stay social while honoring your commitments to yourself.

HAVE SOMETHING FOR GUESTS TO NIBBLE ON when they arrive while you finish the rest of the food prep. All of the elements for the Salmon–Sweet Potato Stacks can be made the night before and stored, covered, in the refrigerator. Let the salmon and sweet potato slices stand at room temperature for 30 minutes before assembling.

OUR MAIN DISHES INCLUDE THE BUFFALO CHICKEN FRITTATA, Sheet-Pan Sweet Potato Hash and Eggs, Taco Breakfast Casserole, or Spinach–Arugula Breakfast Hash. They're easy to size up, too . . . just add more eggs, or make more than one main.

DON'T FORGET THE COFFEE AND TEA! Offer a selection of caffeinated coffee, coffee alternatives like MUD\WTR or Rasa, or Four Sigmatic Chai or Matcha. I don't drink caffeine, so I also appreciate when my host has an herbal tea or decaf offering as well. (Don't forget the Nutpods!)

buffalo chicken frittata

SERVES 8

Love Buffalo chicken wings? This is your breakfast. This frittata is packed with shredded chicken, celery, onion, garlic, and that Buffalo-sauce flavor you love. It's not very spicy, so even the heat-averse can enjoy it. Add an extra drizzle of hot sauce at the end if you're looking to up the temperature.

······································

PREP: 10 MINUTES **COOK:** 5 MINUTES **BAKE:** 15 MINUTES
STAND: 10 MINUTES **TOTAL:** 40 MINUTES

······································

2 tablespoons extra-virgin olive oil

¼ cup diced yellow onion

2 stalks celery, diced

1 clove garlic, minced

1½ cups shredded cooked chicken

10 large eggs

⅓ cup Whole30-compliant hot sauce, plus more for serving

¼ teaspoon salt

¼ teaspoon cayenne pepper

Sliced green onions (optional)

PREHEAT the oven to 400°F.

IN a 10-inch cast iron or other ovenproof skillet, heat the olive oil. Add the onion, celery, and garlic. Cook, stirring frequently, until tender, 5 to 7 minutes. Remove from the heat. Spread in the skillet and top with the chicken.

IN a large bowl, whisk together the eggs, hot sauce, salt, and cayenne. Pour over the chicken. Bake until the middle is set, 15 to 20 minutes.

LET stand for 10 minutes. Run a knife around the edge of the pan. If desired, top with the green onions and additional hot sauce. Cut into wedges.

spinach-arugula breakfast hash

SERVES 8

This is my go-to breakfast because it takes 25 minutes from start to finish. It's a total crowd pleaser with crispy golden potatoes, plenty of greens, garlic, and fried eggs. You can't go wrong with this one!

....

PREP: 10 MINUTES **COOK:** 15 MINUTES
TOTAL: 25 MINUTES

....

3 tablespoons extra-virgin olive oil

4 large Yukon Gold potatoes, diced

1 medium yellow onion, diced

½ teaspoon salt

¼ teaspoon black pepper

2 cloves garlic, minced

1 (5-ounce) container spinach and arugula salad blend

8 large eggs

IN a large nonstick pan, heat the olive oil over medium-high heat. Add the potatoes and onion; sprinkle with the salt and pepper. Cook, stirring frequently, until the potatoes are tender and browned, 8 to 9 minutes. Add the garlic and salad greens; stir to combine. Cover and cook until the greens wilt, 2 to 3 minutes.

MAKE 8 indentations in the hash, and carefully break an egg into each indentation. Cover and cook just until the egg whites are set, 5 to 6 minutes. Season to taste.

skillet breakfast potatoes

SERVES 8

The trick to perfect skillet potatoes with crispy outsides and soft insides is to be careful not to overfill your pan. Spread the potatoes evenly in the pan to create a single layer. Also—and this is may be the most important part—don't cover the potatoes until you've achieved that golden crispy brown you want on the outside. After browning is complete you can cover for an additional few minutes if necessary.

....

PREP: 10 MINUTES **COOK:** 10 MINUTES
TOTAL: 20 MINUTES

....

3 tablespoons extra-virgin olive oil

4 medium Yukon Gold potatoes, diced

1 medium yellow onion, diced

¾ teaspoon coarse salt

½ teaspoon black pepper

Fresh thyme leaves or chopped fresh cilantro or parsley (optional)

HEAT the olive oil in a large heavy skillet over medium-high heat. Add the potatoes and onion. Cook, stirring occasionally, until tender and browned, about 10 minutes. If the potatoes are browned but not tender, cover, reduce the heat to medium, and cook an additional 2 to 3 minutes. Sprinkle with salt and pepper. Top with herbs, if desired.

balsamic peach-arugula salad

SERVES 8

I love a salad that perfectly balances sweet and savory, and this salad does just that. Roasting frozen peaches (yes, frozen!) with a little ghee and balsamic vinegar brings out their sweetness and makes this dish accessible even when peaches are out of season!

PREP: 20 MINUTES **COOK:** 15 MINUTES **TOTAL:** 35 MINUTES

FOR THE PEACHES AND VEGETABLES

3 ripe peaches, peeled and sliced, or
1 (16-ounce) bag frozen peaches, thawed

2 tablespoons Clarified Butter
(page 241) or ghee, melted

2 tablespoons balsamic vinegar

1 small red onion, thinly sliced into rings

2 teaspoons extra-virgin olive oil

¼ teaspoon salt

¼ teaspoon black pepper

24 thin asparagus spears, trimmed

FOR THE ARUGULA SALAD

½ cup balsamic vinegar

3 (5-ounce) containers baby arugula

3 tablespoons extra-virgin olive oil

½ teaspoon salt

¼ teaspoon pepper

½ cup coarsely chopped roasted pistachios

PREHEAT the oven to 425°F. Line two large rimmed baking pans with parchment paper.

MAKE THE PEACHES AND VEGETABLES: Arrange the peach slices on half of one pan; brush with the butter. Drizzle vinegar over the slices. Arrange the onion on the other half of the pan. Drizzle with 1 teaspoon olive oil. Sprinkle with ⅛ teaspoon each salt and pepper. Roast for 5 minutes.

MEANWHILE, arrange the asparagus on the other pan. Drizzle with 1 teaspoon olive oil. Sprinkle with the remaining ⅛ teaspoon each salt and pepper. Add the asparagus to the oven. Stir the onions. Roast both pans 10 minutes more.

MAKE THE ARUGULA SALAD: Meanwhile, in a small saucepan, bring the vinegar to a boil over medium-high heat. Reduce the heat to medium-low and simmer until reduced by half, 8 to 10 minutes. Cool completely.

PLACE the arugula in an extra-large bowl. Drizzle with the olive oil and sprinkle with ½ teaspoon salt and ¼ teaspoon pepper; toss to coat.

DIVIDE the arugula, asparagus, peaches, and onions among 8 salad plates. Drizzle the salads with about 1 teaspoon of the reduced vinegar. Sprinkle with the pistachios.

salmon–sweet potato stacks with lemon-dill sauce

SERVES 8

These stacks of sweet potato, flaky salmon, arugula, and a creamy lemon-dill sauce are perfect as an appetizer for brunch or any kind of entertaining. They pack a lot of wow and obliterate the notion that Whole30 food is boring. They make any occasion feel special!

....

PREP: 15 MINUTES   **ROAST:** 10 MINUTES
STAND: 20 MINUTES   **TOTAL:** 45 MINUTES

....

FOR THE SWEET POTATO STACKS

1 large (12- to 16-ounce) sweet potato, peeled, narrow ends trimmed

1 (6-ounce) salmon fillet

1 tablespoon extra-virgin olive oil

¼ teaspoon salt

⅛ teaspoon black pepper

FOR THE LEMON-DILL SAUCE

¼ cup Basic Mayonnaise (page 240) or Whole30-compliant mayonnaise

2 teaspoons chopped fresh dill

1½ teaspoons Whole30-compliant almond milk

1½ teaspoons fresh lemon juice

¾ teaspoon grated lemon zest

Pinch salt

¾ cup chopped arugula or spinach

PREHEAT the oven to 425°F. Line a large rimmed baking pan with parchment paper.

MAKE THE SWEET POTATO STACKS: Slice the sweet potato into eight ¼-inch slices. Arrange the slices in a single layer on half of the pan, and place the salmon on the other half. Brush the salmon and sweet potato with olive oil. Sprinkle the salmon with salt and pepper.

ROAST for 10 to 12 minutes, until the salmon just barely starts to flake when pulled apart with a fork, and the sweet potato rounds are tender. Let cool to room temperature, about 20 minutes. Remove the skin and coarsely flake the salmon.

MAKE THE LEMON-DILL SAUCE: Meanwhile, in a small bowl, whisk together the mayonnaise, dill, almond milk, lemon juice, lemon zest, and salt.

TO serve, arrange the sweet potato rounds on a serving platter. Top each round with a heaping tablespoon of the arugula, about 2 tablespoons salmon, and 1½ teaspoons sauce.

taco breakfast casserole

SERVES 8

This breakfast casserole is much lighter than the kind I grew up eating. It doesn't require milk or cheese and it truly doesn't need either. The trick is the salsa that's stirred into the egg mixture before baking. It makes every bite super-flavorful. Plus, it's incredibly easy to throw together.

••••••••••••••••••••••••••••••••

PREP: 15 MINUTES   **COOK:** 10 MINUTES   **BAKE:** 30 MINUTES
STAND: 10 MINUTES   **TOTAL:** 1 HOUR 5 MINUTES

••••••••••••••••••••••••••••••••

2 tablespoons extra-virgin olive oil

½ cup diced yellow onion

1 pound lean ground beef or turkey

1 teaspoon Whole30-compliant chili powder

½ teaspoon onion powder

½ teaspoon garlic powder

½ teaspoon dried oregano

¼ teaspoon smoked paprika

¼ teaspoon ground cumin

¾ teaspoon salt

10 large eggs

¾ cup Whole30-compliant salsa, plus more for serving (optional)

½ teaspoon black pepper

1 avocado, halved, pitted, peeled, and sliced (optional)

Chopped fresh cilantro (optional)

PREHEAT the oven to 350°F.

IN a large skillet, heat 1 tablespoon of the olive oil over medium-high heat. Add the onion and meat. Cook, stirring with a wooden spoon to break up the meat, until browned, about 10 minutes. Add the chili powder, onion powder, garlic powder, oregano, paprika, cumin, and ¼ teaspoon of the salt. Stir and set aside.

CRACK the eggs into a large bowl; whisk until blended. Add the remaining ½ teaspoon salt, the salsa, and the pepper. Stir to combine.

LIGHTLY coat the sides and bottom of a 2-quart baking dish with the remaining 1 tablespoon olive oil. Spread the cooked meat and onion on the bottom of the pan. Pour the egg mixture over the meat. Bake for 30 to 35 minutes, until cooked through (160°F).

LET stand for 10 minutes before serving. Run a knife around the edge of the dish. Cut into squares. To serve, top with avocado slices, salsa, and/or cilantro, if desired.

sheet pan sweet potato hash and eggs

SERVES 8

This dish combines the natural sweetness of sweet potatoes with delectable runny eggs and fresh herbs. It's an entire meal on a single baking pan! Enjoy as is or serve with a simple salad of greens, chopped macadamia nuts or almonds, tomatoes, salt, pepper, and a squeeze of lemon juice.

PREP: 15 MINUTES **ROAST:** 25 MINUTES **TOTAL:** 40 MINUTES

3 large (12- to 16-ounce) sweet potatoes, cut into ½-inch cubes

1 small yellow onion, diced

2 tablespoons extra-virgin olive oil or avocado oil

½ teaspoon salt

¼ teaspoon black pepper

8 large eggs

Chopped fresh parsley or cilantro (optional)

PLACE a rack in the center of the oven. Preheat the oven to 400°F. Line a large rimmed baking pan with parchment paper.

IN a large bowl, combine the sweet potatoes and the onion. Drizzle with the olive oil and sprinkle with the salt and pepper. Toss to coat. Spread the onion and sweet potato cubes in a single layer on the prepared pan.

ROAST for 20 minutes, stirring halfway through. Make eight indentations in the hash and carefully break an egg into each indentation. Roast until the egg whites are set, 5 to 7 minutes more.

TO serve, season to taste and sprinkle with parsley or cilantro, if desired.

pink sunrise mocktail

SERVES 8

This fizzy mocktail is the prettiest shade of pink and made with simple ingredients. While it absolutely looks like a fruity cocktail, it isn't syrupy sweet at all and won't compromise your Whole30 experience. More good news—this recipe will make enough fruit puree for 8 servings so you can whip up a batch when entertaining guests, mix what you need with sparkling water, and refrigerate the remaining puree for later.

PREP: 10 MINUTES **TOTAL:** 10 MINUTES

1 (6-ounce) container fresh raspberries

½ cup peaches, fresh or frozen

⅔ cup fresh orange juice

Whole30-compliant orange-flavored sparkling water

Ice

PLACE the raspberries, peaches, and orange juice in a blender. Cover and blend until smooth.

PLACE a fine-mesh strainer over a large bowl. Pour the fruit mixture into the strainer. Gently press the fruit with the back of a large spoon to remove the seeds. Discard the seeds and pulp.

TO serve, add 3 tablespoons fruit puree and 1 cup sparkling water to each ice-filled glass. Store the fruit puree in an airtight container in the refrigerator for up to 1 week.

basics

basic mayonnaise
clarified butter
whole30 sriracha
cashew cream

basic mayonnaise

MAKES 1½ CUPS

PREP: 10 MINUTES **TOTAL:** 10 MINUTES

1¼ cups light-tasting olive oil

1 large egg, at room temperature (see Tip)

½ teaspoon dry mustard

½ teaspoon salt

Juice of ½ lemon

PLACE ¼ cup of the olive oil, the egg, dry mustard, and salt in a blender, food processor, or mixing bowl. Blend, process, or mix thoroughly. While the food processor or blender is running (or while mixing in a bowl with an immersion blender), slowly drizzle in the remaining 1 cup olive oil until the mayonnaise has emulsified. Add the lemon juice and blend on low or stir to incorporate.

tip: THE KEY TO THIS EMULSION is making sure all the ingredients are at room temperature. Leave your egg out on the counter for an hour, or let it sit in a bowl of hot water for 5 minutes before mixing. Keep one lemon on the counter at all times for the express purpose of making mayo—trust us, you'll be making a lot of this. The slower you add the oil, the thicker and creamer the emulsion will be. You can slowly pour the oil by hand out of a spouted measuring cup, or use a plastic squeeze bottle to slowly drizzle it into the bowl, food processor, or blender. If you're using an immersion blender, pump the stick up and down a few times toward the end to whip some air into the mixture, making it even fluffier.

clarified butter

MAKES 1½ CUPS

Plain old butter isn't allowed on the Whole30 because it contains traces of milk proteins, which may be problematic for dairy-sensitive individuals. Clarifying butter is the technique of simmering butter slowly at a low temperature to separate the milk solids from the pure butterfat. The end result is a delicious, pure, dairy-free fat, perfect for flavoring dishes or cooking (even on high heat).

....

PREP: 5 MINUTES **COOK:** 20 MINUTES
TOTAL: 25 MINUTES

....

1 pound (4 sticks) unsalted butter

CUT the butter into 1-inch cubes. In a small pot or saucepan, melt the butter over medium-low heat and let it come to a simmer without stirring. As the butter simmers, foamy white dairy solids will rise to the surface. With a spoon or ladle, gently skim the dairy solids off the top and discard, leaving just the pure clarified butter in the pan.

ONCE you've removed the majority of the milk solids, strain the butter through cheesecloth into a glass storage jar, discarding the milk solids and cheesecloth when you are done. Allow the butter to cool before storing.

CLARIFIED butter can be stored in the refrigerator for up to 6 months or at room temperature for up to 3 months. (With the milk solids removed, clarified butter is shelf-stable for a longer period of time than regular butter.)

ghee

You'll also see ghee suggested in the recipes—ghee is just a different form of clarified butter. To make ghee, simply simmer the butter longer, until the milk proteins begin to brown, clump, and drift to the bottom of the pan. Ghee has a sweeter, nuttier flavor than clarified butter.

You can also purchase pastured organic ghee online. While it's not part of our official Whole30 rules, we always encourage you to look for pastured organic butter when making your own clarified butter or ghee. Common brands available at health food stores nationwide include Straus, Kerrygold, Kalona SuperNatural, and Organic Valley.

whole30 sriracha

MAKES 1½ CUPS

This spicy condiment has been all the rage for years now, but the bottled stuff contains sugar. This totally compliant version gets a touch of sweetness from a single dried date—so go crazy with it!

PREP: 15 MINUTES **COOK:** 10 MINUTES
TOTAL: 25 MINUTES

1 pound Fresno chiles, seeded and roughly chopped

5 cloves garlic, smashed and peeled

2 tablespoons apple cider vinegar

2 tablespoons Whole30-compliant tomato paste

1 medium dried Medjool date, pitted

2 tablespoons Whole30-compliant fish sauce

½ teaspoon salt

IN a high-power blender (see Tip), combine all the ingredients and process until smooth.

TRANSFER to a small saucepan and bring to a boil. Reduce the heat and simmer, stirring occasionally, for 10 minutes. Taste the sauce and adjust for salt. If the sauce is too thick, add water, 1 tablespoon at a time, until it reaches the desired consistency. Let cool.

USE immediately, or store in an airtight container in the refrigerator for up to 1 week.

tip: IF USING A REGULAR BLENDER, chop the peppers into smaller pieces and mince the garlic for a smoother consistency.

cashew cream

MAKES 2 CUPS

PREP: 10 MINUTES **STAND:** 4 HOURS
TOTAL: 4 HOURS 10 MINUTES

1 cup raw unsalted cashews, rinsed and drained

⅛ teaspoon salt

PLACE the cashews in a medium bowl and add water to cover by 1 inch. Cover the bowl and let stand for 4 hours or up to overnight. Drain the cashews and rinse under cold water. Place the cashews, 1 cup fresh water, and salt in a high-speed blender. Cover and blend until smooth, about 5 minutes. Use immediately or cover and store in an airtight container in the refrigerator for up to 1 week.

whole30 resources

This first part of this resources section includes websites, cookbooks, and social media feeds we really like, from people with whom I have developed close personal relationships. They're smart, talented community members who are Whole30 experts in their own right. They've done the program, offer specific resources for your Whole30 success, and really *get* the spirit and intention of the program.

Not everything in these websites, cookbooks, and social media feeds is Whole30 compliant. They don't eat Whole30 all the time, and as I explain in *The Whole30's Food Freedom Forever*, neither will you. I'm just pointing this out because you have to read website content, recipes, and social media hashtags just as carefully as you have to read labels. Anybody on the Internet can say a meal or ingredient is "#Whole30," but it's your job to determine whether that's actually true.

Unless it's coming from me (the Whole30 website, my books, or our social media feeds), one of our Whole30 Certified Coaches, or one of our Whole30 Endorsed cookbooks, don't take a "Whole30 compliant" label at face value. Read your labels/ingredients/recipes carefully, and when in doubt, leave it out. It's only 30 days.

WEBSITES

Whole30
whole30.com

Home of the official Whole30 program. This is where you'll find the program rules, meal planning help, free recipes, testimonials, our Whole30 forum, Whole30 Approved partners, our Certified Coaches, and more Whole30-related articles than you could possibly read in thirty days.

> Facebook: whole30
> Instagram: @whole30, @whole30recipes, @whole30approved
> Twitter: @whole30
> YouTube: whole30
> Pinterest: @whole30

Whole Mamas
Wholemamasclub.com

Whole Mamas is the daughter site of Whole30, an online platform devoted to supporting you through all stages of motherhood from a Whole30 perspective. We know how hard it can be to find reliable information to gracefully navigate the physical, emotional, and psychological aspects of parenting. Whole Mamas offers current research from leading experts; resources for preconception, pregnancy, postpartum, breastfeeding, and family (including resources for your Whole30 every step of the way); and a Whole Mamas pregnancy video course.

Facebook: wholemamasclub
Instagram: @wholemamasclub
Twitter: @wholemamasclub
Pinterest: @wholemamasclub

No Crumbs Left:
Teri Turner

nocrumbsleft.net

Teri loves cooking for her family and friends and filling her life with food-related adventures, including cooking, writing, researching, appreciating, photographing, and talking about food. She's a master collaborator, blogger, food columnist, regular contributor to Whole30, and editor @thefeedfeed.

Facebook: nocrumbsleft
Instagram: @nocrumbsleft
YouTube: nocrumbsleft
Pinterest: nocrumbsleft

The Whole Smiths:
Michelle Smith

thewholesmiths.com

Michelle Smith is passionate about eating real food and creating a sustainable food system that everyone can enjoy for many years to come. Her recipes focus on minimally processed and sustainable foods that are easy to prepare, taste great, and make us feel good again.

Facebook: thewholesmiths
Instagram: @thewholesmiths
Twitter: @thewholesmiths
Snapchat: @thewholesmiths
Pinterest: thewholesmiths

Danielle Walker
(Against All Grain)

againstallgrain.com

Danielle Walker is a *New York Times* best-selling author and photographer who shares her grain-free and gluten-free recipes on her blog and in her cookbooks, *Against All Grain*, *Meals Made Simple*, *Celebrations*, and *Eat What You Love*. With her acquired culinary skills, love for food, and deeply touching personal story, she is a go-to source for those suffering from all types of diseases and allergies.

Facebook: againstallgrain
Instagram: @daniellewalker
Twitter: @againstallgrain
YouTube: againstallgrain
Pinterest: @againstallgrain

Nom Nom Paleo:
Michelle Tam

nomnompaleo.com

Since 2010, Michelle Tam has been religiously taking pictures of her Whole30 meals and sharing her Whole30 meal plans and recipes. She also penned the *New York Times* best-selling cookbooks *Nom Nom Paleo* and *Ready or Not!*, both of which feature a large number of Whole30-friendly meals.

Facebook: nomnompaleo
Instagram: @nomnompaleo
Twitter: @nomnompaleo
Pinterest: nomnompaleo

Alex Snodgrass
(The Defined Dish)

thedefineddish.com

Alex Snodgrass is a recipe developer, food stylist, and the founder of the popular blog and social media outlet The Defined Dish. Alex was voted as the reader's choice at the *Saveur Magazine* 2018 blog awards in the category of "Most Inspired Weeknight Dinners."

Facebook: thedefinedish
Instagram: @thedefineddish
Twitter: @thedefineddish
YouTube: thedefineddish
Pinterest: @thedefineddish

COOKBOOKS

There are only a handful of books in which 100 percent of the recipes featured are officially Whole30 Approved. You're reading one of them right now—the others are *The Whole30: The 30-Day Guide to Total Health and Food Freedom*, *The Whole30 Cookbook*, *The Whole30 Fast and Easy*, and *The Whole30 Slow Cooker*.

THE HOW-TO FOR THE WHOLE30

Although *The Whole30* features more than 100 delicious and totally compliant recipes, it's more than just a cookbook—it's a complete Whole30 handbook start to finish and includes planning and preparation tips, an extensive FAQ, and Whole30 kitchen basics. If you're loving the recipes in *The Whole30 Friends and Family* but want a game plan to help you maximize your Whole30 success, *The Whole30* is all you'll need.

THE HOW-TO FOR FRIENDS AND FAMILY

While there are no recipes in *The Whole30's Food Freedom Forever*, there are three (count 'em) chapters about talking to friends, family, and coworkers about the Whole30 and your new healthy habits once you complete the program. Combine those strategies for discussion, gaining support, and dealing with pushback with the menus in this book and you have a comprehensive plan for Whole30 success that covers all your bases.

However, there are other cookbooks that feature delicious, Whole30-compliant recipes (either labeled as such or not) or Whole30-friendly recipes that could easily be adapted for compliance. You'll still need to be on the lookout for noncompliant ingredients, however, and save the baked goods, desserts, and treats sections for life after your Whole30.

The Whole Smiths Good Food Cookbook

By Michelle Smith

An official Whole30 Endorsed cookbook featuring 150 recipes (80 of which are Whole30-compliant) to help you prepare delicious, healthy meals during your Whole30 and in your food freedom.

No Crumbs Left

By Teri Turner

One of the toughest things about completing the Whole30 is figuring out what to eat during the other 335 days of the year. Teri Turner, author of this Whole30 Endorsed cookbook, has healthful and great tasting answers in these over 100 recipes, most of which are Whole30-compliant.

The Defined Dish Wholesome Weeknights

(coming January 2020)

By Alex Snodgrass

The third in our series of Whole30 Endorsed cookbooks, *The Defined Dish* offers gluten-free, dairy-free, and grain-free recipes that sound and look way too delicious to be healthy. Each dish is clearly marked for Whole30 compliance, and Alex includes creative variations to ensure recipes can work for almost any diet.

Against All Grain: Meals Made Simple, Celebrations, and Eat What You Like

By Danielle Walker

Danielle's best-selling cookbooks provide grain-free, dairy-free, and Whole30-friendly family meals, quick and easy dinners, and complete holiday and special event menus. (She also offers downloadable PDFs labeling the Whole30-compliant recipes in each of her books!)

Nom Nom Paleo: Food for Humans and Ready or Not: 150+ Make-Ahead, Make-Over, and Make-Now Recipes

By Michelle Tam and Henry Fong

Whether you're a planner or an improviser, these cookbooks feature family-friendly recipes (many of which are Whole30-compliant) and step-by-step instructional photographs for everything from make-ahead feasts to lightning-fast leftover makeovers.

WHOLE30 CERTIFIED COACHES

coach.whole30.com/coaches

Our Whole30 Certified Coaches are a wealth of Whole30 knowledge and expertise. Some have professional credentials (like R.D., M.D., or Ph.D.) that allow them to incorporate the Whole30 into their healthcare practices, while others specialize in Whole30 for families; Whole30 in conjunction with yoga or fitness programs; meal planning and grocery shopping; Whole30 on a budget; Whole30 over 50; and more. Connect with a Whole30 Certified Coach in your area for in-person social support, accountability, resources, and community.

whole30 inspiration

Our special guest contributors to *The Whole30 Friends and Family* have drool-worthy websites, social media feeds, and YouTube channels with hundreds of Whole30-compliant recipes, meal-planning strategies, kitchen tips, family resources, and food freedom guidance to keep you happy and healthy long after your Whole30 journey is over. Again, not everything they create or share is Whole30-compliant; read your recipes carefully, and save sweets and treats for your food freedom.

First and Full:
Marissa Allen
firstandfull.com

Marissa Allen believes in the power of good food to connect people. She creates delicious, approachable recipes using real ingredients to bring family and friends to the dinner table.

Facebook: firstandfull
Instagram: @firstandfull
Pinterest: firstandfull

Physical Kitchness:
Chrissa Benson
physicalkitchness.com

Chrissa Benson is a self-proclaimed "kitchen ninja" with a mission to make healthy eating quicker and easier for busy women. Her recipes are focused on simple, family-friendly meals so you can make healthy living fun and sustainable.

Facebook: physicalkitchness
Instagram: @physicalkitchness
Twitter: @physicalkitch
Pinterest: physicalkitchness

Whole Kitchen Sink:
Bailey Fischer
wholekitchensink.com

Bailey Fischer is a Whole30 Certified Coach, writer, and cookbook author passionate about developing easy recipes that create lifestyle changes through food. Beginning from a need to teach herself to cook real, good-tasting food in ways that didn't stress her limited time or budget, she is now dedicated to helping others find health and healing.

Facebook: wholekitchensink
Instagram: @wholekitchensink
Pinterest: wholekitchensink

Healthy Little Peach:
Ashley McCrary
healthylittlepeach.com

In 2014, the Whole30 program completely transformed Ashley's life and allowed her to successfully fight polyscystic ovarian syndrome (PCOS) and to take back her health.

Now she is passionate about sharing her success story and budget-friendly recipes that the whole family will love. Today, she is a Whole30 Certified Coach and loves supporting and encouraging the Whole30 community with tips, tricks, and free resources.

Instagram: @healthylittlepeach

Little Bits of Real Food: Kelsey Preciado
littlebitsof.com

Kelsey Preciado loves to share real-food recipes perfect for everyone from babies to grown-ups. She wants everyone to find joy in their kitchen and their life, and she finds hers somewhere between baked sweet potato fries and a dance party.

Facebook: littlebitsof
Instagram: @littlebitsof_realfood
Pinterest: littlebitsofrealfood

The Whole Cook: Christina Shoemaker
thewholecook.com

Christina Shoemaker is the creator of *The Whole Cook*, a blog dedicated to real-food recipes made from wholesome ingredients. She credits the Whole30 program with setting her down the path of eating and serving nutrient-dense food to her family. Now she creates easy-to-prepare recipes your whole family can love too!

Facebook: wholecook
Instagram: @thewholecook
Twitter: @thewholecook
Pinterest: thewholecook

Thyme and Joy: Valerie Skinner
thymeandjoy.com

Valerie Skinner is a professionally trained holistic chef who shares healthy recipes and easy cooking tips that make time in the kitchen approachable and fun. Valerie passionately shares her thoughts on attaining a balanced mindset around food, relationships, and lifestyle on her blog, and creates Whole30 Approved meals for her community through her personal chef services.

Facebook: thymeandjoy
Instagram: @thymeandjoy
Pinterest: thymeandjoy

Every Last Bite: Carmen Sturdy
everylastbite.com

Carmen Sturdy is a passionate foodie who created her blog, *Every Last Bite*, after achieving remission from an autoimmune disease through dietary changes. She is now a passionate advocate for healthy eating and showing others that regardless of your dietary restrictions, you can still make delicious meals that won't leave you feeling deprived.

Instagram: @everylastbite_
Facebook: everylastbite1
Pinterest: everylastbite
Twitter: @everylastbite1

Cook by Color Nutrition: Stephanie Vanlochem
cookbycolornutritition

Stephanie Vanlochem (BA, nutritional therapy practitioner, and Whole30 Certified Coach) is the founder of Cook by Color Nutrition, a practice that teaches the power of cooking real food as nourishment for both mind and body. Stephanie believes in eating for both health and pleasure, and helps clients create an individualized, sustainable, colorful lifestyle.

> Facebook: @cookbycolor
> Instagram: @cookbycolor

MEAL PLANNING
Real Plans
w30.co/w30realplans

Delicious, totally compliant Whole30 meals in a weekly plan to fit your taste and schedule. Fully customizable; choose which days of the week and meals to plan, exclude ingredients to which you are allergic or just don't like, prioritize recipes using specific kitchen gadgets like a slow cooker or Instant Pot, and generate an automated shopping list and meal prep instructions for each week. Features more than 1,000 Whole30-compliant recipes to build into your family's perfect weekly meal plan.

HEALTH CARE
SteadyMD
steadymd.com/whole30

No co-pays. No office visits. No waiting. Just 24/7 access to your own personal Whole30 doctor, completely online. For the first time ever, you can now partner with a primary care doctor to support and encourage you during your Whole30 journey and beyond. You'll be able to securely text your doctor for a quick answer or have more in-depth conversations over the phone or video chat. With SteadyMD, you'll get dedicated personal attention without the hassles of a traditional clinic, and true preventative care tailored to your medical needs and lifestyle.

whole30 approved®

This is a list of our official Whole30 Approved partners, with the addition of some Whole30-friendly products from brands we love. These companies make a variety of products to support your Whole30 journey, but in many cases, not every product they make fits our guidelines. Read your labels, or look for the official Whole30 Approved logo on their website or packaging. We add to our list of Whole30 Approved partners every week, so visit whole30.com/whole30-approved for the full roster.

WHOLE30 CURATED KITS

Thrive Market Whole30 Curated Kits (l.thrv.me/whole30-25p1): Whole30 Approved curated kits, "Melissa's Picks" featuring her favorite Whole30 products, and more than 100 compliant pantry staples delivered to your door, all at up to 50 percent off retail. New members get a 30-day free trial and 25 percent off their first order with our affiliate link.

Barefoot Provisions Whole30 Kits (w30.co/w30bpkits): Whole30 Approved curated kits for emergency foods, healthy fats, and pregnancy nutrition, shipped throughout the world, no membership required.

Natura Market Canada Whole30 Kits (w30.co/w30natura): Your Canadian source for Whole30 Approved curated kits and over 100 compliant items delivered to your door.

ON-THE-GO AND TRAVEL FOOD

DNXBar (dnxbar.com/whole30): Six delicious flavors of grass-fed-meat bars packed with organic ingredients to fuel your on-the-go lifestyle.

EPIC (epicbar.com): Grass-fed/pastured jerky bars, bits, and strips, and bacon bites for salads and soups. Most varieties are Whole30 compliant (read your labels).

Chomps Snack Sticks (gochomps.com): Grass-fed and free-range beef, venison, and turkey snack sticks.

Brooklyn Biltong (brooklynbiltong.com): Seasoned, all-natural dried beef snacks.

Nick's Sticks (nicks-sticks.com): 100-percent grass-fed beef and free-range turkey meat snack sticks.

Elements Meals (getyourelements.com): Freeze-dried, whole food meals on the go. Simply add hot water and enjoy.

Seasnax (seasnax.com): Nutrient-packed roasted seaweed sheets in a variety of flavors.

RXBar (rxbar.com): Egg white protein-based bars. Most flavors are Whole30 compliant; read your labels and don't use these as treats, please.

MEAT AND PRODUCE

Applegate (applegate.com/whole30): More than 20 Whole30 Approved natural and organic humanely raised meat products. No antibiotics and no GMO ingredients ever.

Butcherbox (butcherbox.com/whole30): 100-percent grass-fed, grass-finished beef, organic chicken, and heritage breed pork, delivered to your door CSA-style for less than $6.50 per meal.

Tribalí Foods (tribalifoods.com): Organic 100-percent grass-fed beef and chicken patties, plus mini breakfast sliders, made with only real ingredients.

Hungry Harvest (hungryharvest.net): Recovered farm-fresh produce and organic produce, delivered to your door CSA-style in the mid-Atlantic states (and rapidly growing).

U.S. Wellness Meats (grasslandbeef.com): Grass-fed and free-range meats from family farmers, including the first-ever Whole30 Approved sugar-free bacon.

Panorama (panoramameats.com): Grass-fed beef from certified organic family farmers.

Verde Farms (verdefarms.com): Pastured grass-fed beef raised according to strict animal welfare protocols.

Pre Brands (eatpre.com): Always grass-fed, grass-finished and raised with care. Available online, on Amazon, and at select retailers.

Teton Waters Ranch (tetonwatersranch.com): Certified humane, 100-percent grass-fed and finished beef hot dogs, dinner sausages, hamburgers, and breakfast sausages in a variety of flavors.

The Honest Bison (honestbison.com): Grass-fed and humanely raised bison offerings, including soup bones.

Primal Cut Natural Sausages UK (primalcut.co.uk): Primal Cut offers hand-crafted, artisan sausages from free-range pork with no added sugars. Exclusively in the UK.

Pederson's Natural Farms (thesimplegrocer.com): Certified humane and sugar-free bacon, sausages, hot dogs, and ham.

Nature's Rancher (naturesrancher.com): Certified humane, all-natural, nitrate-/nitrite-free pork, beef, poultry, and lamb.

Northstar Bison (northstarbison.com): Bison raised on native grasslands and field harvested for zero stress. Offering a wide variety of meats, shipped nationally.

Naked Bacon (nakedbaconco.com): Sugar-free, nitrate-/nitrite-free, all-natural bacon and breakfast sausage.

Sizzlefish (sizzlefish.com): Online seafood market for hand-selected and perfectly portioned seafood.

Cece's Veggie Noodle Co. (cecesveggieco.com): Fresh, riced veggies from cauliflower and broccoli and raw spiralized veggie noodles made from zucchini, butternut squash, sweet potatoes, and beets.

Serenity Kids Baby Food (myserenitykids.com): Pureed organic vegetables and pastured-raised meat from small American family farms.

NATURAL FATS

Primal Kitchen Avocado Oil and Mayo (primalkitchen.com): Heart-healthy avocado oil and avocado oil-based sugar-free mayonnaise, in original and chipotle flavors.

Tin Star Ghee (tinstarfoods.com): Cultured, handmade pastured ghee and brown butter ghee made from the milk of grass-fed cows.

Pure Indian Foods Ghee (pureindianfoods.com): Grass-fed, organic, non-GMO ghee and cooking oils.

Omghee (omghee.com): Small-batch, grass-fed, organic, non-GMO ghee.

Fatworks (fatworksfoods.com): Traditional handcrafted cooking fats, including tallow (beef, buffalo, and lamb), lard, leaf lard, duck fat, goose fat, and chicken schmaltz.

Georgia Grinders (georgiagrinders.com): Handcrafted, premium almond, cashew, pecan, and hazelnut nut butters made out of simple, all-natural ingredients.

PANTRY STAPLES

Safe Catch (safecatch.com): Wild-caught tuna in cans and pouches, featuring the lowest mercury content of any brand—safe even for pregnant women.

Cucina Antica Pasta Sauces (cucina-antica.com): Cooking sauces made with imported Italian San Marzano tomatoes.

Monte Bene (montebene.com): Pasta sauces made without preservatives, added sugar, gluten, water, or tomato paste.

Organico Bello (organicobello.com): USDA organic- and non-GMO-verified pasta sauces, salsas, and canned tomatoes made with 100-percent imported organic Italian tomatoes.

Lucina Italia (lucini.com): The leading producer of premium Italian extra virgin olive oils, and the creator of organic, Italian-made tomato sauces.

Big Tree Farms Coconut Aminos (bigtreefarms.com): A soy sauce substitute made from brewed and naturally fermented coconut blossom nectar and sea salt.

Red Boat Fish Sauce (redboatfishsauce.com): All-natural, first-press, "extra-virgin" Vietnamese fish sauce made without MSG or preservatives.

Kettle & Fire (kettleandfire.com): Grass-fed, organic beef and chicken bone broth in shelf-stable packaging.

Epic Broth (epicbar.com): The first-ever ready-to-heat pasture-raised and grass-fed beef, chicken, and turkey broth, from their Whole Animal Project.

Bonafide Provisions (bonafideprovisions.com): Organic, grass-fed, pasture-raised chicken and beef bone broth and soups.

Osso Good (ossogoodbones.com): Pasture-raised and grass-fed, all-natural chicken and beef sippable, organic bone broths and soups.

Bare Bones (barebonesbroth.com): Nutritious, pasture-raised, grass-fed, organic chicken and beef bone broths.

Brodo (brodo.com): High-quality ingredients and century-tested craftsmanship create the finest bone broth available. Available online and in four NYC shop locations.

Primal Palate Organic Spices (primalpalate.com): Organic, gluten-free, non-GMO, non-irradiated high-quality spices and spice blends, including an AIP-friendly spice pack.

Paleo Powder Seasonings (paleopowderseasoning.com): All-purpose Paleo, MSG-free, and gluten-free seasonings.

FREEZER AND FRIDGE STAPLES

Great Value Freezer Meals (walmart.com): Available exclusively at Walmart, Whole30 Approved Great Value freezer meals come in eight varieties.

Grandcestors Meals (grandcestors.com): Individual serving sizes of prepared frozen meals with hearty portions.

True Fare (truefare.com): The first Whole30 Approved meal delivery company, with meals now found in the frozen section of select Costco stores.

Primitive Feast (primitivefeast.com): Hearty, flavorful frozen entrees, shipped nationwide.

Medlie Soups (medlie.com): Ready-to-sip nutrient-dense soups containing over four servings of whole, organic vegetables per bottle.

Tio Gazpacho (tiogazpacho.com): Chef-crafted drinkable soups made with super clean non-GMO ingredients.

Farmhouse Culture (farmhouseculture.com): Organic, probiotic-rich krauts, Gut Shots, and vegetables with zingy, zesty flavors.

DRESSINGS AND SAUCES

Noble Made Marinades, Cooking Sauces, and Dressings (thenewprimal.com): Classic, citrus herb, and spicy marinades; five varieties of Buffalo and BBQ sauces for meat and veggies; and four varieties of salad dressings, from The New Primal.

Primal Kitchen Dressings (primalkitchen.com): An extensive variety of avocado oil-based, sugar-free dressings and marinades.

Tessemae's All Natural (tessemaes.com): All-natural and certified organic dressings, sauces, condiments, and marinades from their family to yours.

Organicville (skyvalleyfoods.com): Organic, all-natural, and fully flavored dressings, condiments, sauces, and marinades.

Yai's Thai Sauces (yaisthai.com): Thai-inspired, hand-crafted salsas, sauces, almond sauce, and curry sauces.

Mesa De Vida Cooking Sauces (mesadevida.com): Healthy cooking sauces and flavor bases inspired by vibrant cuisines from around the globe.

Good Food for Good (goodfoodforgood.ca): Organic ketchup, BBQ sauces, and cooking sauces. Available in Canada and on Thrive Market in the US.

BEVERAGES

Waterloo (drinkwaterloo.com): A bold taste on sparkling water, focusing on true-to-fruit flavor and aroma and delivering a rich, authentic taste in 100-percent BPA-free cans.

Spindrift (spindriftfresh.com): Sparkling water made with only real squeezed fruit, water, and bubbles.

Hint Water (drinkhint.com): Pure, unsweetened water infused with truly natural fruit flavors. Available in more than 25 refreshing flavors, in still and sparkling.

LaCroix Water (lacroixwater.com): Sugar- and calorie-free naturally flavored sparkling waters.

Rethink Water (drinkrethinkwater.com): The first-ever zero-sugar, zero-sweetener, zero-calorie, USDA-certified-organic flavored water for kids.

Sound (drinksound.com): Sparkling water infused with organic tea botanicals and fruit extracts. Completely unsweetened and certified organic.

Nutpods (nutpods.com): Unsweetened, carrageenan-free almond and coconut milk coffee creamers in four delicious varieties and seasonal offerings.

New Barn Organics (newbarnorganics.com): Unsweetened almond milk with only four simple, organic ingredients and veggie-based almond dips in a variety of delicious flavors.

Four Sigmatic (foursigmatic.com): Functional mushroom powders to help you relax, be well, reenergize, and be more productive.

MUD\WTR (mudwtr.com): Made with organic, earth-grown ingredients, MUD\WTR is packed with adaptogenic mushroom compounds for optimal health and performance benefits.

Rasa Koffee (wearerasa.com): Three delicious varieties of nourishing, adaptogenic coffee and coffee alternative blends created with great-tasting herbs to provide lasting energy.

LIFESTYLE

Vital Proteins (vitalproteins.com): Pasture-raised collagen peptides and gelatin for healthier skin, nails, and hair; to promote joint and bone health; and to aid in athletic performance.

Mindbodygreen (mindbodygreen.com): Organic sea veggies and antioxidants to balance hormones and blood sugar; organic grass-fed bovine collagen; plus essential nutrients to support beauty, gut health, and inflammation.

Doc Parsley's Sleep Remedy (docparsley.com): Developed by sleep expert Dr. Kirk Parsley, Sleep Remedy aims to lay the foundation for the best sleep possible.

Lyteline Electrolytes (lyteline.com): Healthier hydration products, including a sports drink, electrolytes, and trace minerals.

RESTAURANTS AND MEAL DELIVERY (NATIONAL)

Zoë's Kitchen (zoeskitchen.com): Fresh-made Mediterranean with a robust Whole30 Approved menu in more than 250 locations nationwide.

Snap Kitchen (snapkitchen.com): Fresh prepared meals from scratch, with dozens of Whole30 Approved options. Pick-up, delivery, and subscriptions to weekly Whole30 meal plans.

True Fare (truefare.com): Chef-prepared, seasonal, and organic breakfasts, lunches, dinners, and snacks shipped frozen across the United States.

The Good Kitchen (thegoodkitchen.com): High-quality, fully prepared Whole30 Approved meals shipped nationally. Farm to table in three minutes.

Kettlebell Kitchen (kettlebellkitchen.com): Whole30 meals designed by nutritionists, prepared by chefs, and delivered nationwide.

Paleo on the Go (paleoonthego.com): Hand-crafted, chef-prepared meals with an AIP focus. Shipped frozen and available across the US.

Visit whole30.com/whole30-approved for dozens of local catering, meal delivery, and restaurant options in every region of the U.S.

whole30 support

Resources to give you Whole30 support, motivation, and accountability.

Do the Thing: A Podcast with Melissa Hartwig Urban
whole30.com/podcast

Eating healthier, exercising, setting boundaries, managing your money, recovering from addiction, healing from trauma, eliminating toxic relationships . . . we all have a thing we've been working on, but despite our best intentions, we just can't make it stick. This podcast explores what's been missing every time you've tried to do the thing, so you can finally change the pattern and level up for good.

Whole30 Day by Day: Your Daily Guide to Whole30 Success
whole30.com/daybyday

Advice, tips, hacks, and inspiration to guide you through every day of your Whole30, with guided reflections, dedicated space to track your non-scale victories and Whole30 meals, and daily check-ins to keep you motivated.

Wholesome
whole30.com/wholesome

Our free weekly newsletter filled with Whole30-related advice, tips, recipes, reader stories, discounts, giveaways, and more.

The Whole30 Forum
forum.whole30.com

If you have a question, we can almost guarantee it's been answered. Find those answers, solicit expert advice from our moderators, and get support from fellow Whole30ers on our free forum.

Whole30 Resources
whole30.com/pdf-downloads

Home to a host of helpful PDF downloads (including our shopping list, meal template, label-reading guide, pantry-stocking guide, and more).

Dear Melissa
whole30.com/category/dear-melissa

My own Whole30 (and life after) advice column, where I answer your questions and share from my own experience.

CONNECT WITH MELISSA

I love hearing your stories, answering your questions, giving you my best Whole30 and food freedom advice . . . and tough-loving you when you need it.

Facebook: hartwig.melissa
Instagram: @melissa_hartwig
Twitter: @melissahartwig_

cooking conversions

Metric weights listed here have been slightly rounded to make measuring easier.

Volume

U.S.	METRIC	IMPERIAL
¼ tsp	1.2 ml	
½ tsp	2.5 ml	
1 tsp	5 ml	
½ tbsp (1½ tsp)	7.5 ml	
1 tbsp (3 tsp)	15 ml	
¼ cup (4 tbsp)	60 ml	2 fl oz
⅓ cup (5 tbsp)	75 ml	2½ fl oz
½ cup (8 tbsp)	125 ml	4 fl oz
⅔ cup (10 tbsp)	150 ml	5 fl oz
¾ cup (12 tbsp)	175 ml	6 fl oz
1 cup (16 tbsp)	250 ml	8 fl oz
1¼ cups	300 ml	10 fl oz (½ pint)
1½ cups	350 ml	12 fl oz
2 cups (1 pint)	500 ml	16 fl oz
2½ cups	625 ml	20 fl oz (1 pint)
1 quart	1 liter	32 fl oz

Weight

U.S.	METRIC
¼ oz	7 grams
½ oz	15 g
¾ oz	20 g
1 oz	30 g
8 oz (½ lb)	225 g
12 oz (¾ lb)	340 g
16 oz (1 lb)	455 g
2 lb	900 g
2¼ lb	1 kg

index

NOTE: Page numbers in *italics* indicate photos.

Ahi Tuna and Salmon Poke with Crudités, 270, *271*

Aioli
  Green Onion-Cracked Pepper, Almond-Crusted Onion Rings with, 92, *92*
  Roasted Garlic, "Patatas Bravas" with Cauliflower and, 280

Alcohol, xvi

Aleppo Pepper-Garlic Prosciutto Crisps, 98, *99*

Almond Butter
  -Coconut Bananas, Chilled, *84*, 85
  -Curry Chicken Salad, 22, *23*
  Dressing, Rainbow Mango Slaw with Fresh Herbs and, 106, *107*

Almond-Crusted Onion Rings with Green Onion-Cracked Pepper Aioli, 92, *92*

Angels on Horseback with Grapefruit-Fennel-Radish Relish, 34, *35*

Apple(s)
  -Bacon Bites, 66
  -Mustard Compote, Tangy, Coriander-Crusted Pork Tenderloin with, *32*, 33
  Slices, Prosciutto-Wrapped, 14
  Warm Spiced, with Nutty Coconut Topping, 205

Approved partners and products, 251-55

Apricots, Peaches, and Plums, Grilled, with Charred Green Onion Vinaigrette, 216

Artichoke-Parsley Dip, Hot, with Roasted Fingerling Dippers, 43

Arugula
  Pesto, Beet-Parsnip Fritters with, 40, *41*
  Salad, Fennel, Citrus and, 198, *199*
  Salad, with Roasted Grapes, Beet Noodles, Walnuts, and Orange-Red Wine Vinaigrette, 282, *283*
  -Spinach Breakfast Hash, 231

Asparagus-Chicken Roll-Ups, 59, *59*

Avocado
  Cucumber Bites, Shrimp and, *154*, 155
  -Jicama Topping, Plantain Crostini with, *44*, 45
  Summer Salad, Peach, Cucumber and, with Dill, Mint, and Almonds, 296, *297*
  Whip, Seared Scallops with, 68, *69*

Bacon
  Angels on Horseback with Grapefruit-Fennel-Radish Relish, 34, *35*
  -Apple Bites, 66
  -Herb Mushrooms, 197
  -Nut Snack Mix, Double Peppered, 9
  -Pesto Potato Salad, 20, *21*
  Sofrito Greens with Peppers and, 281
  -Wrapped Stuffed Peppers, 182, *183*
  -Wrapped Sweet Potato Bites, 130, *131*
  -Wrapped Trees with Roasted Red Pepper-Almond Dip, 140, *141*
  -Wrapped Turkey Jalapeño Poppers, 88, *89*

Balsamic Peach-Arugula Salad, 232, *233*

Bananas, Chilled Coconut-Almond Butter, *84*, 85

Barbecue Meatballs, 184

Basic Mayonnaise, 240

Basil-Balsamic Cucumber Bites, 12, *13*

Beef. *See also* Steak
  Peppered, Fajita Bowls, *176*, 177
  Smoky Barbecue Brisket, 226, *227*
  Spanish-Style Surf and Turf, 286, *286*
  Teriyaki, -Cauliflower Rice Cabbage Cups, 50, 51
  Toasts with Caramelized Onions and Horseradish Sauce, *272*, 273

Beet
  Chips, Oven-Roasted, with Caramelized Onion-Chive Dip, 93
  Noodles, Arugula Salad with Roasted Grapes, Walnuts, and Orange-Red Wine Vinaigrette, 282, *283*
  -Parsnip Fritters with Arugula Pesto, 40, *41*

Berry(-ies)
  -Coconut Cream Shots, 102, *103*
  and Grapes, Roasted, with Sesame-Pistachio Crumble, 52, *53*
  -Melon Lemonade, Fizzy, 178

Beverages, Approved, 254-55

BLT Potato Skins, 2, *3*

Botanical extracts, xvii

Brisket, Smoky Barbecue, 226, *227*

Broccoli
  Bacon-Wrapped Trees with Roasted Red Pepper-Almond Dip, 140, *141*

Breakfast Skillet, Sweet Plantain, Sausage, and, 112, *113*
Salad, Creamy Cauliflower and, 184
Brussels/Brussels Sprouts
    and Butternut Squash, Dijon, 67
    Snackable Spicy Garlic, 58
Buffalo Chicken
    Frittata, 230
    Patties, 185
Buffalo Dip, Creamy, 127
Butter, Clarified, xvii, 241
Butternut Squash, Dijon Brussels and, 67

Cabbage Rolls, Mini, 275
Cajun-Rubbed Chicken Wings, 220, *221*
Campfire Grilled Peaches, *116*, 117
Caponata, Grilled, 294
Caramelized Onion-Chive Dip, Oven-Roasted Beet
    Chips with, 93
Cardamom-Ginger Poached Pears, *206*, 207
Carrageenan, xvii
Cashew
    Cream, 242
    Hummus, Roasted Pepper-Garlic, 62
Cauliflower
    and Broccoli Salad, Creamy, 184
    -Garlic Dip, Smoky Roasted, 212, *213*
    "Patatas Bravas" with Roasted Garlic Aioli and, 280
    Rice, Mexican, 159
    Rice-Teriyaki Beef Cabbage Cups, 50, 51
Celery Root Tortillas, Orange and Cumin Pork
    Carnitas in, 160, *161*
Celery Soup, Creamy Roasted Garlic and, 274
Champagne Vinaigrette, Tiny Tomato Salad with, 210,
    211
Charred Green Onion Vinaigrette, Grilled Apricots,
    Peaches, and Plums with, 216
Charred Pepper Steak Tacos with Citrus Chimichurri,
    5
Chicken
    -Asparagus Roll-Ups, 59, *59*
    Burgers, Hawaiian, *80*, 81
    Casserole, Jalapeño Popper, 126
    Cobb Spears, *24*, 25
    Collard Green Enchiladas, Saucy, *156*, 157
    Curried, Drumsticks with Pineapple-Pepper Salsa,
        292, 293
    Frittata, Buffalo, 230
    Grilled Cilantro Shrimp and, 186, *187*

Kabobs, Roasted Garlic-Ranch, 224, *225*
Lime-Garlic Hot Wings with Green Chile Sauce,
    90, 91
Marinated, Pineapple, and Vegetable Foil Packets,
    109
Patties, Buffalo, 185
Peppery Pecan, Drumsticks with Cider Barbecue
    Sauce, 8, *8*
Salad, Almond Butter-Curry, 22, *23*
Salad, Masala-Mango, Lettuce Cups, 46
Salad, Sonoma, 120, *121*
Salad, Sun-Dried Tomato and Basil, with Pepitas,
    114
Tenders, Sub-Lime, with Confetti Ranch, 144, *145*
Wings, Cajun-Rubbed, 220, *221*
Chili-Lime Roasted Zucchini, 78
Chilled Coconut-Almond Butter Bananas, *84*, 85
Chimichurri, Citrus, Charred Pepper Steak Tacos with,
    5
Chipotle Slaw, Crispy Pulled Pork Potato Skins with,
    222, 223
Choco-Vanilla Rooibos Tea, 17
Chorizo Filling, Roasted Turkey Breast with, 202, *203*
Cider Barbecue Sauce, Peppery Pecan Chicken
    Drumsticks with, 8, *8*
Cinnamon
    -Orange Dip, 171
    -Toasted Oranges with Pistachios, 14, *15*
Citrus
    Chimichurri, Charred Pepper Steak Tacos with, 5
    Kale Salad, *70*, 71
    -Pickled Vegetables, 268
    Salad, Arugula, Fennel, and, 198, *199*
Citrusy Watermelon Strawberry Shortcakes, *148*, 149
Clarified Butter, xvii, 241
Cobb Spears, *24*, 25
Coconut
    -Almond Butter Bananas, Chilled, *84*, 85
    Ambrosia Salad, 75
    aminos, xvii
    Cream, Vanilla, 179, *179*
    Cream-Berry Shots, 102, *103*
    Topping, Nutty, Warm Spiced Apples with, 205
Coleslaw
    Piña Colada, 82
    Ranch, 192, *192*
Collard (Greens)
    Enchiladas, Saucy Chicken, *156*, 157
    Roll-Ups, Spicy, with Macadamia Hummus, 47

Confetti Ranch, Sub-Lime Chicken Tenders with, 144, *145*

Converting weights and measures, 257

Coriander-Crusted Pork Tenderloin with Tangy Apple-Mustard Compote, *32*, 33

Crab-Stuffed Mushrooms, 269

Cranberry-Pear Rooibos Iced Tea, *16*, 17

Crazy Water, Fish in, 36

Cream
    Cashew, 242
    Horseradish, Roasted Root Vegetables with, 36
    Vanilla Coconut, Fruit with, 179, *179*

Creamy Buffalo Dip, 127

Creamy Cauliflower and Broccoli Salad, 184

Creamy Roasted Celery and Garlic Soup, 274

Creole Shrimp, 100, *100*

Crisp Prosciutto-Topped Deviled Eggs, *168*, 169

Crispy Pulled Pork Potato Skins with Chipotle Slaw, *222*, 223

Crunchy Asian Noodle Salad, 217

Cucumber
    Bites, Basil-Balsamic, 12, *13*
    Bites, Shrimp and Avocado, *154*, 155
    Cups with Red Curry Shrimp Salad, 42
    -Lime Infused Water, 171
    Summer Salad, Peach, Avocado and, with Dill, Mint, and Almonds, 296, *297*

Curried Chicken Drumsticks with Pineapple-Pepper Salsa, *292*, 293

Dairy, xvi, xvii

Dates, Sweet Potato-Stuffed, Wrapped in Prosciutto, 83, *83*

Desserts, xiii

Deviled Eggs
    Crisp Prosciutto-Topped, *168*, 169
    Pimenton, 285, *286*

Dijon Brussels and Butternut Squash, 67

Dip
    Caramelized Onion-Chive, Oven-Roasted Beet Chips with, 93
    Cinnamon-Orange, 171
    Confetti Ranch, Sub-Lime Chicken Tenders with, 144, *145*
    Creamy Buffalo, 127
    Herb-Garlic, Veggies with, 174
    Hot Artichoke-Parsley, with Roasted Fingerling Dippers, 43
    Layered Mexican, 6

Muhammara, 101, *101*

Roasted Red Pepper-Almond, Bacon-Wrapped Trees with, 140, *141*

Smoky Roasted Cauliflower-Garlic, 212, *213*

Double Peppered Bacon-Nut Snack Mix, 9

Dressing(s)
    Almond Butter, Rainbow Mango Slaw with Fresh Herbs and, 106, *107*
    Approved, 254
    Dijon, Brussels and Butternut Squash, 67
    Green Goddess, Green Bean and Red Potato Salad with Egg and, 295
    Lime-Cilantro, Spicy Mexican Slaw with, 159
    Whole30 Ranch, *132*, 133
    Whole30 Ranch, Zucchini Coins with, 132, *132*

Egg(s)
    Deviled, Crisp Prosciutto-Topped, *168*, 169
    Green Bean and Red Potato Salad with Green Goddess Dressing and, 295
    Pimenton Deviled, 285, *286*
    Sheet Pan Sweet Potato Hash and, *238*, 239
    Turkey Sausage Scotch, 115

Enchiladas, Saucy Chicken Collard Green, *156*, 157

Fajita Bowls, Peppered Beef, *176*, 177

Fall Sangria, 207

Fats, Approved, 252-53

Fennel, Arugula, and Citrus Salad, 198, *199*

Fingerling Potatoes with Parsley Pesto, 74

Fish in Crazy Water, 36

Fizzy Melon-Berry Lemonade, 178

Flower Power Punch, *54*, 55

Food Freedom Forever, xiii

Freezer staples, Approved, 254

Frittata, Buffalo Chicken, 230

Fritters, Beet-Parsnip, with Arugula Pesto, 40, *41*

Fruit
    and RXBAR Kabobs, 193
    Salad, Melon Ball, with Lime, Mint, and Chile, 163
    Salad, with Lemon-Poppy Seed Vinaigrette, *26*, 27
    with Vanilla Coconut Cream, 179, *179*

Fruit juice, xvii

Garlic
    Mayo, Smashed Potatoes with Everything Seasoning and, 7
    -Roasted Lamb, 72, *73*
    Soup, Creamy Roasted Celery and, 274

Ghee, xvii

Ginger-Pineapple Barbecue Sauce, Hot Dog Bites in, 143

Grains, xvi

Grapefruit-Fennel-Radish Relish, Angels on Horseback with, 34, *35*

Grapes
  and Berries, Roasted, with Sesame-Pistachio Crumble, 52, *53*
  Roasted, Arugula Salad with Beet Noodles, Walnuts, and Orange-Red Wine Vinaigrette, 282, *283*

Green Bean(s), xvii
  and Red Potato Salad with Egg and Green Goddess Dressing, 295

Green Chile
  Pulled Pork, *214*, 215
  Sauce, Lime-Garlic Hot Wings with, *90*, 91

Green Goddess Dressing, Green Bean and Red Potato Salad with Egg and, 295

Green Onion-Cracked Pepper Aioli, Almond-Crusted Onion Rings with, 92, *92*

Grilled Apricots, Peaches, and Plums with Charred Green Onion Vinaigrette, 216

Grilled Caponata, 294

Grilled Cilantro Chicken and Shrimp, 186, *187*

Grilled Pineapple, 224

Grilled Steak and Peach Salad, *188*, 189

Guacamole, Jicama Chips with, 79, *79*

Hamburger
  Meatball Kabobs, Mile-High, with Special Sauce, 142, *142*
  Skillet, 122, *123*
  Sliders, Tostones, 190, *191*

Hawaiian Chicken Burgers, *80*, 81

Herb-Garlic
  Butter, Smashed Potatoes with, 204
  Dip, Veggies with, 174

Hibiscus-Cherry Italian Soda, 296

Horseradish
  Cream, Roasted Root Vegetables with, 36
  Sauce, Beef Toasts with Caramelized Onions and, *272*, 273

Hot Artichoke-Parsley Dip with Roasted Fingerling Dippers, 43

Hot Dog Bites in Ginger-Pineapple Barbecue Sauce, 143

Hummus
  Cashew, Roasted Pepper-Garlic, 62
  Macadamia, Spicy Collard Roll-Ups with, 47

Indian-Spiced Lamb Chops with Raita Sauce, 276, *276*

Iodized salt, xvii

Jalapeño Popper(s)
  Bacon-Wrapped Turkey, 88, *89*
  Chicken Casserole, 126

Japanese Sweet Potato Hash, 108

Jicama
  -Avocado Topping, Plantain Crostini with, *44*, 45
  Chips with Guacamole, 79, *79*

Kale
  Chips, Mexican-Style Dino, 146
  Lemon Butter-Garlic Sautéed, 82
  Salad, Citrus, *70*, 71

Lamb
  Chops, Indian-Spiced, with Raita Sauce, 276, *276*
  Garlic-Roasted, 72, *73*

Layered Mexican Dip, 6

Legumes, xvi

Lemon
  Butter-Garlic Sautéed Kale, 82
  -Dill Sauce, Salmon-Sweet Potato Stacks with, *234*, 235
  -Garlic Shrimp Kabobs, *60*, 61
  -Poppy Seed Vinaigrette, Fruit Salad with, *26*, 27

Lemonade, Fizzy Melon-Berry, 178

Lifestyle Approved partners/products, 255

Lime
  -Cilantro Dressing, Spicy Mexican Slaw with, 159
  -Garlic Hot Wings with Green Chile Sauce, *90*, 91

Macadamia Hummus, Spicy Collard Roll-Ups with, 47

Mango
  con chile y limon (Mango with Chile and Lime), 162, *162*
  -Masala Chicken Salad Lettuce Cups, 46
  Slaw, Rainbow, with Almond Butter Dressing and Fresh Herbs, 106, *107*

Marinated Chicken, Pineapple, and Vegetable Foil Packets, 109

Masala-Mango Chicken Salad Lettuce Cups, 46

Mayo(nnaise)
    Basic, 240
    Garlic, Smashed Potatoes with Everything
        Seasoning and, 7
Meal delivery, Approved, 255
Measuring yourself, xvii
Meatballs
    Barbecue, 184
    Meatloaf, 102
Meatloaf Meatballs, 102
Meats, Approved, 252
Melon
    Ball Salad, with Lime, Mint, and Chile, 163
    -Berry Lemonade, Fizzy, 178
Mexican
    Cauliflower Rice, 159
    Dip, Layered, 6
    Slaw, Spicy, with Lime-Cilantro Dressing, 159
    -Style Dino Kale Chips, 146
Mile-High Hamburger Meatball Kabobs with Special
    Sauce, 142, *142*
Milk, Spicy Golden, 37
Mini Cabbage Rolls, 275
Mocktail, Pink Sunrise, 239
Mocktail Mule, 75
MSG, xvii
Muhammara Dip, 101, *101*
Mushrooms
    Bacon-Herb, 197
    Crab-Stuffed, 269

Noodle Salad, Crunchy Asian, 217
Nut-Bacon Snack Mix, Double Peppered, 9
Nutty Coconut Topping, Warm Spiced Apples with,
    205

Olive(s)
    and Pesto-Stuffed Mini Bell Peppers, 70
    Warm Spiced, 197
Onion(s)
    Caramelized, and Horseradish Sauce, Beef Toasts
        with, 272, *273*
    Rings, Almond-Crusted, with Green Onion-
        Cracked Pepper Aioli, 92, *92*
On-the-go food, 251
Orange(s)
    -Cinnamon Dip, 171
    Cinnamon-Toasted, with Pistachios, 14, *15*

and Cumin Pork Carnitas in Celery Root Tortillas,
    160, *161*
    Juliet, 135
    -Red Wine Vinaigrette, Arugula Salad, with
        Roasted Grapes, Beet Noodles, Walnuts, and,
        282, *283*
Oven-Roasted Beet Chips with Caramelized Onion-
    Chive Dip, 93
Oven-to-Grill Baby Back Ribs with Peach-Chipotle
    Sauce, 290, *291*

Pantry staples, Approved, 253
Parsley Pesto, Fingerling Potatoes with, 74
Parsnip-Beet Fritters with Arugula Pesto, 40, *41*
"Patatas Bravas" with Cauliflower and Roasted Garlic
    Aioli, 280
Peach(es)
    Campfire Grilled, *116*, 117
    -Chipotle Sauce, Oven-to-Grill Baby Back Ribs
        with, 290, *291*
    Grilled, Apricots, Plums and, with Charred Green
        Onion Vinaigrette, 216
    Salad, Grilled Steak and, *188*, 189
    Summer Salad, Cucumber, Avocado and, with Dill,
        Mint, and Almonds, 296, *297*
    Tea, 193
Pear(s)
    Cardamom-Ginger Poached, *206*, 207
    -Cranberry Rooibos Iced Tea, *16*, 17
Pecans, Smoky, 196
Pepper(s)
    Bacon-Wrapped Stuffed, 182, *183*
    Mini Bell, Olive- and Pesto-Stuffed, 70
    -Pineapple Salsa, Curried Chicken Drumsticks
        with, *292*, 293
    Sofrito Greens with Bacon and, 281
Peppered Beef Fajita Bowls, *176*, 177
Peppery Pecan Chicken Drumsticks with Cider
    Barbecue Sauce, 8, *8*
Pesto
    Arugula, Beet-Parsnip Fritters with, 40, *41*
    -Bacon Potato Salad, 20, *21*
    and Olive-Stuffed Mini Bell Peppers, 70
    Parsley, Fingerling Potatoes with, 74
Pimenton Deviled Eggs, 285, *286*
Piña Colada Coleslaw, 82
Pineapple
    -Ginger Barbecue Sauce, Hot Dog Bites in, 143
    Grilled, 224

Marinated Chicken, and Vegetable Foil Packets, 109
-Pepper Salsa, Curried Chicken Drumsticks with, *292*, 293
Spritzer, Sparkling, 85
Pink Sunrise Mocktail, 239
Pistachio(s)
Cinnamon-Toasted Oranges with, 14, *15*
-Sesame Crumble, Roasted Berries and Grapes with, 52, *53*
Pizza Bites, Zoodle Sausage-Pepper, 138, *139*
Plantain
Crisps, Tuna Ceviche with, 158
Crostini, with Avocado-Jicama Topping, *44*, 45
Planter's Punch, 277
Plums, Apricots, and Peaches, Grilled, with Charred Green Onion Vinaigrette, 216
Pork
Carnitas, Orange and Cumin, in Celery Root Tortillas, 160, *161*
Chili Verde, *124*, 125
Crispy Pulled, Potato Skins, with Chipotle Slaw, *222*, 223
Green Chile Pulled, *214*, 215
Oven-to-Grill Baby Back Ribs with Peach-Chipotle Sauce, 290, *291*
Tenderloin, Coriander-Crusted, with Tangy Apple-Mustard Compote, *32*, 33
Potato(es)
Fingerling, with Parsley Pesto, 74
"Patatas Bravas" with Cauliflower and Roasted Garlic Aioli, 280
Red, Salad, Green Bean and, with Egg and Green Goddess Dressing, 295
Roasted Fingerling Dippers, Hot Artichoke-Parsley Dip with, 43
Salad, Pesto-Bacon, 20, *21*
-Sausage Breakfast Bites, 175, *175*
Skillet Breakfast, 231
Skins, BLT, 2, *3*
Skins, Crispy Pulled Pork, with Chipotle Slaw, *222*, 223
Smashed, with Everything Seasoning and Garlic Mayo, 7
Smashed, with Herb-Garlic Butter, 204
Produce, Approved, 252
Prosciutto
Crisps, Aleppo Pepper-Garlic, 98, *99*
Sweet Potato-Stuffed Dates Wrapped in, 83, *83*

-Topped Deviled Eggs, *168*, 169
-Wrapped Apple Slices, 14
Pumpkin
Power Bites, Spicy, 63, *63*
-Spiced Sweet Potatoes, 178
Punch
Flower Power, *54*, 55
Planter's, 277
Raspberry-Lime Sparkling, 146, *147*

Rainbow Mango Slaw with Almond Butter Dressing and Fresh Herbs, 106, *107*
Ranch Coleslaw, 192, *192*
Raspberry-Lime Sparkling Punch, 146, *147*
Re-creating unapproved foods, xvii
Red Curry Shrimp Salad, Cucumber Cups with, 42
Red Zinger Tonic, 287
Refrigerator staples, Approved, 254
Relish, Grapefruit-Fennel-Radish, Angels on Horseback with, 34, *35*
Restaurants, Approved, 255
Roasted Berries and Grapes with Sesame-Pistachio Crumble, 52, *53*
Roasted Garlic Aioli, "Patatas Bravas" with Cauliflower and, 280
Roasted Garlic-Ranch Chicken Kabobs, 224, *225*
Roasted Pepper-Garlic Cashew Hummus, 62
Roasted Red Pepper-Almond Dip, Bacon-Wrapped Trees with, 140, *141*
Roasted Root Vegetables with Horseradish Cream, 36
Roasted Sweet Potato Soup, *200*, 201
Roasted Turkey Breast with Chorizo Filling, 202, *203*
Root Vegetables, Roasted, with Horseradish Cream, 36
RXBAR, and Fruit Kabobs, 193

Salad
Almond Butter-Curry Chicken, 22, *23*
Arugula, Fennel, and Citrus, 198, *199*
Arugula, with Roasted Grapes, Beet Noodles, Walnuts, and Orange-Red Wine Vinaigrette, 282, *283*
Citrus Kale, *70*, 71
Coconut Ambrosia, 75
Crunchy Asian Noodle, 217
Fruit, with Lemon-Poppy Seed Vinaigrette, *26*, 27
Grilled Steak and Peach, *188*, 189
Summer Peach, Cucumber, and Avocado, with Dill, Mint, and Almonds, 296, *297*
Tiny Tomato, with Champagne Vinaigrette, 210, *211*

Salmon
 and Ahi Tuna Poke with Crudités, 270, *271*
 Rillettes, Smoky, with Caramelized Shallots, *48*, 49
 -Sweet Potato Stacks with Lemon-Dill Sauce, *234*, 235
Salt, xvii
Sangria, Fall, 207
Sauce(s)
 Approved partners/products, 254
 Cider Barbecue, Peppery Pecan Chicken Drumsticks with, 8, *8*
 Green Chile, Lime-Garlic Hot Wings with, *90*, 91
 Horseradish, Beef Toasts with Caramelized Onions and, *272*, 273
 Lemon-Dill, Salmon-Sweet Potato Stacks with, *234*, 235
 Peach-Chipotle, Oven-to-Grill Baby Back Ribs with, 290, *291*
 Pineapple-Ginger Barbecue, Hot Dog Bites in, 143
 Special, Mile-High Hamburger Meatball Kabobs with, 142, *142*
Saucy Chicken Collard Green Enchiladas, *156*, 157
Sauerkraut-and-Sausage-Loaded Sweet Potatoes, 94, *95*
Sausage
 -and-Sauerkraut-Loaded Sweet Potatoes, 94, *95*
 -Pepper Zoodle Pizza Bites, 138, *139*
 -Potato Breakfast Bites, 175, *175*
 Sweet Plantain, and Broccoli Breakfast Skillet, 112, *113*
 Turkey, Scotch Eggs, 115
Sautéed Snap Peas with Lemon and Tarragon, 30, *31*
Scallops
 Angels on Horseback with Grapefruit-Fennel-Radish Relish, 34, *35*
 Seared, with Avocado Whip, 68, *69*
Sesame-Pistachio Crumble, Roasted Berries and Grapes with, 52, *53*
Shallots, Caramelized, Smoky Salmon Rillettes with, *48*, 49
Sheet Pan Sweet Potato Hash and Eggs, *238*, 239
Shrimp
 and Avocado Cucumber Bites, *154*, 155
 Creole, 100, *100*
 Grilled Cilantro Chicken and, 186, *187*
 Kabobs, Lemon-Garlic, *60*, 61
 Salad, Red Curry, Cucumber Cups with, 42
 Spanish-Style Surf and Turf, 286, *286*
Skillet Breakfast Potatoes, 231

Smashed Potatoes
 with Everything Seasoning and Garlic Mayo, 7
 with Herb-Garlic Butter, 204
Smoky Barbecue Brisket, 226, *227*
Smoky Pecans, 196
Smoky Roasted Cauliflower-Garlic Dip, 212, *213*
Smoky Salmon Rillettes with Caramelized Shallots, *48*, 49
Snackable Spicy Garlic Brussels Sprouts, 58
Snack Mix
 Double Peppered Bacon-Nut, 9
 Sweet and Savory, 133
Snap Peas, xvii
 Sautéed, with Lemon and Tarragon, 30, *31*
Snow peas, xvii
Social situations, xii-xiii
Soda, Hibiscus-Cherry Italian, 296
Sofrito Greens with Bacon and Peppers, 281
Sonoma Chicken Salad, 120, *121*
Soup
 Creamy Roasted Celery and Garlic, 274
 Roasted Sweet Potato, *200*, 201
Spanish-Style Surf and Turf, 286, *286*
Sparkling Lemon Iced Tea, 27
Sparkling Pineapple Spritzer, 85
Special Sauce, Mile-High Hamburger Meatball Kabobs with, 142, *142*
Spicy Collard Roll-Ups with Macadamia Hummus, 47
Spicy Golden Milk, 37
Spicy Mexican Slaw with Lime-Cilantro Dressing, 159
Spicy Pumpkin Power Bites, 63, *63*
Spinach-Arugula Breakfast Hash, 231
Sriracha, Whole30, 242
Staples, Approved, 253-54
Steak
 Charred Pepper, Tacos with Citrus Chimichurri, 5
 Fajitas Foil Packets, *110*, 111
 and Peach Salad, Grilled, *188*, 189
Strawberry Shortcakes, Citrusy Watermelon, *148*, 149
Sub-Lime Chicken Tenders with Confetti Ranch, 144, *145*
Sugar, xvi
Sulfites, xvii
Summer Peach, Cucumber, and Avocado Salad with Dill, Mint, and Almonds, 296, *297*
Sun-Dried Tomato and Basil Chicken Salad with Pepitas, 114
Sweet and Savory Snack Mix, 133

Sweet Plantain, Sausage, and Broccoli Breakfast
Skillet, 112, *113*
Sweet Potato(es)
Bites, Bacon-Wrapped, 130, *131*
Hash, Japanese, 108
Hash and Eggs, Sheet Pan, *238,* 239
Pumpkin-Spiced, 178
Roasted, Soup, *200,* 201
-Salmon Stacks with Lemon-Dill Sauce, *234,* 235
Sausage-and-Sauerkraut-Loaded, 94, *95*
-Stuffed Dates Wrapped in Prosciutto, 83, *83*

Taco(s)
Breakfast Casserole, 236, *237*
Charred Pepper Steak, with Citrus Chimichurri, 5
Walking, 134, *134*
Tea
Choco-Vanilla Rooibos, 17
Iced, Cranberry-Pear Rooibos, *16,* 17
Iced, Sparkling Lemon, 27
Peach, 193
Teriyaki Beef-Cauliflower Rice Cabbage Cups, 50, 51
Tiny Tomato Salad with Champagne Vinaigrette, 210,
211
Tomato
Gazpacho Shots, 152, *153*
Tiny, Salad, with Champagne Vinaigrette, 210, *211*
Tortillas, Celery Root, Orange and Cumin Pork
Carnitas in, 160, *161*
Tostones Hamburger Sliders, 190, *191*
Travel food, 251
Tuna
Ahi, and Salmon Poke with Crudités, 270, *271*
Ceviche with Plantain Crisps, 158
Lettuce Wraps, Spicy, 166, *167*
Turkey
Breast, Roasted, with Chorizo Filling, 202, *203*
Jalapeño Poppers, Bacon-Wrapped, 88, *89*
Sausage Scotch Eggs, 115

Vanilla Coconut Cream, Fruit with, 179, *179*
Vegetables, Citrus-Pickled, 268
Veggies with Herb-Garlic Dip, 174
Vinaigrette
Champagne, Tiny Tomato Salad with, 210, *211*
Charred Green Onion, Grilled Apricots, Peaches,
and Plums with, 216
Lemon-Poppy Seed, Fruit Salad with, *26,* 27
Orange-Red Wine, Arugula Salad, with Roasted
Grapes, Beet Noodles, Walnuts, and, 282, *283*
Vinegar, xvii

Walking Tacos, 134, *134*
Warm Spiced Apples with Nutty Coconut Topping,
205
Warm Spiced Olives, 197
Water, Cucumber-Lime Infused, 171
Watermelon
and Lime Sparkling Refresher, 163
Strawberry Shortcakes, Citrusy, *148,* 149
Weighing yourself, xvii, xxi
Whole30, xiv-xv
Approved partners and products, 251-55
getting started with, xix-xxi
information resources for, 244-47
inspiration for, 248-50
rules for, xvi-xviii
support resources for, 256
Whole30 Curated Kits, 251
Whole30 Ranch Dressing, *132,* 133
Zucchini Coins with, 132, *132*
Whole30 Sriracha, 242

Zoodle Sausage-Pepper Pizza Bites, 138, *139*
Zucchini
Chili-Lime Roasted, 78
Coins, with Whole30 Ranch Dressing, 132, *132*
Zoodle Sausage-Pepper Pizza Bites, 138, *139*

new year's eve

So many people start their Whole30 on January 1st groggy, headache-y, and craving sugar thanks to their New Year's Eve festivities. WHY? New Year's is an end *and* a beginning, so start the new year right by celebrating in a way that honors your health commitments and goals. (I didn't have a sip of alcohol this past holiday season, and I enjoyed the festivities even more because I felt clear-headed, energetic, and *free*.) You won't even miss the champagne because this menu is a celebration on its own. It's astonishingly elegant—classic old-school dishes such as roast beef with horseradish sauce and crab-stuffed mushrooms—with fresh and modern twists.

....

citrus-pickled vegetables

crab-stuffed mushrooms

**ahi tuna and salmon
poke with crudités**

**beef toasts with caramelized
onions and horseradish sauce**

creamy roasted celery and garlic soup

mini cabbage rolls

**indian-spiced lamb chops
with raita sauce**

planter's punch

happy new year!

Lots OF PEOPLE ARE SOBER-CURIOUS these days (or just plain sober), and will appreciate a "zero-proof" celebration environment. Entice friends with a few mentions of what's on the menu, and plan a follow-up fun activity for New Year's Day. (Attendance will be high, as no one will have to "sleep it off.")

As THE SIGNATURE MOCKTAIL FOR THE EVENING, the Planter's Punch knocks it out of the park. If you want to clink glasses at midnight with something bubbly, consider serving chilled Spindrift (sparkling water with a touch of real fruit juice) in champagne flutes.

YOU DON'T NEED ALCOHOL TO SNAP FUN PICTURES, and best of all, you won't regret seeing them on social media the next day. Provide guests with photo booth props—handlebar mustaches and hot lips on sticks, silly hats, and glasses—for even more fun.

USE THE INVITATIONS to mention you're starting the Whole30 a little bit early, and ask if anyone wants to join you. There's fun in numbers, and kicking off your New Year's together like this sets a fantastic intention for the whole new year.

citrus-pickled vegetables

SERVES 10

These mildly spicy pickled veggies provide a splash of color on the appetizer buffet and a palate-cleansing break from the heavier foods of the holiday season.

....

PREP: 20 MINUTES **CHILL:** 2 HOURS
TOTAL: 2 HOURS 20 MINUTES

....

Grated zest and juice of 1 lime

Grated zest and juice of ½ lemon

2 tablespoons fresh orange juice

1 teaspoon coconut aminos

1 teaspoon Whole30-compliant fish sauce

3 tablespoons rice vinegar

2 tablespoons minced fresh cilantro

¼ teaspoon salt

¼ teaspoon red pepper flakes

10 asparagus spears, ends trimmed, cut into 2-inch pieces

5 radishes, trimmed and cubed

1 medium cucumber, peeled and cut into ¼-inch slices

2 medium carrots, peeled and cut diagonally into ¼-inch slices

IN a large resealable plastic bag, combine the lime zest and juice, lemon zest and juice, orange juice, coconut aminos, fish sauce, vinegar, cilantro, salt, and red pepper flakes. Add the asparagus, radishes, cucumber, and carrots. Seal the bag; chill for 2 hours.

DRAIN the vegetables in a colander. To serve, arrange on a serving platter.

crab-stuffed mushrooms

SERVES 10

Reducing the balsamic vinegar intensifies the flavor and gives it a syrupy consistency, which helps the drizzle cling to the mushrooms and the filling.

PREP: 20 MINUTES **COOK:** 5 MINUTES
BAKE: 20 MINUTES **TOTAL:** 45 MINUTES

20 (1½- to 2-inches wide) baby portobello mushrooms

3 tablespoons Clarified Butter (page 241) or ghee

3 cloves garlic, minced

¾ teaspoon dried thyme

¼ teaspoon salt

¼ teaspoon black pepper

1½ tablespoons finely chopped green onions

⅔ cup finely chopped lump crab meat

1 tablespoon tapioca flour

3 tablespoons finely chopped walnuts

¼ cup balsamic vinegar

2 tablespoons minced fresh parsley

PREHEAT the oven to 375°F.

REMOVE and reserve the stems from the mushrooms. Use a small spoon to remove the mushroom gills. Finely mince the stems to make ½ cup. Discard the remaining stems. Use a damp paper towel to wipe the mushrooms clean.

IN a large nonstick skillet, melt 1 tablespoon butter over medium-high heat. Add the chopped stems, garlic, thyme, salt, and pepper. Cook, until the stems are tender, 3 to 5 minutes. Remove from the heat and place in a medium bowl. Stir in the green onions, crab meat, and tapioca flour.

IN a small glass bowl, melt the remaining 2 tablespoons butter in the microwave. Pour into a 9 × 13-inch baking dish; tilt to coat the bottom. Fill the mushroom caps with the crab filling and arrange in the baking dish. Sprinkle the filling with walnuts. Bake for 20 to 25 minutes, until the filling is heated through.

MEANWHILE, in a saucepan, bring the vinegar to a boil over medium-high heat; reduce heat. Simmer, until the vinegar is reduced by half, 3 to 4 minutes. Remove from the heat and let cool.

TO serve, arrange the mushrooms on a serving platter. Sprinkle with the parsley and drizzle with the reduced vinegar.

ahi tuna and salmon poke with crudités

SERVES 10

Poke (*POH-keh*)—a native Hawaiian specialty that features diced raw sushi-grade fish that's seasoned with soy and/or fish sauce, chile, sesame, green onions, and salt—has taken the mainland by storm in the last few years. It makes an elegant appetizer for a New Year's gathering.

....

PREP: 30 MINUTES   **CHILL:** 30 MINUTES
TOTAL: 60 MINUTES

....

8 ounces sushi-grade Ahi tuna,
cut into ¼-inch dice

8 ounces sushi-grade fresh salmon,
cut into ¼-inch dice

½ medium cucumber, peeled
and cut into ¼-inch dice

1 serrano chile, seeded and minced

3 green onions, thinly sliced

¼ cup coconut aminos

1 tablespoon sesame oil

½ teaspoon Whole30 compliant fish sauce

½ teaspoon sesame seeds, toasted (see Tip)

½ teaspoon black sesame seeds

½ teaspoon salt

¼ teaspoon black pepper

1 cucumber, peeled and diced

1 daikon radish, peeled and sliced into matchsticks

1 green bell pepper, sliced into matchsticks

1 large carrot, peeled and sliced into matchsticks

20 (2-ounce) shooter glasses or cups

IN a large bowl, combine the tuna, salmon, cucumber, serrano, and green onions. Set aside.

IN a small bowl, stir together the coconut aminos, sesame oil, fish sauce, sesame seeds, salt, and pepper. Pour over the fish; stir to combine. Place the bowl in a shallow pan filled with ice and chill for 30 minutes.

TO serve, spoon 1½ tablespoons of the poke into each glass. Arrange the glasses and vegetables on serving platters.

tip: To TOAST THE SESAME SEEDS, heat in a dry skillet over medium heat, stirring, until fragrant and lightly browned, about 2 minutes.

beef toasts with caramelized onions and horseradish sauce

SERVES 10

The "toasts" for these compliant canapés are thin slices of crisp-roasted potatoes—a perfect pairing with grilled strip steak, sweet caramelized onions, and heady horseradish sauce.

PREP: 25 MINUTES   **BAKE:** 30 MINUTES
COOK: 20 MINUTES   **TOTAL:** 1 HOUR 15 MINUTES

FOR THE POTATOES

5 (2- to 3-inch-wide) Yukon Gold potatoes, cut into ¼-inch slices (20 slices total)

2 tablespoons extra-virgin olive oil

¼ teaspoon garlic powder

¼ teaspoon salt

¼ teaspoon black pepper

FOR THE ONIONS

2 tablespoons extra-virgin olive oil

1 large yellow onion, thinly sliced (see Tip)

¼ teaspoon salt

¼ teaspoon black pepper

FOR THE HORSERADISH SAUCE

¾ cup Whole30-compliant coconut milk (see Tip)

2 teaspoons Whole30-compliant prepared horseradish

1½ teaspoons fresh lemon juice

1½ teaspoons tamarind paste

¼ teaspoon salt

¼ teaspoon black pepper

FOR THE STEAK

1 tablespoon Whole30-compliant steak and burger seasoning

1 pound New York strip steak

3 tablespoons chopped fresh chives

MAKE THE POTATOES: Preheat the oven to 425°F. Line a large rimmed baking pan with parchment paper or foil. Place the potato slices on the baking pan. In a small bowl, stir together the olive oil, garlic powder, salt, and pepper. Brush both sides of the potato slices with the oil mixture. Bake for 30 to 35 minutes, turning once halfway through, or until the potatoes are golden brown on both sides. Keep warm until serving.

MAKE THE ONIONS: Heat the olive oil over medium heat in a large nonstick skillet. Add the onion, salt, and pepper. Reduce the heat to medium-low and cook, stirring frequently, until tender and golden, 20 to 25 minutes.

MAKE THE HORSERADISH SAUCE: In a small bowl, stir together the coconut milk, horseradish, lemon juice, tamarind paste, salt, and pepper until smooth. Set aside.

MAKE THE STEAK: Preheat the grill to medium-high. Season both sides of the steak with the steak seasoning. Grill, turning once, until an instant-read thermometer reaches 145°F for medium doneness, 8 to 10 minutes. Tent the steak with foil for 3 minutes before thinly slicing.

TO serve, arrange the potato slices on a large serving platter. Top with the beef slices and onions. Drizzle each beef toast with about 1 teaspoon of the horseradish sauce. Sprinkle with the chives. Hold on a warming plate or serve immediately.

tips: A MANDOLINE set at ⅛ inch makes quick work of thinly slicing the onion.

CANNED COCONUT MILK SEPARATES IN THE CAN, with the cream rising to the top. Make sure to whisk the coconut milk well before measuring.

creamy roasted celery and garlic soup

SERVES 10

Celery root—also called celeriac—is a gnarly looking and highly underappreciated vegetable. When cooked and pureed with broth, it creates a delightfully creamy soup with a mild celery flavor.

PREP: 25 MINUTES   **ROAST:** 25 MINUTES
COOK: 10 MINUTES   **TOTAL:** 60 MINUTES

1 small yellow onion, diced

1 large celery root, peeled and chopped

3 stalks celery, chopped

1 (10-ounce) package cauliflower florets (about 3 cups)

¼ cup extra-virgin olive oil, plus more for garnish

¾ teaspoon salt

½ teaspoon ground white pepper

1 head garlic

4 cups Whole30-compliant vegetable broth

2 tablespoons fresh lemon juice

Pomegranate arils for garnish

PREHEAT the oven to 450°F. Line a large rimmed baking pan with parchment paper.

ARRANGE the onion, celery root, celery, and cauliflower in a single layer on the baking pan. Drizzle with 3 tablespoons of the olive oil. Sprinkle with ¼ teaspoon salt and ¼ teaspoon white pepper. Set aside.

SLICE ¼-inch off the top of the garlic, exposing the cloves, and place in a 4-inch square piece of foil. Drizzle with the remaining 1 tablespoon olive oil; fold up the sides and seal. Place on the baking pan along with the vegetables. Roast, stirring halfway through, until the vegetables are tender, 25 to 30 minutes.

IN a large pot, bring the vegetable broth and 1 cup water to a boil over medium-high heat. Add the roasted vegetables. Squeeze the garlic cloves into the pot. Boil for 2 minutes. Add the remaining ½ teaspoon salt, remaining ¼ teaspoon white pepper, and lemon juice.

CAREFULLY transfer the soup to a blender, in batches, and let cool briefly. Pulse a few times, then blend until smooth, adding additional water if necessary to desired consistency. (Or use an immersion blender to blend the soup directly in the pot.)

TOP each serving with a few pomegranate arils and drizzle with olive oil.

mini cabbage rolls

SERVES 10

Cabbage rolls in tomato sauce—a classic old-school supper—are shrunk down to appetizer size in this recipe. Instead of green cabbage, delicate leaves of napa cabbage hold the pork, mushroom, and potato filling flavored with garlic, dill, marjoram, and thyme.

....

PREP: 25 MINUTES   **COOK:** 2 MINUTES
BAKE: 40 MINUTES   **TOTAL:** 1 HOUR 7 MINUTES

....

20 large napa cabbage leaves (from 2 large heads)

¾ pound ground pork

1 cup finely chopped mushrooms

1 cup Whole30-compliant hash browns, thawed if frozen

6 cloves garlic, minced

1¼ teaspoons dried dill

½ teaspoon dried marjoram

1 teaspoon dried thyme

1 teaspoon salt

1 teaspoon black pepper

1 (14.5-ounce) can Whole30-compliant crushed tomatoes

2 cups Whole30-compliant vegetable broth

PREHEAT the oven to 375°F.

BRING a large pot of water to a boil. Prepare a large bowl of ice water. Place half of the cabbage leaves in the boiling water to cook for 1 minute; transfer to the ice water. Let stand 2 minutes. Drain well and pat leaves dry with a paper towel. Repeat with the remaining leaves.

IN a large bowl, combine the pork, mushrooms, hash browns, garlic, ¼ teaspoon dill, marjoram, ½ teaspoon thyme, ½ teaspoon salt, and ½ teaspoon pepper. Mix well.

FOR each cabbage roll, place a leaf on a clean work surface. Spoon about 2 tablespoons of the filling in the center of the leaf. Fold the top of the leaf over the meat. Fold in the sides and roll tightly to the bottom of the leaf. Place, seam side down, in a 9 × 13-inch baking pan.

IN a medium bowl, stir together the tomatoes, broth, and the remaining 1 teaspoon dill, ½ teaspoon thyme, ½ teaspoon salt, and ½ teaspoon pepper. Pour the tomato mixture over the cabbage rolls. Bake, uncovered, until the cabbage rolls are cooked through (160°F), 40 to 50 minutes.

indian-spiced lamb chops with raita sauce

SERVES 10

"Frenching" a chop refers to scraping the meat, fat, and other tissue from the end of the rib bone to expose it and create a clean, aesthetically pleasing presentation. It also provides a handy and perfectly acceptable way to eat these tasty "lollipop" lamb chops—simply picking them up by the bone and nibbling away.

PREP: 20 MINUTES **CHILL:** 30 MINUTES
COOK: 5 MINUTES **TOTAL:** 1 HOUR

1 medium cucumber, peeled and shredded (about ½ cup)

1 cup Basic Mayonnaise (page 240) or Whole30-compliant mayonnaise

½ cup fresh lemon juice

2 tablespoons chopped fresh mint

2 tablespoons fresh dill

3 cloves garlic, minced

1 teaspoon salt

1 teaspoon black pepper

2 teaspoons smoked paprika

1 teaspoon garlic powder

1 teaspoon onion powder

1 teaspoon ground cumin

½ teaspoon ground allspice

½ teaspoon ground coriander

½ teaspoon ground turmeric

20 frenched lamb rib chops

¼ cup extra-virgin olive oil

⅓ cup chopped fresh parsley

PRESS the shredded cucumber between paper towels to remove excess liquid; place in a medium bowl. Stir in the mayonnaise, 3 tablespoons lemon juice, mint, dill, garlic, and ¼ teaspoon salt. Cover and refrigerate until ready to serve.

IN a small bowl, stir together the remaining ¾ teaspoon salt and the black pepper, paprika, garlic powder, onion powder, cumin, allspice, coriander, and turmeric. Season both sides of the lamb chops with the spice mixture.

COMBINE the olive oil, remaining 5 tablespoons lemon juice, and parsley in a 9 × 13-inch baking dish. Add the lamb chops and turn to coat. Cover and marinate in the refrigerator for at least 30 minutes.

PREHEAT the grill to medium-high. Grill the lamb chops, turning once halfway through, until 145°F (medium), 5 to 7 minutes.

TRANSFER to a serving platter; tent with foil and let rest for 3 minutes. Serve with raita sauce.

planter's punch

SERVES 10

The recipe for traditional Planter's Punch was created in the rum-rich Caribbean—probably Jamaica—centuries ago and since then has been stirred up in countless iterations. While this cinnamon and star anise–infused libation isn't traditional, it is absolutely delicious.

PREP: 10 MINUTES   COOK: 5 MINUTES   STAND: 10 MINUTES
CHILL: 30 MINUTES   TOTAL: 55 MINUTES

1 cup black cherry juice

2 cinnamon sticks

2 star anise

1 medium orange, thinly sliced

1 medium blood orange, thinly sliced

1 lemon, thinly sliced

1 (8-ounce) can pineapple chunks in juice, undrained

1 bottle (2 liters) Whole30-compliant sparkling water, chilled

Ice

IN a medium saucepan, bring the cherry juice, cinnamon sticks, and star anise to a boil over medium-high heat. Reduce the heat and simmer 2 minutes. Remove from the heat and let cool for 10 minutes. Remove and discard the cinnamon sticks and star anise.

MEANWHILE, place the oranges, lemon, and pineapple in a 3- to 4-quart pitcher. Add 6 cups of the seltzer water. Once cool, add the cherry juice. Chill in the refrigerator for 30 minutes.

TO serve, remove and discard the fruit. Pour the punch into ice-filled cocktail glasses. Top with a splash of sparkling water.

valentine's day date night

Valentine's Day at a restaurant can be tough even when you're not on the Whole30. Reservations are hard to get, menus are overpriced, and there's so much pressure to spring for the wine/caviar/truffles. Why not stay in and make a romantic meal together? This Spanish-themed menu starts with smoked-paprika deviled eggs, then moves on to a very simple preparation of surf and turf—seared and oven-roasted beef tenderloin fillets and zesty sautéed shrimp. We've also included spicy roasted potatoes, sautéed greens, and a gorgeous salad that glows with vibrant shades of red. Light some candles, throw on a sexy playlist . . . and save the dishes for the morning, if you know what I mean.

. . . .

"patatas bravas" with cauliflower and roasted garlic aioli

sofrito greens with bacon and peppers

arugula salad with roasted grapes, beet noodles, walnuts, and orange–red wine vinaigrette

pimenton deviled eggs

spanish-style surf and turf

red zinger tonic

be mine

ODDS ARE THAT VALENTINE'S DAY FALLS ON A WEEK-NIGHT, but you can still make the entire menu if you get a few things done the day before. Make the deviled eggs and the aioli for the potatoes; cover each separately and refrigerate. Wash and thoroughly dry the collard greens; slice into ribbons and store in the refrigerator in an airtight container. Finally, make the vinaigrette for the salad, storing in the fridge and shaking vigorously before using.

OFFER SUGGES-TIONS if your partner normally brings you choco-lates and is stuck on an alternative small gesture. Flowers, a bottle of your favorite compli-ant kombucha, or making a romantic playlist ahead of time are great sub-stitutions. (Offering to do the dishes works, too.)

EVEN IF YOU'VE DONE A FAIR AMOUNT OF PREP WORK AHEAD, get your sweetie in on the cooking action. Cooking together as a team feels good, and provides the time and space for deep conversa-tions—the kind you couldn't get with a waiter interrupting you every four min-utes. (Or, just keep it light and fun—no work talk, kid talk, or dentist appoint-ment reminders.)

"patatas bravas" with cauliflower and roasted garlic aioli

SERVES 2

"Spicy potatoes," as they are known in their native Spain, are a traditional tapas or bar snack. On this side of the ocean, they have been adapted by many chefs as a side dish—and why not? They're a perfect accompaniment to Spanish-Style Surf and Turf.

PREP: 15 MINUTES   BAKE: 30 MINUTES
COOK: 15 MINUTES   TOTAL: 60 MINUTES

FOR THE AIOLI

1 head garlic, halved crosswise

1 tablespoon extra-virgin olive oil

½ cup Basic Mayonnaise (page 240) or Whole30-compliant mayonnaise

2 teaspoons sherry vinegar

1 teaspoon fresh lemon juice

⅛ teaspoon salt

⅛ teaspoon black pepper

FOR THE POTATOES

1 tablespoon extra-virgin olive oil

6 ounces Yukon Gold potatoes, halved (quartered, if large)

1½ cups small cauliflower florets

½ (14-ounce) can Whole30-compliant whole peeled tomatoes, undrained

3 cloves garlic, thinly sliced

1 teaspoon smoked paprika

¼ teaspoon red pepper flakes

¼ teaspoon ground cumin

Dash Whole30-compliant hot sauce or Whole30 Sriracha (page 242)

¼ teaspoon coarse salt

2 tablespoons chopped fresh parsley

PREHEAT the oven to 350°F.

MAKE THE AIOLI: Place the garlic halves in a 4-inch square piece of foil. Drizzle with olive oil; fold up sides and seal. Place on a baking pan. Bake, until the cloves are tender, 30 minutes. Let the garlic cool. Squeeze one garlic half over a small bowl (use the other half for the Pimenton Deviled Eggs, see Tip, page 263). Mash the cloves with the back of a fork. Add the mayonnaise, sherry vinegar, and lemon juice. Sprinkle with the salt and pepper; set aside until ready to serve. (The aioli may be made up to 2 days ahead. Cover and refrigerate; bring to room temperature before serving.)

MAKE THE POTATOES: In a large nonstick skillet, heat the olive oil over medium-high heat. Add the potatoes; reduce the heat to medium. Cook, stirring occasionally, until the potatoes are browned but not quite tender, about 5 minutes.

MEANWHILE, place the cauliflower, tomatoes, garlic, red pepper flakes, cumin, and hot sauce in a food processor. Cover and pulse until the tomatoes are coarsely chopped (do not puree). Add to the potatoes. Cover and cook for 5 minutes. Remove the cover. Cook, stirring frequently, until the vegetables are tender, about 5 minutes more. Transfer to a serving dish and sprinkle with coarse salt and parsley. Drizzle with the aioli.

sofrito greens with bacon and peppers

SERVES 2

In Spain, "sofrito" is a sauce—usually of onion, garlic, peppers, and tomato—that has all kinds of applications. Here, a tomato-less sofrito (plus bacon!) flavors a mess of glossy greens.

....

PREP: 10 MINUTES   **COOK:** 15 MINUTES   **TOTAL:** 25 MINUTES

....

2 slices Whole30-compliant bacon, finely chopped

½ cup minced onion

¼ cup minced pimiento

2 cloves garlic, minced

½ teaspoon smoked paprika

½ teaspoon dried oregano

¼ teaspoon black pepper

1 bunch (8 ounces) collard greens, stemmed and sliced into ¼-inch ribbons

½ cup Whole30-compliant vegetable broth or water

IN a large nonstick skillet, cook the bacon over medium heat until crisp, 5 to 7 minutes. Add the onion, pimiento, garlic, paprika, oregano, and pepper. Cook until the onion is translucent and tender, about 5 minutes. Stir in the collard greens and broth. Cook, stirring frequently, until the greens are tender but still bright green, 3 to 4 minutes.

arugula salad with roasted grapes, beet noodles, walnuts, and orange–red wine vinaigrette

SERVES 2

Think of Valentine's Day and you see red—the color, that is. This elegant salad celebrates that warm hue with a mélange of curly red beet noodles, red grapes that are roasted to enhance their natural sweetness, and a final touch of juicy pomegranate arils.

PREP: 15 MINUTES   **ROAST:** 10 MINUTES   **TOTAL:** 25 MINUTES

1 cup red grapes

1 small beet, peeled and spiralized or cut into matchsticks

1 tablespoon extra-virgin olive oil

¼ teaspoon salt

¼ teaspoon black pepper

½ cup coarsely chopped walnuts

FOR THE VINAIGRETTE

3 tablespoons fresh orange juice

3 tablespoons red wine vinegar or white balsamic vinegar

1 tablespoon minced shallot

1 teaspoon Whole30-compliant Dijon mustard

⅛ teaspoon salt

⅛ teaspoon black pepper

¼ cup extra-virgin olive oil

FOR THE SALAD

3 cups arugula

¼ cup pomegranate arils

¼ cup torn fresh mint leaves

PREHEAT the oven to 400°F. Line a large rimmed baking pan with parchment paper.

PLACE the grapes and beet on the baking pan. Drizzle with the olive oil and sprinkle with the salt and pepper. Roast for 7 to 8 minutes, until the grapes wrinkle slightly. Stir gently; sprinkle with the walnuts. Roast for 3 to 5 minutes more, until the walnuts are toasted and the beets are tender. Remove from the oven and let stand until ready to assemble the salads.

MAKE THE VINAIGRETTE: In a small bowl, whisk the orange juice, vinegar, shallot, mustard, salt, and pepper. Slowly drizzle in the olive oil, whisking constantly, until emulsified.

MAKE THE SALAD: Place the arugula in a large bowl; drizzle with 3 to 4 tablespoons of the vinaigrette to lightly coat. Drizzle 2 tablespoons of the vinaigrette over the beet-grape mixture. Divide the greens and beet-grape mixture between two salad plates. Sprinkle the salads with the pomegranate arils and mint leaves.

tip: STORE LEFTOVER VINAIGRETTE in an airtight container in the refrigerator for up to 1 week.

pimenton deviled eggs

Long before it was commonly referred to as "smoked paprika," it was called *pimenton* in Spain—an almost magical ingredient made from wood-smoked and dried red peppers. Most smoked paprika in this country is sweet (*dolce*), but there is a hot (*picante*) version too.

PREP: 10 MINUTES   **COOK:** 5 MINUTES
STAND: 30 MINUTES   **TOTAL:** 45 MINUTES

2 large eggs

3 tablespoons Basic Mayonnaise (page 240) or Whole30-compliant mayonnaise

1 teaspoon roasted garlic (see Tip)

¾ teaspoon sherry vinegar

¼ teaspoon smoked paprika

Pinch salt and black pepper

2 tablespoons chopped fresh parsley

Small strips of pimiento (optional)

PLACE the eggs in a small saucepan; add cold water to cover by 1 inch. Bring the water to a rolling boil. Remove from the heat. Let stand, covered, 15 minutes. Drain the eggs. Add cold water to the pan to cover the eggs. Add a few handfuls of ice cubes. Let stand until the eggs are cool enough to handle, about 15 minutes. Drain the eggs and peel.

CUT the eggs in half lengthwise and place the yolks in a small bowl; reserve the whites. Mash the yolks with the mayonnaise; stir in the garlic, vinegar, paprika, salt, and pepper. Use a small spoon to fill the reserved egg whites with the filling.

TO serve, sprinkle with parsley and top with strips of pimiento, if using.

tips: USE THE LEFTOVER ROASTED GARLIC from the "Patatas Bravas" with Cauliflower and Roasted Garlic Aioli, page 258.

TO PIPE THE FILLING into the reserved egg whites, spoon the filling into a sandwich-size resealable plastic bag. Snip a corner off the bag and pipe.

spanish-style
surf and turf

"Surf and turf"—which pairs shrimp, prawns, crab, or lobster with beef—is the ultimate old-school entrée. The first known reference to the phrase is from 1961, in the *Los Angeles Times*, and not long thereafter it became associated with luxurious dining. It's prepared simply—the flavors of the meat and shellfish are rich enough not to require much enhancement.

PREP: 10 MINUTES **COOK:** 8 MINUTES
ROAST: 7 MINUTES **TOTAL:** 25 MINUTES

2 tablespoons extra-virgin olive oil
2 beef tenderloin fillets (about 6 ounces each)
¼ teaspoon salt
¼ teaspoon black pepper
8 medium peeled and deveined shrimp
4 cloves garlic, sliced
1 bay leaf
Pinch red pepper flakes
1 tablespoon sherry vinegar
1 tablespoon fresh lemon juice
2 tablespoons chopped fresh parsley

PREHEAT the oven to 400°F.

IN a large ovenproof skillet, heat 1 tablespoon of the olive oil over medium-high (see Tip). Sprinkle the fillets with salt and pepper and place in the hot skillet. Cook the fillets on one side until deep brown, about 4 minutes. Use tongs to turn the fillets over; transfer the skillet to the oven. Roast for 7 to 8 minutes, until the fillets are 145°F (medium), or to desired doneness. Carefully remove the skillet from the oven (the handle will be very hot). Transfer the fillets to a plate and loosely tent with foil. Let rest for 5 minutes while preparing the shrimp.

IN the same skillet, heat the remaining 1 tablespoon olive oil. Add the shrimp, garlic, bay leaf, and pepper flakes. Cook until the shrimp are pink and curled, 4 to 5 minutes. Add the vinegar and lemon juice. Sprinkle with the parsley.

SERVE the fillets with the shrimp.

tip: A CAST IRON SKILLET is perfect for going from stovetop to oven.

red zinger tonic

SERVES 2

Hot peppermint tea flavored with pomegranate juice, cinnamon, orange, and lemon makes a zippy sipper when you're avoiding alcohol—and it's anything but boring.

· ·

PREP: 5 MINUTES **STAND:** 3 MINUTES
TOTAL: 10 MINUTES

· ·

½ cup 100% pomegranate juice

1 cinnamon stick

Peel of 1 orange

Peel of 1 lemon

2 peppermint tea bags

IN a small saucepan, combine 2 cups of water, pomegranate juice, cinnamon stick, orange peel, and lemon peel. Heat until steaming. Divide the mixture between two cups; add a tea bag to each cup. Steep for 3 to 4 minutes. Remove the tea bags and serve.

independence day

Every Fourth of July, people all over the country march in parades, swoon at fireworks, and gather around the grill to celebrate America's independence with cheeseburgers, potato chips, popsicles, and cherry pie. But what if you're working toward a different kind of freedom . . . what I call food freedom? Every recipe on this menu fits perfectly into this classic American celebration—and fits your Whole30 too. We've got baby back ribs, potato salad, chicken drumsticks, and fresh, crisp salad . . . and cherries make an appearance in a refreshing sparkling Italian soda.

. . . .

oven-to-grill baby back ribs with peach-chipotle sauce

curried chicken drumsticks with pineapple-pepper salsa

grilled caponata

green bean and red potato salad with egg and green goddess dressing

summer peach, cucumber, and avocado salad with dill, mint, and almonds

hibiscus-cherry italian soda

bring on the sparklers!

ANY SORT OF BACK-YARD COOKOUT lends itself naturally to the Whole30— grilled meat, veggies, fruit, and a sparkling beverage are all you need to make any crowd happy. (And we've chosen meat that isn't normally eaten on a bun anyway!)

IF YOUR GUESTS WANT TO CON-TRIBUTE A DISH, be specific about what you need, so you don't end up with four fruit salads. (Although a fruit or garden salad sans croutons or cheese is a great idea; it's almost always Whole30-compliant as-is, and you can provide a Whole30 dressing on the side.)

PROVIDE A SEPAR-ATE COOLER if guests want to BYOB, so you're not constantly reaching past your favorite ale for a can of Waterloo.

IF YOU'RE LOOKING FOR a fun and festive way to end the meal, try grilling your favorite fruit! Grapes (left on the bunch), watermelon, pineapple, peaches, or cherries take on a smoky, caramelized flavor when grilled, and it's fun for kids to eat fruit off kabob sticks.

oven-to-grill baby back ribs with peach-chipotle sauce

SERVES 8

These ribs are roasted in the oven and then given a quick turn on the grill before serving to get some smoke, charring, and a generous basting of barbecue sauce. You can roast the ribs and make the sauce up to 2 days ahead.

....

PREP: 20 MINUTES   **BAKE:** 2 HOURS   **COOK:** 30 MINUTES
TOTAL: 2 HOURS 50 MINUTES

....

FOR THE RIBS

2 tablespoons coarse salt

2 teaspoons black pepper

1 teaspoon chipotle chile powder

1 teaspoon ground coriander

7 pounds pork baby back ribs, membrane removed (see Tip)

FOR THE SAUCE

3 tablespoons extra-virgin olive oil

1 pound fresh ripe peaches, pitted and sliced

1 ripe mango, diced (see Tip)

1 medium yellow onion, diced

3 cloves garlic, minced

1 teaspoon chipotle chile powder

¾ cup Whole30-compliant chicken broth

¼ cup Whole30-compliant tomato paste

3 tablespoons cider vinegar

1 teaspoon coconut aminos

PREHEAT the oven to 300°F. Line 4 large rimmed baking pans with foil.

MAKE THE RIBS: In a small bowl, combine the salt, black pepper, chipotle powder, and coriander. Rub both sides of the ribs with the spice mixture. Arrange the ribs on the baking pans; add water to a depth of ½ inch; cover tightly with foil. Bake the ribs until tender and cooked through, 2 to 2½ hours. (The ribs may be roasted up to 2 days ahead. Wrap in foil and refrigerate until ready to grill.)

MAKE THE SAUCE: In a large saucepan, heat the olive oil over medium heat. Add the peaches, mango, onion, garlic, and chipotle powder. Cook, stirring often, until the onion is translucent and the fruit begins to break down, about 8 minutes. Add the broth, tomato paste, vinegar, and aminos; simmer for 10 minutes. Use an immersion blender (or transfer to a stand blender) to blend until smooth, adding water 1 tablespoon at a time to thin, if necessary.

PREHEAT the grill to medium-high. Place the cooked ribs on the grill and brush liberally with sauce. Grill, covered, brushing with additional sauce and turning once halfway through, until the ribs are slightly charred and heated through, about 10 minutes. Serve with the remaining sauce.

tips To REMOVE THE MEMBRANE (silver skin) from the back of the ribs, start at one end of the rack and slide a table knife under the membrane. Lift and loosen the membrane. Use a paper towel to grab the edge of the membrane and pull it off. Or you can ask the butcher to do this for you.

To CUT A MANGO, use a "Y" peeler to peel it., then use a sharp knife to trim the stem. Set the mango on one of its narrow sides and, holding the mango in one hand and a knife in the other, slice through the flesh slightly off center to avoid the pit. Repeat with the other side. Dice the cut fruit.

curried chicken drumsticks with pineapple-pepper salsa

SERVES 8

What would a Fourth of July celebration be without firing up the grill? These curried drumsticks served with pineapple salsa are a nice departure from the standard burgers and hot dogs.

PREP: 20 MINUTES **COOK:** 40 MINUTES
TOTAL: 60 MINUTES

FOR THE SALSA

1½ cups diced fresh pineapple

¾ cup diced red bell pepper

¼ cup finely chopped red onion

¼ cup chopped fresh cilantro

3 tablespoons fresh lime juice

½ medium jalapeño, seeded and finely chopped

⅛ teaspoon salt

Dash Whole30-compliant hot sauce

FOR THE CHICKEN

3 tablespoons Whole30-compliant curry powder

½ teaspoon red pepper flakes

½ teaspoon salt

½ teaspoon black pepper

8 chicken drumsticks

Extra-virgin olive oil

¼ cup chopped fresh cilantro

FOR THE SAUCE

½ cup plus 2 teaspoons unfiltered apple juice

1 teaspoon tapioca flour

PREHEAT the grill to medium heat.

MAKE THE SALSA: In a medium bowl, stir together the pineapple, bell pepper, onion, cilantro, lime juice, jalapeño, salt, and hot sauce. Set the salsa aside until ready to serve.

MAKE THE CHICKEN: Add the curry powder, red pepper flakes, salt, and black pepper to a large resealable plastic bag. Add the drumsticks and toss to coat; reserve any remaining spices. Transfer the drumsticks to a large plate or baking pan and drizzle with olive oil. Arrange the drumsticks on the grill rack. Grill, covered, turning once, until 165°F, about 25 minutes.

MAKE THE SAUCE: Meanwhile, in a small saucepan, bring ½ cup of the apple juice and the remaining spices to a boil over medium-high heat, about 4 minutes. In a small bowl, stir together the tapioca flour and the remaining 2 teaspoons of the apple juice until smooth. Whisk the tapioca mixture into the boiling apple juice. Reduce the heat and simmer until thickened, 1 to 2 minutes. Brush the apple syrup onto the drumsticks and grill 5 minutes more.

TRANSFER the drumsticks to a platter; sprinkle with the cilantro. Serve with the pineapple salsa.

grilled caponata

SERVES 8

Caponata—a mélange of eggplant, bell peppers, onion, tomatoes, olives, capers, golden raisins, and vinegar—is a Sicilian invention that showcases the country's love of sweet-and-sour flavors. It is most often cooked on the stovetop, but this grilled version adds a wonderful touch of smoke to the finished dish.

PREP: 20 MINUTES   **COOK:** 10 MINUTES
TOTAL: 30 MINUTES

1 medium eggplant, sliced into 1-inch-thick rounds

2 red bell peppers, halved

1 medium red onion, cut into wedges, root end intact

4 medium ripe tomatoes, halved crosswise

4 tablespoons extra-virgin olive oil

½ teaspoon coarse salt

½ teaspoon black pepper

1 cup unsulfured golden raisins

½ cup halved, pimiento-stuffed, Whole30-compliant green olives

1 tablespoon Whole30-compliant drained capers

½ cup chopped fresh parsley

½ cup chopped fresh basil leaves

3 tablespoons balsamic vinegar

1 tablespoon unsweetened cocoa powder

PREHEAT the grill to medium-high.

PLACE the eggplant, bell peppers, onion, and tomatoes on a large rimmed baking pan. Brush both sides of the vegetables with 2 tablespoons of the olive oil; sprinkle with ¼ teaspoon each salt and pepper.

ARRANGE the vegetables on the grill rack. Grill, turning once halfway through, until lightly charred and tender, about 10 minutes. Remove the vegetables from the grill and let cool slightly, then chop into bite-size pieces. Transfer to a large bowl and add the raisins, olives, and capers; gently stir to combine.

IN a small bowl, stir together the parsley, basil, remaining 2 tablespoons of the olive oil, 2 tablespoons of the vinegar, and the cocoa powder. Pour the mixture over the vegetables and gently stir. Season with the remaining ¼ teaspoon each salt and pepper, and the remaining 1 tablespoon of vinegar.

tip: FOR THE BEST FLAVOR, let the salad stand at room temperature for 30 minutes before serving.

green bean and red potato salad with egg and green goddess dressing

SERVES 8

The star of green goddess dressing is tarragon—a fragrant, anise-flavored herb. The dressing totally makes this summery salad, but if you are not a fan of tarragon, you can substitute fresh basil.

PREP: 15 MINUTES **COOK:** 15 MINUTES
TOTAL: 30 MINUTES

FOR THE DRESSING

4 green onions, trimmed and cut into 1-inch pieces

¼ cup chopped fresh tarragon

¼ cup chopped fresh parsley

¼ cup white wine vinegar

¼ cup Basic Mayonnaise (page 240) or Whole30-compliant mayonnaise

1 tablespoon Whole30-compliant Dijon mustard

⅛ teaspoon salt

⅛ teaspoon black pepper

FOR THE SALAD

1 pound red potatoes, halved (quartered, if large)

3 large eggs

¼ teaspoon salt

1 pound fresh green beans, trimmed

MAKE THE DRESSING: In a food processor, combine the green onions, tarragon, and parsley; pulse until minced. Add the vinegar, mayonnaise, mustard, salt, and black pepper; pulse to blend. Set aside.

MAKE THE SALAD: Place the potatoes, eggs (in their shells), and salt in a large pot of water to cover by 1 inch. Bring to a boil; reduce the heat to a simmer. Cook until the potatoes are just fork-tender, about 10 minutes. Add the green beans. Continue cooking until the beans are tender-crisp, about 3 minutes more. Drain. Remove the eggs and place in a bowl with ice water. When the eggs are cool, peel and coarsely chop.

TRANSFER the potatoes and beans to a large serving bowl; drizzle with some of the dressing and gently toss to coat. Sprinkle the chopped eggs on the salad and drizzle with the remaining dressing.

summer peach, cucumber, and avocado salad with dill, mint, and almonds

SERVES 8

One of summer's greatest gifts is fresh, ripe peaches. They are the centerpiece of this light and very fresh salad—just the thing to serve alongside hearty grilled meats.

PREP: 25 MINUTES TOTAL: 25 MINUTES

⅓ cup fresh lemon juice

½ cup thinly sliced green onions

¼ cup avocado oil or extra-virgin olive oil

⅛ teaspoon salt

⅛ teaspoon black pepper

4 ripe fresh peaches, pitted and diced

2 English cucumbers, halved lengthwise and thinly sliced crosswise

2 ripe avocados, halved, pitted, peeled, and diced

½ cup chopped fresh dill

½ cup chopped fresh mint

¾ cup sliced almonds, toasted (see Tip)

IN a large bowl, whisk the lemon juice, green onions, oil, salt, and pepper. Add the peaches, cucumber, avocado, dill, mint, and almonds. Carefully stir to combine. Transfer to a large serving bowl.

tip: TO TOAST THE NUTS, heat in a dry skillet over medium heat, stirring, until fragrant and lightly browned, about 2 minutes.

hibiscus-cherry italian soda

SERVES 8

Basil and sweet cherries have a real affinity for each other—there's something about the lightly peppery, licorice-like taste of basil that enhances the sweetness of the cherries. The combo infuses this refreshing sparkling drink with amazing flavor.

PREP: 10 MINUTES STAND: 5 MINUTES
CHILL: 2 HOURS 30 MINUTES TOTAL: 2 HOUR 45 MINUTES

8 Whole30-compliant hibiscus tea bags

4 cups fresh or frozen pitted dark sweet cherries, slightly thawed if frozen

2 (0.8-ounce) containers fresh basil (about 2½ cups), plus sprigs for garnish, if desired

Ice

2 cups Whole30-compliant sparkling water

Whole30-compliant almond milk (optional)

PLACE the tea bags in a heatproof 4-quart pitcher. Pour 4 cups of boiling water over the tea bags and let steep for 6 minutes. Remove the bags and add 4 cups cold water to the tea. Chill for 2 hours or until the tea is cold.

ADD the cherries and basil to the tea; gently mash with a potato masher or large spoon until the cherries are crushed and the basil is bruised. Chill for 30 minutes. Strain and discard the cherries and basil.

TO serve, pour 1 cup of the tea mixture over ice-filled tall glasses; top with sparkling water and a splash of the almond milk, if desired. Garnish with basil sprigs, if desired.

CHANGE YOUR LIFE WITH
THE BEST-SELLING BOOKS FROM

THE **WHOLE30**®

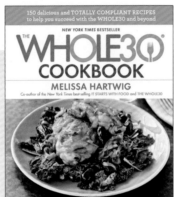

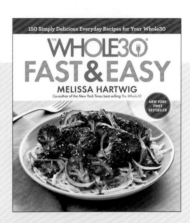

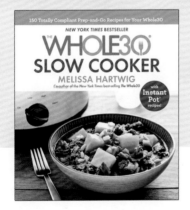

HMH

WHOLE30.COM